Biblical Characters
and the Enneagram

Images of Transformation

There have been many books written on the theory, the psychological implications and the social uses of the Enneagram. But Biblical Characters and the Enneagram *provides another whole layer of understanding. This book not only provides new insights into the process of human development: it gives it human validity and spiritual ground as well. By using popular scriptural figures to demonstrate each of the personalities described,* Biblical Characters *enables the reader to see a model of the type in action. The effects of the linkage are to enhance both psychological development and the spiritual life at the same time. The Scripture comes alive with current meaning and human development becomes a very spiritual thing. This book puts flesh on theory. Theorists, personal growth groups and retreatants will all see the Enneagram come alive here.*

    – **Joan Chittister**, O.S.B., lecturer, columnist, and author of 21 books including her most recent, *The Friendship of Women: A Spiritual Tradition*

A most welcome result of the Second Vatican Council (1962-1965) is greater use of the Bible by Roman Catholics for study, spiritual reading and prayer. Less known and more controversial is the proposal by some spiritual directors that the Enneagram is a useful "modern compass" for the journey of personal transformation. This book combines these two movements by using the Enneagram to explore the spiritual journeys of 18 women and men met in Bible stories, thereby suggesting new ways "to lose ourselves in order to find ourselves" (Matthew 10:39).

    – **Bernard Daly**, Ottawa, publisher emeritus of *The Catholic Register*

I recommend this book to people who wish to be transformed in their relationship with the Divine. The book might well be entitled "A Meditation for Spiritual Knowledge of Self." By using various personalities of the Bible it invites us "to penetrate, to probe, and to experience in new ways the patterns of divine communication with

*human beings in all their complexity, frailty and strength, their
sinfulness and their amazing potential, and their ultimate
grandeur." May you find it as enlightening as I did.*
  – **John English**, S.J., Director of Spiritual Exercises Programs,
    Winnipeg, and author of *Spiritual Freedom: From the
    Experience of the Ignatian Exercises to the Art of Spiritual
    Guidance*

*The book masterfully weaves Enneagram insights with biblical
characters revealing God's gentle hand in transforming compulsion
into the image of God.*
  – **Carol Ann Gotch**, Enneagram teacher, co-author of *Soul Stuff*

*Combining their probing interpretation of the nine personality types
of the Enneagram with their lifelong love of the people we encounter
in the Bible, the authors of this book have created a masterpiece of
wisdom and insight. In their deft hands, the characters of the Bible
become mirrors for ourselves, so that we come to know ourselves and
discover the richness of experiencing God. Read this book and luxu-
riate in a personal awareness of God's love for humanity.*
  – **Kathy Hurley** and **Theodorre Donson**, Enneagram teachers
    and authors of *Discover Your Soul Potential, What's My Type?*
    and *My Best Self: Using the Enneagram to Free the Soul*

*This is a breakthrough book, representing a dialogue between
Biblical figures and the archetypal personality types of the
Enneagram. It uses Biblical characters as models and mentors to
lead us into greater insight into the human quest for the Divine. By
investigating the psychology of Biblical figures, the authors take us
to a new level of appreciation of both the Bible and the Enneagram.
This book opens new and exciting paths for our continuing search
for wisdom.*
  – **Don Richard Riso** and **Russ Hudson**, Enneagram teachers,
    authors of *The Wisdom of the Enneagram* and *Personality
    Types*

Biblical Characters and the Enneagram *incisively cuts into our personalities and helps us to see how we are — or are not — a reflection of the Creator. With biblical characters as our reference point, we learn how even our simple daily gestures take on a new meaning. The Enneagram is a useful tool in energizing us to build a spiritual transformation within ourselves. The object is the merging of our true self with God. This book takes us on an exciting, and mystical, journey.*
  - **Senator Douglas Roche**, O.C.

Like the dragnet of Jesus, these authors are pulling from the great sea things both old and new. This is very traditional teaching in a fresh and compelling form. A very helpful contribution to Judeo-Christian enneagram studies.
  - **Richard Rohr**, O.F.M, Center for Action and Contemplation, Albuquerque, N.M., author of *The Enneagram: A Christian Perspective*

For those interested in a psychological reading of Scripture, Biblical Characters and the Enneagram *will be a helpful resource. While not everyone will agree with such an approach, everyone will be challenged by this skilfully argued form of biblical interpretation.*
  - **Elisabeth Schüssler Fiorenza**, Krister Stendahl Professor of Scripture and Interpretation, Harvard University Divinity School

The Enneagram has proved a valuable tool for penetrating the healthy and unhealthy things that motivate me and my loved ones. In lucid language, this book creatively broadened my understanding of the Enneagram's nine personality types. Written by three clear-headed practitioners (including a legendary Canadian bishop), it makes compelling links between the Enneagram's personality types and major Biblical figures. It led me deeper into self-understanding and the Scriptures.
  - **Douglas Todd**, Religion and Ethics Writer, *The Vancouver Sun*

The Authors

Diane Tolomeo received her Ph.D in English Literature from Princeton University. She currently teaches in both the English Department and the Humanities Diploma Program at the University of Victoria, Canada. Her talks and retreats focus on biblical literature, archetypes, and the tradition of Christian meditation.

Pearl Gervais has extensive experience in education and counselling. She holds degrees from the University of Manitoba and the University of Wisconsin, and has studied at the Tantur Institute in Jersusalem. She is a certified Enneagram teacher and gives workshops and retreats in the areas of personal growth, spirituality and business.

Remi J. De Roo, STD, received his doctorate from the Angelicum, Rome and is Bishop Emeritus of the Diocese of Victoria, Canada. He is a Vatican II Council Father and a certified Enneagram teacher. He holds five honourary degrees and is an internationally known lecturer and retreat leader. He has co-authored or authored six books including *Even Greater Things: Hope and Challenge after Vatican II*.

For Tess,
Blessings of health,
peace and joy!
Fraternally,
Remi

Biblical Characters
and the Enneagram

Images of Transformation

May you
continue to
journey in faith
& courage!
Pearl

Diane Tolomeo
Pearl Gervais
Remi J. De Roo

Pearl Gervais
Remi J. De Roo

Newport Bay Publishing Limited • Victoria, B.C., Canada

National Library of Canada Cataloguing in Publication Data

Tolomeo, Diane, 1948-
 Biblical characters and the enneagram

 Includes bibliographical references.
 ISBN 0-921513-13-5

 1. Bible--Psychology. 2. Enneagram. 3. Bible--Biography.
I. Gervais, Pearl. II. De Roo, Remi J. III. Title.
BS645.T64 2002   220.6'01'9   C2001-911698-5

Published by   Newport Bay Publishing Limited
                    356 Cyril Owen Place
                    Victoria, British Columbia, Canada   V9E 2B6

International Standard Book Number 0-921513-13-5

Printed in Canada

The New Revised Standard Version (Oxford Univ. Press) of the Bible was
used in references and quotations for this book.

Acknowledgements

Many people throughout Canada and the United States have assisted us in the writing of this book through their participation in workshops and retreats, and through generously providing either their written or their verbal comments at various stages in its writing. This book would not have been possible without their stories, their insights, and their humour.

We offer a special note of appreciation to the following: Jill Aigner, Muriel Allen, Elaine Beatch, Pat Brady, Margaret Baumann, Bonnie Brennan, Beverley Brown, Joan Chittister, Muriel Clemenger, Laura Distaso, Donna Dolan, Elizabeth Eede, John English, Jim and Joan Felling, Maria Fernau, Mary Ann Gisler, Patricia Grell, Peggy Hughes, Laura and Michael Hargreaves, Robert Kaiser, Bill Lawrence, Phyllis McGrath, Ron MacIsaac, Valin Marshall, Bob Martens, Margaret Mary Miller, Rosemary Moskal, Rochelle Pearce, Steve Ratkai, Richard Rohr, Douglas Roche, Elisabeth Schüssler Fiorenza, Murray Smith, Ray and Betty Anne Smith, Anita Tavera, Mary Anne and Ron Tinney, Douglas Todd, Terry Totzke, and Andrew Twiddy.

Our deep appreciation and gratitude also go to those who taught us Scripture and the Enneagram and who continue to call us to live the tenets of both: Don Riso and Russ Hudson, whose friendship we treasure and whose wisdom nourishes us; Kathy Hurley and Theodorre Donson, for their friendship and their efforts to unfold the spiritual reality of the Enneagram; David Walsh and Carol Ann Gotch, who in faith and courage devoted their life to "soulstuff"; Helen Palmer, whose leadership continues to stimulate growth and depth; and the Tantur staff in Jerusalem for their knowledge and their love of the Word.

We also offer our humble gratitude to the Creator, the Lord of the Dance who faithfully feeds our souls with the calm of the sea, the beauty of the sunrises, the soaring eagles and the groundedness of the deer, and who in our writing of this book taught us so much about the sharing of a deep and rich spirituality, as well as patience, wisdom and forgiveness, during this most enriching experience.

Special thanks also go to Donna Lindenberg, who so ably helped us see this project through to its publication, and to the many other friends and family who encouraged us to begin and continue this work, and who supported us with love, casseroles, prayers, space to work, listening ears, and celebrations. They know who they are.

Table of Contents

Preface: Stories of Transformation

This is a book that wanted to be written. Several years ago, the authors offered a series of workshops to 35 persons involved in different ministries at St. Andrew's Cathedral in Victoria, Canada. Participants were invited to reflect on some of the stories in the Bible in the light of their own particular ministry within the community. Each week, three different biblical characters, whom we referred to as 'mentors,' were presented as models for ministry. We explored how we discover and respond to God's presence in our very different personalities, and how we could attempt to build teams in our ministries which utilize our different energies and gifts. Participants came to appreciate more clearly their interdependency and complementarity in the work they shared. The result was an overwhelming desire of the participants to return to the Bible and see in its characters people like ourselves who could offer us models to guide us in our spiritual growth and in our ministry.

The context for each session was based on the Bible, and knowledge of the Enneagram or of one's Enneagram type was not a prerequisite for the workshops. In fact, the Enneagram was barely mentioned during the eight-week course, though the authors themselves used it as the background and structure for each session.

Encouraged by the overwhelming responses of people who were eager to return to familiar biblical stories to shed light on their own lives and ministries, we decided to take the project one step further. We invited 18 people who were already familiar with their own Enneagram profile to spend a weekend exploring biblical characters whom we felt represented their types. The rewards were rich: as we worked and prayed and ate together, we experienced how we need one another to complement our different energies and insights. Deeper perceptions of the scriptures and ourselves opened as participants identified characteristics of their biblical mentors and compared them with their own lives. We reflected on the ways in which God interacts with our diverse personality patterns, and we marvelled at the depth of insight people were able to provide for those biblical characters or archetypes who shared their own Enneagram 'space.' The Bible took on a renewed luminosity and energy in relation to our everyday life and work. Scriptural passages became even more life-giving than before as they spoke to and threw light upon our personally experienced realities. One person reported that, having set aside the Bible years earlier as of little interest and relevance, there was now an excitement about opening it once again to meet more of the wonderful friends discovered in its pages. Some of the comments expressed by those who shared their reflections with us during our study have been incorporated into the chapters which follow.

Many requests for workshops followed on the heels of that weekend, and people from other places began to seek more information on opening the Bible more fully by using the insights gained from studying the Enneagram and discovering treasures in the scriptures that had been too long hidden to them. A number of people asked if we were going to write all this down somewhere. That is why we claim that this book wanted, finally, to be written.

There are some who may feel nervous about using the Enneagram as a tool for reading and opening the Bible more fully as well as for using it for their own spiritual growth. For some, the Enneagram is perceived as a system without a Christian basis. This is an assumption that needs to be addressed seriously. As Christians ourselves, we are seeking to work within this context with the utmost fidelity to and respect for the Christian tradition. The Christian teaching has never been hostile to diversity in approaching and reading scripture. It has also always endorsed diverse practices in meditation and prayer. When we discover a tool or a method which leads us closer to God and encourages our own inner transformation and growth, it will be a friend and not a foe on our spiritual path.

The Enneagram is such a tool, and it may in fact be closer to the Christian tradition than has previously been thought. Recent work on the sources of the Enneagram has uncovered a history which may go back at least to the time of the Desert Fathers and Mothers in the 4th century.[1]

As early as the fourth century, Augustine of Hippo wrote that wherever truth is found, it belongs to God. Writing about how the Israelites took the gold from the Egyptians when they fled, he developed the notion of "Egyptian gold" to refer to anything precious which can be found in places other than the Christian tradition, and which may freely be utilized for the sake of the people of God.[2] The Enneagram is only one form of this "Egyptian gold," but a very rich one which may in fact turn out to have roots closer to home than previously thought.

Gregory of Nyssa, another fourth century theologian, wrote that the soul is covered over through neglect so that its similarity to its Archetype is hidden and that once unclouded, the eye of the soul will be able to perceive the holiness, simplicity, and all other aspects of the divine nature. This is precisely the work of the Enneagram, which helps us discover how our individual personality development has layered over our divine image, and how we can help our own transformation into union with its divine source by experiencing the many ways in which God is hidden, waiting to be discovered in the human form.

Nearer to our own time, the Second Vatican Council (1962-65), in the document entitled *Dei Verbum* (*On Divine Revelation*), stated that, since in the sacred scripture God speaks through humans in human fashion, those who interpret and comment on the scriptures must pay close attention to, among other things, the particular literary forms, or genres, which occur in the Bible. This entails examining forms of narration which prevailed at the time of the writing and respecting the conventions which people of the time used in dealing with one another.[3] By using the Enneagram as a tool to help us read and deepen our understanding of the biblical narratives, we are attempting to do that very thing. For example, bringing insights gained from reading and analyzing literary texts to a study of John's Gospel helps us recognize and interpret patterns and images in the gospel in a deeply metaphorical as well as a literal sense. Our knowledge of how motifs and repetitions work in literary genres opens up the gospel in ways which a strictly literal reading cannot do.

Our experience of presenting the Bible to groups of people who were wanting to read the scriptures at a deeper level has proven to us that the Enneagram provides a way into the biblical stories which helps people understand the numerous ways in which divine intervention may come in our lives. Even without knowing where they fit within the Enneagram types, those who took the matter to heart found that the biblical characters did indeed become their personal mentors and companions. Their stories entwined with those of Abraham and Sarah, Ruth and Nicodemus, and helped them become more aware of the ordinary and extraordinary ways God meets us exactly where we are and leads us in the direction we need to go for healing and wholeness.

To do this we may need to let go of some of our old ideas and 'unlearn' what is no longer helpful and which may in fact be holding us back in our spiritual growth. The anonymous 14th century author of the mystical treatise on prayer called *The Cloud of Unknowing* tells us that when we first begin this work we may feel as if we are entering the darkness of a "cloud of unknowing." This cloud or "lack of knowing" seems to stand between us and God but is in reality the only way in which we will feel and see God in this life. We cannot think of God, for he is beyond thought: we can only love him.[4] The brief epigraphs from *The Cloud* which appear in the opening chapter are there to remind us of this as we progress.

It is only through love that our transformation can begin and continue.

While we do present some introductory material for those who are unfamiliar with the Enneagram, this is not primarily an Enneagram book. It is not structured to help you find out what type you are (though after reading it you might have a clearer sense of which one seems closest). Nor does it deal with "wing" theories or subtypes, or levels of development. Other writers have examined these areas well, and there are many good books on all of these aspects.[5] This book is and remains a book on characters from the Bible, one which examines their stories and shows them to be images or archetypes of different aspects of the human soul. While this is a helpful beginning, it becomes merely an intellectual exercise unless we integrate their stories into our own and awaken to our own being and the many possibilities of divine interaction in our own lives. This, then, is ultimately a book about transformation, and therefore it is also a book about love. If these stories of biblical persons stir you to think new thoughts of wholeness, feel new feelings of love, and do deeds of kindness and justice, it has served its purpose well.

Diane Tolomeo
Pearl Gervais
Remi J. De Roo

Biblical Characters and the Enneagram: Images of Transformation

The Bible and the Enneagram

Transforming the Soul

> "Since you will it, and desire it, obviously
> you already have it."
>
> *– Cloud of Unknowing*, ch. 34.

Spiritual transformation is a paradox. We strive for it, yet we cannot make it happen any more than we can make the acorn grow into an oak tree. We long for it even as its work is already going on within us. Its outcome is already assured but we are not yet at its completion. This paradox is well known in all the great spiritual traditions. Too often, we live in a limiting fashion while the work of the transformation of the soul moves like the breath and the wind and the dance. There are many ways to begin this work, many paths up the mountain, but from the top the view is the same.

When we speak of transforming our souls, it may sound as if we are trying to *do* something, as if we are undertaking a program which will guarantee that at the end of it, we are more loving and more peaceful, more resilient and better able to bear all of life's burdens. In fact, the most that we can really do is ready ourselves to be present to the ongoing encounter with the Divine. This encounter occurs in our deepest centre and never ceases, but most of us go about our daily lives unaware that we bear within us the image of God. Certain moments wake us temporarily from our sleep — intense joy, suffering or longing are their most common forms — but eventually we return to our normal condition of sleep-walking.

Transformation is a process of waking up. For some people, it may be instantaneous, a single life-changing experience after which they are more loving and more present to others and to the world. For most people, however, the journey is slower, a gradual unfolding of insights, feelings and actions which draw them closer to their divine core, sometimes called their Essence. Underneath all the layers of our personality — composed of all our likes and dislikes, our habits and preferences — lies something which is deeper, more profound, and lasting. Made in the image of God, we bear in ourselves the divine likeness. It unfolds according to its own rhythms and reasons. Our task, our work, is to cooperate with this unfolding, to say 'yes' to its workings, and to remove whatever obstacles in us hinder its freedom to flow through our hearts and outward into the world.

The Bible is full of stories of people who have allowed the divine image in them to have its way, to heal them of their frailties and vices, and to fill them with a love which radiates to others. As the first letter of John tells us, "what we will be has not yet been revealed. What we do know is this: when he is revealed, we will be like him, for we will see him as he is. And all who have this hope in him purify themselves" (1 John 3:2-3). We are destined to be like God, and our work is to undertake the necessary healing of those parts of ourselves which are not whole. The biblical narratives provide us with many models of people who have consented to this transforming work, and we can learn from them by allowing them to act as our mentors. There are many tools we can use as we begin our instruction from these teachers. One such tool is the Enneagram which is based on an understanding of the relationships and balances between the human being's three centres of the Head, the Heart, and the Body.

How can we understand the Bible more fully and profoundly by approaching it through the insights offered by the Enneagram? How can we use our understanding of the Enneagram to lead us into deeper reflection on the characters we encounter in the Bible? The wisdom of the Bible can be perceived in many ways, and the Enneagram is a particularly useful method for both reflecting and respecting the biblical stories at the same time that it shines a new kind of light on them. The Enneagram offers us ways to work with the thinking, doing, and feeling aspects of ourselves. Its insights help us to understand the layers of personality we have acquired since our birth and how they so often get in the way of our spiritual transformation. By applying its wisdom to the people we encounter in the Bible, we can learn how the soul struggles and grows, and how the Divine encounters us in each of our various situations, offering life, healing, and wisdom.

The Enneagram is thus a tool that assists us in opening the Bible, itself a uniquely inspired instrument of Revelation. Perhaps the most central prayer of Judaism, which Jesus probably prayed daily, is: "Hear, O Israel: The LORD is our God, the LORD alone. You shall love the LORD your God with all your heart, and with all your soul, and with all your might" (Deuteronomy 6:4-5). This core assertion proclaims that anyone or anything which claims the centrality due to God alone is an idol to be rejected. Such an idol need not be external to ourselves: we can and do make idols of our attitudes, our attachments, our principles, and our wants. By using the Enneagram to uncover the illusions which our personalities have created, we are able to name the idols which have stood between us and the divine reality. Once they are uncovered, they are disempowered, seen for what they really are — pale and fabricated imitations of the Divine which have deceived us into thinking they represent who we really are. If the Enneagram invites us to genuine honesty about ourselves, it does so to liberate us from our idols and help us commune more fully with the deeper reality that lies within us, our true Essence. The power of truth found in the Enneagram is its revelation of that Essence which is more beautiful than any illusion or fantasy we may have about ourselves. When we are in touch with our Essence, we are filled with serenity and love. Its nature is reflected in the Divine Name which God revealed to Moses in the burning bush: "I AM", the pure Essence of divinity which is also shared with humanity.

In pointing us to our Essence, the Enneagram intersects with and reinforces the Bible. Both seek to celebrate and deepen our experience of human life in the heights and the depths of its reality. In contemplating and portraying the image of a divine Source of all that is, and which is our true Essence, both the Bible and the Enneagram attempt to indicate and transcend the many false idols which we unintentionally create, as we continue to make gods in our own image. These idols are like will-o'-the-wisps, leading us away from our true centre. We wander off, following a false sense of ourselves, and come to believe that is who we really are. By clinging to a narrow image of God which is defined by and endorses our own limitations, we can easily settle into a comfortable life which does not challenge us to the personal work of transformation. It may even have religious elements in it. We can live our entire lives thinking we are getting somewhere simply because the external events of our lives change. But if our responses to those events remain the same all our lives and we do not see each moment as new, we will not break out of our habitual ways of feeling and thinking and doing. Spiritual training in all the major religions demands that we transcend old ways of being and open ourselves to a deeper and more profound wisdom. This is not something we are born knowing how to do, but something which needs to be learned.

In these first years of the third millennium, there exists an intense interest in such learning and in finding ways to connect to our true nature. We see it in the hunger for a readily available variety of self-improvement techniques offered in books, workshops, and various exercises and disciplines of mind, heart and body. Some of these offer speedy results; others demand long and intensive dedication to specific disciplines. Many if not most of them appeal to a desire to help the individual acquire a greater sense of meaning and purpose in life. However, achieving the common good requires more than just the individual's perfection. Social structures also require transformation. Personal growth needs to go hand in hand with cooperative efforts aimed at benefiting the larger group. When a large number of humans undertakes this sort of journey, their intensified energy radiates outward to benefit the planet.

All the wisdom traditions agree that the collective human consciousness profits from every effort of inner work, and that the individual can learn to live from within in a way which will be in harmony with the energy of the universe. This was realized several thousand years ago when the Deuteronomist wrote, "the word is very near to you; it is in your mouth and in your heart for you to observe" (Deuteronomy 30:14). That "word" is the same which spoke Creation into being in the "let there be" commands of the opening verses of Genesis. Now it is said to be interior and able to be observed. If we observe ourselves carefully, therefore, we have the possibility of discovering this generative, creative, and powerful source of all creation within our own being. Aligned with it, we will allow our inner development to grow in harmony with its divine Source.

However, humans also have the ability to hinder or curtail this growth. Finding the direction in which lies our transformation individually and collectively (for they are not really the same thing, although they are interwoven and interdependent) leads to joy and wholeness. Obstructing or avoiding it may lead to depression, illness, and a perceived sensation of meaninglessness in our lives and in our world. The Bible and the Enneagram confront these possibilities in different but complementary ways. They both urge us to allow the work of transformation to begin and to continue on its path so that we will experience the fullness of life. If studying the Bible through the Enneagram brings us pleasure but not wisdom, ideas but not transformation, then we have not grown in our love of God, self and neighbour, which is the only thing that really matters (1 Corinthians 13:1-3).

Theologians and Mentors

> "Only to our intellect is God incomprehensible:
> not to our love."
>
> – *Cloud of Unknowing*, ch. 4

The 20th-century theologian Karl Rahner (1904-1984) is considered by many to be one of the greatest modern existentialist thinkers.[6] He used both scripture and pastoral experience to assert that God's self-communication to the human person is in fact our deepest meaning, which is simply to be the recipient of God's self-communication.[7] The assumption that this is both true and possible lies at the very core of the Bible. The experience of the divine sharing of Self is thus at the heart of human existence, and to consider the human in depth is ultimately to encounter God. It is also an axiom in theology that grace builds upon nature. If considering the human being more deeply leads us naturally into an encounter with the Divine, one could justifiably argue that disciplines like the Enneagram can become valuable tools in the pursuit of authentic spirituality. Experienced grace would then become the foundation of both spirituality and theology, which in our day are often presented as alternatives, but which were never really meant to be separated from each other.

Rahner also claims that learning to pray presupposes human psychology. Intensifying our awareness and ability to focus is necessary if we want to become adept at anything, and so too is it with the practice of recollection, that is, recalling who we are, in prayer. On one hand, it demands a real distance from the superficialities of life, and, on the other hand, it requires us to take the multiplicity of thoughts, tasks, cares, disappointments, and joys, to God and in a sense to recollect them there. Just as one must ski to learn skiing, so one can learn prayer by praying.[8] While prayer is a divine gift, it is also true that every human being is called to be a mystic, one who can recognize the presence of the transcendent in the humdrum of daily existence. To do this we must awaken to and develop the awareness of being alive, of thinking, feeling, acting, ultimately of just being in a conscious relationship with the Divine present in the universe and in our personal relationships. Through this gradual process, Rahner anticipates the transformation of the entire universe into the perfection of heaven, seen not as a place or a static condition, but as the fulfilment of perfect and dynamic relationships between the Creator and the universe. Hence by individual conversion and transformation, as well as by our interaction with others and with our environment, we can participate in the transformation of all of reality – past, present, and future. Our individual renewal then aligns itself with the renewal of society and of the cosmos.

As we look for ways to understand this exciting possibility, we often turn to the great archetypes, heroes or saints of all ages, who can serve as valuable models and mentors for us. In these personages we are likely to find examples of people in whom we see the least distortion of the relationship between the human person and the reality we call God. In admiring these heroes and heroines, we awaken our own sense of magnitude and we are encouraged to follow their example. The biblical heroes provide us with a special clarity, intensity, and ability to demonstrate the relationship everyone can grow to experience with God. In an age when God often appears to be absent, it is more important than ever to be able to find examples which reflect humanity's personal experiences with God.

Awakening to the True Self:

> "Therefore strain every nerve in every possible way
> to know and experience yourself as you really are."
>
> – *Cloud of Unknowing*, ch. 14

By awakening people to their personal potential for conversion and growth, by initiating them into the mystery of their own spiritual depths, the Enneagram can help open doors and provide tools for transformation no matter what our background or how severe our current problems. It can help us to purify and amplify the barely audible and often distorted experience of God, which nevertheless continues to be present in all human beings. It can transcend all boundaries or limitations imposed by human culture or creeds, and it can lead us more clearly to an authentic worship of the Divine which is rooted in knowledge of the real Self. Even more, moving beyond all individual beings, we can obtain a better perception of the very ground or source of all being to which we attribute the name God.

The Enneagram, in its lists of human ideals of excellence, in its efforts to describe the essence of what constitutes the human searching for perfection, leads those who use it into a deeper understanding of the human spirit. In its application it touches nine spheres of longing: the seemingly unquenchable thirst for love, the hunger for meaning, the compelling drive towards achievement, the undeniable need for personal identity and recognition, the awe and ecstasy inspired by true beauty, the compelling force of truth, the irresistible appeal of excellence, the radical joy found in the little things of ordinary life, and the unutterable bliss of total peace. The yearning for these qualities of Essence is found in every human heart. By opening a path into the inner chambers of the human psyche, exploring the forest of complex human motivations, and clearing away the wild growth that obscures the broader patterns to allow for easier movement, the Enneagram helps to free us to become who we are meant to be. It provides us with a way to weave our own complex patterns together in harmony, and it also casts bridges across the voids which inhibit our communication with others.

We can and often do choose to relate to others by following a code of obedience to socially acceptable rules. According to this code, we might be doing 'all the right things', such as paying our taxes, going to church, and pursuing a healthy lifestyle, but we might feel empty within, as if there has to be more to life than just keeping going. However, if we come to understand that loving relationships are meant to constitute our very being as humans, the search for perfection shifts away from moral imperatives to the development of our capacity to love, from rational prose to love sonnets. We then realize that the Essence of which the Enneagram speaks can be recognized in the ancient teaching as the *imago Dei* or image of God, the mysterious Source from which all creation flows. This imprint of the Divine is engraved in our very core, written into what the scriptures call the heart:

> The mouths of the righteous utter wisdom,
> and their tongues speak justice.
> The law of their God is in their hearts;
> their steps do not slip.

> — Psalm 37:30-31

God also tells Jeremiah,

> I will give them a heart to know that I am the LORD; and they shall be my people and I will be their God, for they shall return to me with their whole heart.

> — Jer. 24:7

To know God in the heart is to know the nature of the *imago Dei* which reminds us of who we are in our innermost being. The *imago Dei* is hardwired into our souls, and is responsible for the unconscious longing for the better which guides us throughout our earthly lives, and the search for perfection that so often drives human beings.

Leading exponents of the Enneagram and indeed of all paths of transformation stress the need for such transformation of the heart as a key to the real meaning and purpose of their disciplines. Moving away from our persona or masks, our false or unreliable personality, in our efforts to regain our lost essence and to attain fulfillment, calls for a constant and courageous pursuit. It can often be a demanding and painful discipline through which we die to our false self in order to awaken to our true Essence. This dying to self constantly reminds us that while we can and do act freely, we are not pure freedom. We have only to recall our hesitant baby steps, our first experience of trying to ride a bicycle, our later efforts to quit some ingrained habit like smoking, or eating too much, to appreciate that often our behaviour seems to control us, and not the other way around. As we become adults, a combination of distorted patterns accumulated since birth acts against our best-intentioned efforts. In our apparently instinctive resistance to change — our often unconscious inertia, the force of habit, or some unknown inner disorder, the patterns of which have long since become almost natural — we experience a disharmony. It is felt in our relationships with the holy ideals, with the Divine, and with other people, to say nothing of the inner turmoil that can affect even our own psyche and our personal lives. We need to find a way to move out of being stuck, a way to embark on a new path.

Metaphorical Truth

> "So for the love of God be careful, and do not
> attempt to achieve this experience intellectually."
>
> – *Cloud of Unknowing*, ch. 4

Relationships are best expressed not in the language of logic but in the language of poetry. Poetic truth does not seek to find exact comparisons or descriptions but points to new and often surprising ways of re-experiencing what we thought we already knew, "what oft was thought, but ne'er so well expressed."[9] Poetry startles us into seeing the old reality with new eyes. It is quite the opposite of formulas and doctrines that sound more like the work of a committee than the language of love.[10] For example, when we try to imagine the Trinity as representing a God who is Three in One, we appreciate the need for a relational language. "Rare is the soul, whatever it says of the Trinity, that knows what it is saying," wrote St. Augustine.[11] It would therefore benefit us greatly to shift our emphasis from the numbers puzzle (how can three be one? how can one be three?) and to focus rather on the aspect of relationship. For the mathematician, one divided by three yields an infinitely repeating decimal. But when we put on our poet's hat, we can see the movement between One and Three as a circulating flow of relationships which has no remainder and can never be understood as a fraction. It is whole, and it is part, but it is never divided. A "doctrine" of this sort can never be some kind of heavenly stuff or fuel poured into us from outside. The doctrine of the Trinity can only be experienced in our own loving relationships, and we cannot impose our experience on anyone else. The Divine Presence as the living source or spiritual soil in which our very being is grounded yields different growth in each human being, and cannot be restricted by human ideas of how things should work.

Our growth in this lifetime can be well-begun but cannot be completed until our return to our Source at the time of our death.

Again, we need to speak of this poetically rather than logically, since we cannot speak from our own experience of death. Traditional Christian theology touches on this transition when it deals with the often misunderstood doctrine of purgatory. Looking into our false self which is dominated by our ego, we recognize the abysmal depths of our unresolved issues or secret conflicts. We see a mass of instincts, a subconscious malaise, and hopes that are not fully integrated into our longing for human perfection. Something inhibits or prevents the giving of our free and total assent to the Divine, and we resist even as we desire to be drawn into the unfathomable, ineffable embrace of eternal love. Faced with the realization that we are not perfect, we acknowledge the need for purification of some sort before we can enter into the presence of the all-holy. We cannot achieve this purification ourselves: it must be done for us and in us.

The metaphor of purgatory (for it must be a metaphor in this life, borrowing from the language of common speech) is useful in describing this condition of both desire and lack. By dying to our old self and moving more fully into God, we become more aware of our sinfulness, disorder, and disharmony. This heightened aware-ness and gradual loss of our ego-self in the loving presence of God may be described as purgatory. This encounter is deeply humili-ating, painful, and purifying for the ego, but it is also the only way by which we can truly die to our old self and be born into our true Self in God. Purgatory *is* in fact God's love purifying, enlighten-ing, liberating, freeing, and bringing us to perfection.[12] When we work with the biblical models of people who have undergone this radical change, we can better understand where the path leads. Similarly, the Enneagram helps us understand where we ourselves are most likely to get 'de-railed' in our attempts to reach wholeness.

To see it this way is to realize that our purification springs not from a need for punishment but out of the depths of Divine Love, which wants to free us from the accumulations of our false identity. Similarly, hell arises out of our freedom to reject what is lovely and good and turn towards what we know to be self-serving. One of the Enneagram's greatest insights is showing us how to reverse this tendency and work to develop the misused aspects of our personalities. Nevertheless, we may indeed fashion our own hell by setting ourselves permanently at odds with the very love of our divine Maker. This condition would then constitute a form of metaphysical schizophrenia in which we reject the divine irrevocable love, and engage in an everlasting struggle to escape the inescapable. Our work in this lifetime is to embrace more and more that which we cannot escape, the love of God, who has been called the "hound of heaven" who pursues us down the narrow alleyways and into our darkest corners. Cornered by such a 'hound', we discover that what we have been running from is in fact our true Essence which is always and ever held in the divine embrace.

Transformation and the World

"God does not ask for help, God asks for you."

– *Cloud of Unknowing*, ch. 2

In combining the many aspects of the work of inner transformation, the Enneagram has a message not only for individuals seeking to find balance in their lives, but also for groups, peoples, and nations in a world fast becoming a global village where instant communication is possible. The Enneagram constitutes a path, a journey, a life and way of living. It has aptly been called "the work," whether for an individual or a community, resulting in transformation and openness. The transformation is accomplished not just through our own efforts but through an awakening of the Divine Spirit which dwells in and through our innermost being.

This is why the author of *The Cloud of Unknowing* could assert with absolute confidence that "God does not ask for help." What is desired instead is *us*, our cooperation with and assent to the Spirit of love and creativity in the world and in our hearts. It has often been said that God helps those who help themselves, but perhaps a clearer statement would be that God helps those who let God help them. This applies to individuals as well as to humanity as a whole. Our individual and our collective transformation allows God to show us more clearly the divine image in which we are made. We discover that we are not our personality. Underneath the layers which form what Merton and others have called the 'false self' lies our true Self, that part of us which bears the divine image. As we live more and more out of our true Self, and do not allow the false self to have its way and encourage our delusions, the divine image in us unfolds like a beautiful flower opening towards the sun.

One tool which can help us cooperate with this process is the Enneagram. In dealing with the whole person, and acknowledging the weaknesses to which we are susceptible, it gives us models for various paths of transformation. In this it is fully compatible with other ways of working on the inner life. For a Christian, observing its movements towards integration and unity will easily align with the desire to model one's life on the fullness of humanity found in Christ, the one in whom all things balance and are complete, and in whom can be found the true destiny of our lives. The Enneagram's focus on undertaking our own movement into wholeness points naturally, therefore, to greater union with Christ. If we integrate our heads, hearts and bodies, focusing on our Essence, then we are truly living an abundant life, transforming ourselves day by day into the image of God which we are.

For some, the popularity of the Enneagram today makes it seem like just another "new age" fad. But for many who have chosen to explore and work with it more deeply, it has been transformative, helping them understand not only their own lives but the complexities of human nature in its great diversity as well. For some people, much of the attraction of exploring the Enneagram lies in a systematic approach to "finding one's number" and then discovering which behaviours are healthy (or unhealthy) for that particular space. Each number, or type, is prone to specific virtues and pitfalls. Often we discover a deep connection between the two, and what had once been our greatest difficulty can be turned into our greatest gift. The preliminary step for most students of the Enneagram is to determine one's basic motivation and from that to work towards discovering one's "type." All of this is a beginning point, but the real work of the Enneagram is to help us understand and discover the path to our wholeness and to begin or continue our work of personal integration and transformation. It is a tool for effecting both personal and social transformations, and requires a sensitivity to the gifts of each person and to the unique challenges each one faces. As early as 1902, the psychologist and student of religious experience William James pointed out that when we are attempting to classify human personalities, "most cases are mixed cases, and we should not treat our classifications with too much respect."[13] We need to bear this caveat in mind when claiming that a person or character (including ourselves!) represents a specific type on the Enneagram.

The Enneagram becomes useful in exploring different characters in the Hebrew and Christian scriptures as representative "types" of each of the Enneagram's nine spaces. The Jewish and Christian traditions, as well as many other world religions, have devoted time and energy to understanding the diversity of what constitutes blessing and sin in our lives. Both the Hebrew and Christian texts in particular have portrayed quite specifically the covenantal relationship between God and humans, and have also lamented the breaking of this relationship at various times in our human history. Other world religions also proclaim the presence of the Absolute within each person, and acknowledge that this Divine Presence is often clouded or even apparently eclipsed by our human nature. Whatever tradition or system we embrace, we encounter some form of description of the rupture of our relationship with the Divine, and how within each person there arises the need for conversion and redemption, what has often been referred to as "doing the Work." Within and outside of traditional religions, the beginning of the new millennium is bursting with movements which invite people to discover their spirituality and to explore it without fear, and to question ideas which have long been accepted but which for some now appear to be addressing questions we are no longer asking.

How this will all settle down cannot be predicted. What we do know, however, is that influencing our world and its future lies in our own power. By cracking open the structures and traditions which have served so many people in the past, many are finding not a rotten core but a germinating seed of new life. Through re-examining their own traditions, free from the fears of questioning what they have been told, these searchers are often rediscovering their spiritual lives and beginning to live them more freely and fully. They begin to know from within what Genesis describes as the Divine Spirit hovering over their inner chaos and bringing forth light and life, knowing that they bear the divine image within their own being. The words they have read take on new meanings and become flesh in their own bodies and psyches, and the teachings they have heard move from laws to life-giving encounters with the Divine Presence within.

The Enneagram is both a practical and useful tool for facilitating this inner work. It embodies truths from the scientific world and metaphors from the poets' views of life. It works with the total person, acknowledging that we are Head, Heart, and Body, and that these three parts of ourselves can be brought into balance and harmony so that our lives will be happy and a source of blessing to others and to our world.

Psychology, Poetry and Physics

"Imagination is the faculty by which we can
picture anything, past as well as present."

– *Cloud of Unknowing*, ch. 65

A great deal of the current interest in both personal and cosmic transformation springs from the work of Carl Jung (1875-1961) and his followers, and more recently from modern physicists, all of whom have helped us appreciate the importance of working towards integration and wholeness, whether through understanding more clearly how archetypes and dreams reveal the workings of the inner self, or through probing the interconnectedness between the nature of matter and energy. We need to examine what modern sciences such as psychology, anthropology, cosmology and physics tell us about what it means to be 'adam', the Bible's name for us as children of earth. Poetry, too, has always known how to address the deepest mysteries of human existence, and teaches us new ways of looking at the world and ourselves.

The increasing compartmentalization found in specialized studies and disciplines today may owe much of its beginning to that time when the new sciences, reacting to biblical literalism (as evidenced in the case of Galileo), prompted the disciplines to drift away into separate paths in pursuit of knowledge. More and more, they lost contact with each other, and in their individual searches for knowledge they often forgot the larger search for wisdom. As Einstein reminded us, "Science without religion is lame; religion without science is blind." The two need each other to maintain a healthy body of experience and knowledge. Pope John Paul II has said that "science can purify religion from error and superstition; religion can purify science from idolatry and false absolutes. Each can draw the other into a wider world, a world in which both can flourish."[14]

At this time in our human history the need for interdisciplinary dialogue could not be greater. We see the fragmentation of disciplines clearly in parts of academia today, in which the multiplication of departments and increased specialization within them often makes it difficult to understand one another. The ivory tower becomes a metaphorical descendant of the Tower of Babel, with its division of peoples and loss of the ability to speak a common language. There is a corresponding symbol, however, which presents the hope of restoration of communication. In the biblical account of Pentecost in the Book of Acts, the wind and flame of the Spirit sweep through the people gathered from many different nations and enable them all to understand each other. The metaphor works on an individual level as well as a communal one: early in our own history we undergo a separation from our original unity and wholeness, and need to find a way towards healthy integration once again. The Enneagram seeks to recreate this return to wholeness by bringing head, heart, and body together into a balanced experience of life. It helps us to return to and remember who we essentially are beyond or beneath our layers of acquired personality.

The approaches of religion, science, and psychology are not therefore as disparate as they might at first seem. Some of the greatest modern scientists, not necessarily known to be believers in a denominational sense, seem to be expressing themselves in terms reminiscent of the great mystics of the past. As a result, discussions in modern physics often sound very close to the language of theology, and psychological explanations often appeal to the order of reason. We hear scientists speak of particles arising spontaneously in a vacuum and think of God creating the universe from nothing. Both the scientists and the storytellers appeal to our imaginations as they attempt in their own ways to render the unseen to us. By providing metaphors which try to explain the inner and outer worlds, they are in fact invaluable allies in accessing the evolving and vast new knowledge and consciousness of the third millennium.

We have learned from both psychology and anthropology that the many symbols of our unconscious, which Jung called archetypes, as well as other projections of our psychic lives, turn up in our dreams and in the myths and fairy tales of every culture and civilization. The biblical stories are not immune from these patterns. They operate in the same way as our dreams and our stories. Jung summed up their power when he explained the potency of archetypes:

> The impact of an archetype, whether it takes the form of immediate experience or is expressed through the spoken word, stirs us because it summons up a voice that is stronger than our own. Whoever speaks in primordial images speaks with a thousand voices; he enthralls and overpowers, while at the same time he lifts the idea he is seeking to express out of the occasional and the transitory into the realm of the ever-enduring. He transmutes our personal destiny into the destiny of [hu]mankind, and evokes in us all those beneficent forces that ever and anon have enabled humanity to find a refuge from every peril and to outlive the longest night.[15]

The Bible is one of the greatest repositories of these stories which stir us and connect our story to a more universal one. Because the mystery of our being is ultimately ineffable, and cannot be directly conveyed by words, the biblical narratives, like other sacred writings, use stories, myths, parables and a variety of images to convey truths too deep for ordinary language. They are multifaceted and cannot be explained by simple equations of meaning. Their archetypes reach deeply into our unconscious and touch our souls at such depths that they may take a long while to rise to the surface. Such momentous stories as those of Adam and Eve in the Garden of Eden, Hagar's banishment, Abraham and Sarah leaving their home, Moses and Miriam being pursued by their enemies and facing the Red Sea, David dancing before the Ark, Mary singing her Magnificat, Peter betraying and confessing his love, and Mary running from the empty tomb to announce the Resurrection touch us at levels beyond our normal fascination with narrative and a good story.

Pointing a Finger at the Moon

> "One can feel this nothing more easily than see it."
>
> – *Cloud of Unknowing*, ch. 65

The stories of these characters, and many others like them in the Bible, speak to us of something more than what they are "about." Written as prose, they cry out to be read as poetry. The distinction we often make between poet and prophet was insignificant for the ancient world. Poetry dealt with serious matters and conveyed them more powerfully than facts ever could.[16] The stories in scripture appeal to our understanding and experience of human beings in diverse emotional states at the same time that they speak to us about ourselves and our inner life. If we see Abraham and Sarah, Moses and Mary, Deborah and Martha, not solely as figures in biblical history but also as representing aspects of ourselves, we begin to understand their stories as intimately connected with our own stories, and they can become mentors in teaching us about our inner lives. Their stories are particular examples of universal narratives about faith and meaning, and all of them point beyond themselves to something much greater than their immediate details. The sacred stories become one of our most significant channels for accessing both the divine Source and the ultimate experience of life.[17]

If we forget to read poetically, we run the risk of turning an icon into an idol.[18] An icon draws us into it and then through it to the mystery beyond itself which it represents. An idol, however, stops with itself, and we concentrate on the object rather than the reality it points to. As with the proverbial finger pointing at the moon, we can focus on the finger and never see the moon. To convey the mysteries of the cosmos, we need indirect and metaphorical language. Beliefs and doctrines can become idols, whereas poetry always knows it is an icon. We cannot use what one writer has called "precision instruments" to dissect the mystery when what is called for is, rather, an "evocative idiom" to probe it.[19]

This has long been known by those who have undertaken the Spiritual Exercises of St. Ignatius. For over 400 years, people have used these exercises to meditate on scriptural events with their minds, their feelings, and their senses. Focusing on the events of the life of Christ, those following this way of prayer, through their thoughts, imagination and 'application of the senses,' are encouraged to enter more fully into the lived experience of the gospels. The scriptures are not read as 'just stories' but as a means for personal conversion and growth. The persons and events come alive in the meditator's own life and transform his or her consciousness into a closer union with the Divine. We need to go beyond many "words about the Word"[20] to actually hearing the voice of the Speaker of the words. This alone keeps one from spiritual deafness and leads to compassion and action. Ultimately, it is not our theology or our hermeneutical methods which will open scripture for us but the degree of love we bring to it and the desire to live out of that love.[21]

Besides the language of poetry and story, we can also look to the insights of physics for help in understanding both the Bible and the Enneagram as potential sources of transformative energy. One of the most exciting aspects of modern physics is the intimate interrelation between matter and energy. As bodily beings, we are not immune from these laws of the physical world. We say that matter is composed of atoms, each of which has a nucleus which contains neutrons and protons, and electrons which orbit around this centre. No one has seen an atom, just as no one has seen an archetype, yet both are patterns which help us understand and interpret reality. We know that the electrons in an atom do not all

lie the same distance from the nucleus of the atom. Like a minia-
ture solar system, they move around the centre at various distances. But unlike the orbital distances in the solar system, the
distances of electrons in an atom from their centre can change.
They can jump from one orbital shell to another. When they are
excited, they jump away from the nucleus; when they settle down,
they return to their own shells. They return at differing rates, and
seem to have a preference for certain shells over others.

If we consider the Enneagram as a sort of atom of the psyche,
we can say that it has nine orbital shells, one for each of its "types".
Like electrons orbiting our centre, we, too, have preferred shells
of movement. These represent where we feel most at home and
how we live our ordinary lives. When some stimulus intervenes,
whether delightful or stressful, our "orbit" of movement may
change. We might become excited or stressed or inspired, and we
can then use that energy to jump out of our familiar orbit and move
into a new way of being. Eventually, when the impulse or stress
is removed, we find that we 'come to ourselves,' and we settle back
into the orbit in which we are most at home.

The model works well for all literary characters, too, not just
those found in the Bible. What makes for plot development in a literary work is the encounter with something extraordinary in the
life of a character. A crisis or intrusion forces the character either
into a new way of being and interacting, or else the character rejects
the encounter and continues in the same old path. Even so-called
'slice of life' stories in which nothing 'happens' follow this pattern,
for what 'happens' in them is the unfolding of a seemingly normal
course of human events. Choosing to do nothing in response is
another form of a character's making a decision, in this case, a decision to not act. The biblical stories, however, most often show an
intervention in the character's life which causes a major overhaul in
how he or she sees things. Frequently, the intervener is God who
intrudes, often suddenly and unexpectedly, into an ordinary life

and demands a change in its direction. Moses encountering the Burning Bush, Samuel hearing the voice of God calling his name at night, and Elizabeth feeling her unborn son leap in her womb, all change direction after this divine "stimulus." None of them returns to the old way of living.

All or Nothing

> "Who is it then who is calling it 'nothing'? Our outer self, to be sure, not our inner. Our inner self calls it 'All', for through it we are learning the secret of all things, physical and spiritual alike, without having to consider every single one separately on its own."
>
> *– Cloud of Unknowing*, ch. 68

Modern physics teaches us that what we perceive as a clear separation between matter and energy is really an illusion. Because something looks 'solid' to us, we think it is more matter than energy. If we bang our foot against a piece of furniture, we find it difficult to believe that we actually encountered more space than solid material. Yet if we were to remove the space in any object of matter, even a very large one, the particles which comprise the object would collapse to an infinitesimally small dot.

Our 'material' world is in fact more space than matter, more nothingness than substance. Out of this nothingness, however, particles arise. What we call a vacuum turns out to be an "all-nourishing abyss"[22] rather than an inert nothingness. Space which appears to us empty is actually not emptiness but fullness, a fullness from which everything arises.[23] The bottom line of the universe seems to be not matter but energy, the 'ultimate stuff of the universe,' and yet it is not really 'stuff' at all. Subatomic particles, it turns out, are not *made* of energy but they *are* energy.[24] The scientific paradox that particles are energy has implications for all fields of human knowledge. If in fact what we cannot see is the very ground of our existence, beyond space and time, then we can take quite literally

St. Paul's statement that "what can be seen is temporary, but what cannot be seen is eternal" (2 Corinthians 4:18).

When we apply these ideas to both the Bible and the Enneagram, we do not find any inconsistencies. The opening chapter of Genesis describes how matter arises out of a "formless void" (Genesis 1:2) by the energy of God's word. Matter proceeds from nothingness and is now seen in the magnificent diversity of all creation. When we look at the diagram of the Enneagram, we see another illustration of this.

FIGURE 1

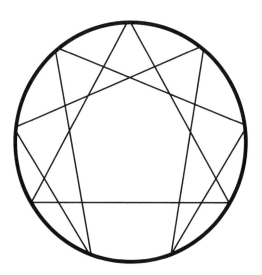

The nine points lie on the outer edges of the diagram. The symbol itself is made up of a circle, a triangle, and a hexad, the angular figure formed by the six lines not included in the triangle. The nine points are fixed. It is not on the points but in the spaces between them, and the variety of possible movements between the numbers, where we ultimately locate our transformational growth. Like matter, the points are static representations; the movement between them, like energy, is what leads us to new places and transformation, not the fixed points on the diagram. The points are places from which we leave; if we allow one to capture us, we will be arrested and imprisoned in our attachment to 'our' number. We will be violating our very nature, which is movement and growth. Caged in our 'type', we may not even realize that the apparent solidity of our familiar space is an illusion which needs to be shattered. Sadly, we can spend our entire lives in our prisons, believing we are free. Yet if energy and movement are the underlying realities of the cosmos, we surely cannot afford to ignore them.

Reading the Bible

"All the visions that we see here in human shape
have spiritual meanings."

– Cloud of Unknowing, ch. 58

Even before the Bible was read, it was narrated, sung, and taught. Since the early days of printing and right up to the present, it has never stopped being a bestseller. But many people are perplexed by it, and are uncertain how to read it. Those who determine to read it through from Genesis to Revelation often bog down somewhere around Leviticus. Even those who persist often wonder if they need to know details of ancient history, language, and archaeology to read it fruitfully. Some find its usefulness chiefly in regarding it as a manual or quick reference book for solving life's problems. There are even editions which prescribe for the reader specific verses to read in various situations or difficulties.

In recent years, however, many people are showing renewed interest in reading the Bible not for its quick solutions but to deepen their understanding of themselves as human beings and to discover their relationship with the Divine. The great literary critic Northrup Frye, borrowing William Blake's phrase, referred to the Bible as "the great code" for deciphering not only western art but all of western civilization. Codes are often puzzles with answers, but the biblical "code" provides us not with easy answers but with hard questions about what constitutes human consciousness. It needs to be read on its own terms, not as history or literature or philosophy, but as sacred story. Its spiritual teachings are hidden in its stories, psalms, and parables. It is not primarily a record of events but a group of stories which have stood the test of time, and each story told "grips the imagination, impregnates the heart, and animates the spirit within."[25] Ultimately, that is what gives any story its staying power, and the biblical stories which have been told and retold for thousands of years survive because they still speak to the human heart today. The scriptures do not idealize human history or cater to current ideologies. People are honestly and frankly presented in the raw, with their weaknesses, distortions and foibles as well as their capacity for scaling sublime heights. A richer or more authentic source of human experience would be very difficult to find.

Enjoying the Kernel

"Therefore let us strip off the husk, and eat
the sweet kernel."

– Cloud of Unknowing, ch. 58

The diverse biblical characters can be seen to represent aspects of ourselves, both savoury and unsavoury; they are brave and beautiful but also fearful and violent. They are loyal, angry, generous, strong, changeable, resentful and inquisitive. Their stories have endured because they are *our* stories, couched in the language of folk-tale and epic, pilgrimage and war. To know their characters is to begin to know ourselves, for we all share the universal human archetype.

This is not a new but rather an ancient way of reading these stories. Philo Judaeus of Alexandria (b. 25 B.C.E.[26]) noticed that the human archetype was certainly present in the book of Genesis.

In his work on the allegorical interpretation of Genesis, he regarded the narratives in Genesis as illustrating a history of the soul from its creation, through its fall, and to its restoration. Each character was seen as representing a stage a person might relate to in terms of the process of her or his own soul's growth. Philo maintained that the soul in its movements often swings between the two poles of having confidence in God and having confidence in the self. The narratives of Genesis would resonate with any point in one's life. In the virtuous person, the soul would know Divine Wisdom as the mother of its goodness. To know Wisdom in this way is to make one's home with her and to be one with God, who is the Source and the ground of all being. The soul would have confidence in God alone. The person who seeks the fullness of life only in the self and in choices made without reference to God, however, is represented in the story of Adam and Eve when they make the choice to disobey God. Thus the opening chapters of Genesis set the stage for reading the biblical stories in a personal and vital way.

To lose sight of this inner dimension and to read these narratives as simple plots involving only historical personages and not our very selves may well be to misread them totally. The richness of these narratives and the whole of the wisdom tradition invite us to probe them for insights into our own lives and to let them steer us towards the wholeness of our beings: bodies, minds, and souls. Growth in our spirituality calls for the involvement of the total person, an inner transformation based on a turning or movement of conversion away from our egocentric compulsions or false personalities and towards the centre or ground of our being. Unless the changes are more than behavioural, we are simply "moving the furniture around."[27]

Along with proclaiming the representative nature of biblical characters goes the assumption that each one reflects some aspect of ourselves, and that their stories are also our stories. Insofar as each one of them 'is' also 'us', as we read their narratives and interpret them, we realize that the stories are also revealing and interpreting *us* to ourselves. This has long been acknowledged in the Passover seder, the great Jewish celebration of freedom. Each year, the festival recalls in story and ritual what God did not only for the Jews who were enslaved in Egypt but also what God *continues to do* for all who celebrate the feast. The release from bondage into freedom did not occur just once in an ancient history but is repeated every time someone throws off an enslavement or obstacle to freedom and inner liberation. God's deliverance is re-enacted in many moments of every day.

This is not a new way of reading scripture. As early as the third century, the Christian theologian Origen commented that "you must not think that all these things happened only in earlier times. In fact, all these things come true in *you* in a mystical way." This method of interpreting scriptural texts (known as scriptural exegesis) which moves from the literal reading to the spiritual meaning or understanding of a text has been popular since at least the time of Origen. This way of reading teaches us to move progressively more deeply into a verse or short passage, moving from the letter to the spirit, which includes the symbolic, the mystical, and the cosmic aspects of the text. This tradition is in keeping with St. Paul's assertion that "the letter kills, but the spirit gives life" (2 Corinthians 3:6). The letter of the law alone can lead to legalism and hardness of heart when it tries to freeze the text into a single meaning. Sacred writing is not one-dimensional but alive and able to inspire us to growth and change. Before the texts were written down and preserved on the scrolls of the synagogues and later on the parchments of many monasteries, they were alive in an oral tradition which nurtured and shaped their hearers. Story-telling, singing, and dancing kept alive the memory of divine intervention in history. The Bible owes its origin to these living traditions which supported the faith of the people.

The writing down of these stories and texts established a uniformity which still retained the sense of the living tradition that inspired them. Though they were read out loud, they still appealed to the imagination and the spirit. The literal sense was the springboard into other levels of reading and hearing the scriptures. Such movement from a literal to a spiritual reading has long been observed in the practice of *lectio divina*, or "divine reading", originally taught in monasteries and now practised by many in the non-monastic world as well. When we undertake this form of reading, we begin with the words on the page. Reading them slowly and deliberately constitutes the *lectio* portion of the process as we address the literal narrative or passage before us. From this first direct reading, we move into *meditatio*, or thinking over what we have read, pondering and discerning its implications for our own lives. This in turn leads to the next stage, *oratio*, in which we follow our impulse to pray over whatever insights or inner movements we might have reached. Finally, we arrive at the last stage, *contemplatio*, the point at which we rest in the Spirit amid all that we have just experienced, and are able to be still in the silent presence of God. *Lectio divina* engages the whole person in its process: we ask ourselves what is being said, what we are thinking, what feelings arise, and what we need to do about them. It is a holistic and transformative process which we undertake again and again as we experience the scriptures as a "living" text. We are doing a very similar exercise when we read the biblical characters through our knowledge of the Enneagram. The Head, Heart, and Body are all engaged as we reflect on their stories as aspects of ourselves and as images which can lead us to our own wholeness.

The first, or literal, sense of scripture is regarded as the most outwardly accessible, while the moral or spiritual sense is perceived inwardly. Whereas history and narrative both tend to point us to the outer world of persons and events, the stories of the Bible, much like similar stories in myths and fairy-tales, direct us to the inner world of growth and maturation. To follow their guidance, we need to move beyond the literal level and into the allegorical or spiritual sense of what we are reading. As St. Gregory the Great (d. 604) put it, "We must seek in the material, or external, words whatever is within...By this means they will become for the reader the pulley by which he is lifted up, not crushed by its weight. The letter covers the inner meaning as the husk covers the seed; to understand in the spirit is to penetrate through the husk to the inner meaning."[28] To limit our comments to a literal understanding of the various narratives of the biblical stories would keep us focused on the surfaces when what we desire are the depths.

Seeing the fuller picture often entails letting go of what we saw the last time we looked at the same picture. The picture itself has not changed but we are not the same as we were then. Even if only a short time has passed since we last looked at a particular biblical passage, we are different, perhaps only slightly, but the change in us is a sign of movement, either into the light or into deeper shadows. The Enneagram is a dynamic symbol of such change and can be a useful tool in reading the biblical narratives. Just as a person does not always occupy the same space in its system but moves from point to point, so, too, the biblical characters can often be assessed as belonging to several different spaces, depending on the perspective from which one views them. They are presented here in the spaces which seem most appropriate for what we are told about them. However, some people may wish to explore how these characters could also be placed in different spaces, and such exploration is to be encouraged. Expanding the possibilities of interpretation encourages us to remain open to the immense complexity of an individual as well as to the vast diversity among human beings.

The biblical characters represent a reliable record of how God has been present in relationships with human beings right from the dawn of humanity. Practically speaking, almost every imaginable human experience is related in the pages of scripture, and the wisdom of centuries is reflected in its stories.

In addition to reading these stories and studying them from the inside out, we can apply them to our own experiences to assist the process of our individual transformation. This requires some genuine knowledge of who we are. The words alone are not enough. The truth of the biblical teaching lies deeper than its obvious surface meanings. We can borrow the "Four Reliances" of Buddhism as a useful reminder to ourselves of how to read the Bible and make it a part of our transformational path:

> Rely on the message of the teacher, not on his personality;
> Rely on the meaning, not just on the words;
> Rely on the real meaning, not on the provisional one;
> Rely on your wisdom mind, not on your ordinary, judgmental mind.[29]

The Enneagram

> "This work demands great serenity, an integrated
> and pure disposition, in soul and in body."
>
> *– Cloud of Unknowing*, ch. 41

It has sometimes been suggested that the great divide which afflicts the Eastern and Western worlds in our time is a split between the head-centred West and the heart-centred East. This may appear an oversimplification in today's context of an emerging global culture but it still has real merit in helping us understand the gift which the Enneagram offers to all cultures. Based on the human being's three centres of Head, Heart, and Body, the work of the Enneagram shows us how to bring them into balance and move ourselves towards wholeness. It unites thoughts, feelings, and actions without privileging one over the others. Yet, in our experiencing the world and the ways in which we address it, we discover that we do in fact usually prefer one of the three centres over the other two. The Enneagram practice shows us how we can begin to integrate the other two centres and undertake our own transformational process. As an instrument useful in personal transformation, the Enneagram seeks to establish or restore the balance between the intellect, the feelings, and the body. Such a restoration is essential to the healing and the integration of the individual and of the community.

FIGURE 2

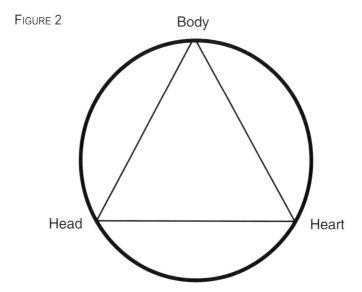

Each Centre has its own unique energy, brain, and purpose:

- the Body: to live, to survive, to move, to create, to do;
- the Heart: to relate, to feel, to be with, to connect with others;
- the Head: to understand, to see, to think, to make sense.

Each Centre is referred to in different terms:

- the Body as the creative, moving, or instinctive centre;
- the Heart as the feeling or relating centre;
- the Head as the intellectual or thinking centre.

Without any one of these centres, we would not be human, and each requires the other two for us to remain alive.

Three is not an arbitrary choice for the number of centres in a person. In classic Greek, three is usually the number for the completion of a process. We see this reflected in the Christian Bible in Jesus' foretelling that he would be raised "on the third day" (Matthew 16:21), in John's gospel telling us that the wedding at Cana occurred "on the third day" (John 2:1), and in Peter's threefold denial of Jesus (John 18:27). In the Hebrew scriptures it is the number of days and nights that Jonah spends inside the belly of the large fish, signifying his encounter with God after running away (Jonah 1:17). G. I. Gurdjieff (b. ca. 1875), who brought the symbol of the Enneagram into the modern world,[30] talked about the "Law of Three" as a basic principle of the physical and cultural world.

In major world religions and belief systems, we also find the number three representing the divine. In Buddhism, there are the Three Jewels or Refuges expressed as Buddha, Dhamma, and Sangha; in Hinduism, there are Brahma, Vishnu, and Shiva; in Christianity, God is Father, Son, and Holy Spirit; in Islam, the qualities of God are expressed as power, knowledge, and life; in Judaism, the Kabbalistic body from the Tree of Life contains Daat, Tiferet, and Yesod. Cosmology also upholds three laws in the fundamental order of the universe: differentiated centres, subjectivity, and communion, of which the absence of any one would cause the universe to collapse.

In the Christian tradition, the Desert Father Evagrius Ponticus (b. 345), in his book on contemplative prayer, pondered the spiritual significance of joining a triangular and a hexagonal figure together and related their numerological meanings to the spiritual life.[31] Later, in the 13th century, the Spaniard Ramón Lull (d. 1315), who was later beatified, developed a diagram of the nine qualities of God, represented in a circle, all of which are linked to one another as well as to the centre of the circle, which represents God's Essence. A second diagram of his depicts a circle containing three triangles which reflect the relative nearness or distance between God and God's creatures. Together, these diagrams may be considered early Christian prototypes of the Enneagram as it is depicted today.[32]

Mathematics also tells us that three is the smallest odd prime number and is associated with stability. For example, a two-legged stool will fall over; it needs the third leg for balance. Similarly, a three-sided figure (triangle) cannot be bent at its vertices because altering its shape will destroy it. A four-sided figure (rectangle), on the other hand, can indeed be altered by collapsing opposite angles in the figure to form a parallelogram or trapezoid.[33]

In the human person, three is also the number for stability and balance. We find it in the traditional language of speaking of the person as being made up of body, mind, and soul. The three Centres of the Enneagram represent the three parts of ourselves that must be aligned and balanced so that we can become persons who are living icons of our creator. We can reverse any personal destabilization by undertaking the serious and often difficult work of transformation of self. We can then begin to align all our energies and gradually bring ourselves back into balance. The Enneagram provides us with an effective model of how to go about doing this.

The Enneagram is most commonly represented by a diagram connecting nine points in the following way:

Figure 3

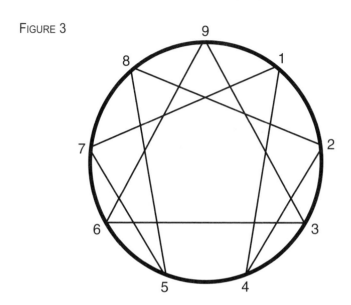

8, 9, 1 : Body energy
2, 3, 4 : Heart energy
5, 6, 7 : Head energy

Each of the three Centres of Head, Heart, and Body on the Enneagram contains three of its nine types. The Head centre is represented by the Fives, Sixes, and Sevens; the Heart centre by the Twos, Threes, and Fours; and the Body centre by the Eights, Nines, and Ones. These are often referred to as the Preferred centres for each type. Many if not most writings and discussions of the Enneagram are organized around the types associated with each of these highly used, or preferred, centres. By regrouping the types in a less familiar but equally effective way, we can perhaps better understand the interplay of energies which we all contain. While one 'number' or 'type' may be considered our home base, we rarely stay there all the time, but wander from energy to energy depending on our situation and our needs.

Our 'number' is like a speed bump on the road: it slows us down when we are there but it does not stop our movement through it to other locations. To incorporate all the nine energies in perfect balance would be to smooth out all our speed bumps. In such a state of inner harmony and balance we would live each moment deeply connected to our divine centre. We would experience the inner rest of knowing we are in that centre, and we would also experience the dynamic movement outwards from that centre into our daily lives.

Each type on the Enneagram is usually described by names or labels which indicate the nature of that particular type. While there is an agreed upon set of characteristics for each type, the labels used may differ:

FIGURE 4

| | Names given to types by | | |
	Hurley-Donson	Palmer	Riso-Hudson
One	Achiever	Perfectionist	Reformer
Two	Helper	Giver	Helper
Three	Succeeder	Performer	Achiever
Four	Individualist	Tragic-romantic	Individualist
Five	Observer	Observer	Investigator
Six	Guardian	Devil's Advocate	Loyalist
Seven	Dreamer	Epicure	Enthusiast
Eight	Confronter	Boss	Challenger
Nine	Preservationist	Mediator	Peace-maker

The nine personality types within the three triads of the Enneagram converge admirably with the call of scripture to turn from vice in all its most basic forms and to strive for the virtues which the Enneagram represents as the nine Faces of God: perfection, loving service, work, creativity, wisdom, loyalty, joy, compassion and peace. The Bible is filled with injunctions to get out of the ego-fixations of the nine spaces (though it does not use such modern language) and to move closer to God. It encourages us to struggle against the distortions or passions that are the common heritage of human beings, and to overcome our instinctive or learned compulsions with the help of divine grace.

Obviously, when using the Enneagram in our daily lives, we can determine more accurately how we ourselves live out of each space than we can do this for anyone else, including characters in a text. Biblical characters may readily be found as exemplars of each of the nine types. We are assuming that each character can be treated as representing a particular space without our necessarily having to know any biographical or historical data connected with that particular personality. When we accept these characters as our mentors, their lives take on a relevance for our own, and their stories illumine the events and choices of our own lives.

We must not forget that the "points" of the Enneagram are merely representational, and that we are not dealing with a two-dimensional system when we speak of the movement from one energy to another. The diagram is a prosaic attempt to depict what must be treated poetically. We need to keep in mind that the Enneagram is about change and growth, and about moving from habitual and lifeless ways of being to awakening to new life within. This is of course consistent with the Bible's continual call to conversion and change of heart. In the gospels, the call to repentance, or conversion, is addressed not to those who are well but to those in need of a (spiritual) physician: not to the righteous but to sinners (Matthew 9:12-13). It involves more than just a behavioural change. The conversion, or metanoia, which scripture speaks of affects all three of our centres. The word *metanoia* includes in its meaning a change of mind, the feeling of pain or remorse, and a turning about for a new beginning. It is both slow and sudden, always transforming us yet bringing about instant changes. One cannot be converted "just a little" any more than one can be "just a little pregnant." While we are transformed gradually, the change in our overall direction is a total about-face.[34] Understood properly, therefore, the biblical insistence on repentance means nothing less than undertaking the transformative work of the entire person in our three centres, slowly over a lifetime, and instantly at each moment.

Things as They Are

> "Work with eager enjoyment rather than with brute force."

> – *Cloud of Unknowing*, ch. 41

In a book which refers to each point on the Enneagram as representing a particular "Holy Idea", A.H. Almaas has succinctly pointed out that all of the Holy Ideas actually constitute a view of reality seen with the great clarity which is only possible from an egoless perspective.[35] Each Holy Idea represents a purging of the false self which allows some aspect of the divine to shine through. Freed from defining ourselves solely by our single point on the Enneagram, we can then absorb the Holy Ideas embodied in the other eight points as well. If we do not cling to our point as if our view were the only reality, then we arrive at an unobscured vision of things as they really are.[36] Reality cannot be limited to our own ideas of what we want it to be; we need to learn to let go of our attachments to our preconceptions, and allow Reality itself to show us what it is. Both Eastern and Western traditions recognize the role of the three centres in the human person, though the West has sometimes tended to minimize the importance of the Body and to elevate the role of the Head, while the East has long used the Body to teach what the Head is not able to know. Both traditions utilize the Heart but in different ways, the West generally preferring to speak of emotions, and the East speaking mostly of compassion.

The Enneagram's way of transformation honours diverse traditions and systems without asking us to abandon our own culture or beliefs. Because it deals with the human person regardless of status or culture, it can go about its work of providing food for the mind, consolation for the heart, and honouring of the body. The great wisdom traditions of both the East and the West have reminded us again and again and in various ways that we ordinarily do not see things as they are: we see things as *we* are. We need to understand who we are and how we got that way, and examine many of our easily held assumptions about ourselves and our world. It is quite difficult to realize that our reality is not also everyone else's. Like the proverbial blind men trying to describe the elephant, we often discover that our experience is very unlike that of another person, even though we have all touched the same elephant. The Enneagram can help us understand how we perceive and respond to the world, and also how other people perceive the same world quite differently. If it did no more than that, it would still be an invaluable tool for promoting peace among families and among nations.

Yearning for the Divine

"Humility is nothing else but a true knowledge
and awareness of oneself as one really is."

– *Cloud of Unknowing*, ch. 13

The humility which derives from knowing we are humus, or earth, opens us to deeper understanding of our relationships to ourselves, each other, our planet, and the universe. Humility goes hand-in-hand with the knowledge that human consciousness, while arising from the earth, is also expanding into an understanding of our interconnectedness to the entire universe and to our divine core. This is not a new concept. The psalms especially remind us that all creation is infused with its divine source:

> When you send forth your spirit, they are created;
> and you renew the face of the ground.

– Psalm 104:30

Or again,

> Let the floods clap their hands;
> let the hills sing together for joy
> at the presence of the LORD, for he is coming
> to judge the earth.

– Psalm 98:8-9

Yearning for union with its creator, all of nature, including human nature, seeks to return to its divine origin in a gradual divinization of the cosmos. Buddhism speaks of the nature of mind, or buddha mind, as "merely the immaculate / Looking naturally at itself."[37] Plato's writings describe the world we see as a shadow of the transcendent. The Athanasian Creed, which dates back to the fifth century C.E., proclaims humanity's union with the Godhead "not by conversion of the Godhead into flesh, but by taking of [humanity] into God."

In our own time, Pope John Paul II has spoken of the need for an anthropology which goes beyond its own limitations and moves towards this goal of the divinization of humanity.[38] This goal is consistent with some of the earliest Christian writings which speak not so much of sin and human weakness as of our being made in the image of God, and restored to the image of God through our union with Christ. As St. Paul writes: "It is no longer I who live, but it is Christ who lives in me" (Gal. 2:20). Being transformed into the image of Christ, which the Eastern Church calls 'deification' or 'divinization', is the goal of the Christian life. Our thirst for who we are, claims Abbot George of Grigoriou, is only satisfied when we achieve the goal of union with our Archetype, God.[39]

Using the Enneagram to awaken us to this possibility and to the direction of our transformation is thus putting it to very good Christian use. The Enneagram is aligned with all these traditions as well as with many others which seek to remind us that at our centre is a divine spark which can be fanned into flame and made to burn brightly both to illumine our inner nature and to enlighten the world in which we live.

A *Question of Balance*

"Take what comes!"

– Cloud of Unknowing, ch. 42

The nine "points" on the Enneagram represent nine different types of energy. We all have all nine energies within, but we do not use them all equally. Once we are able to discover which ones are misused, we can begin to develop them and bring them into balance with the ones we favour. Achieving such an internal balance promotes wholeness and happiness. The Enneagram's nine points are equally divided among three aspects, or centres, of the human person: the Head, Heart, and the Body, or Thinking, Feeling, and Doing. It should be obvious that everyone thinks, feels, and does, but what may be less apparent is that everyone also prefers one of the three centres, uses another to support it, and misuses the third. This third will be misused in such a way that it hinders our growth, and it is there that we must look closely to begin our work of transformation.

This book is therefore organized around our misused (sometimes referred to as repressed) centres. When a centre is misused, this does not mean it is unconscious or *un*used in an individual. It simply means that, of the three centres, the misused one is less developed than the centre we prefer and in which we feel at home. Because each type "lives" in a particular (preferred) centre, the other two centres are, in varying degrees, supportive of the first. Of these two other centres, one is usually more supportive while the other remains more in the background. Rather than enjoying its strength, our misused centre is best recognized through its underside, which may also be a part of what Jung refers to as our shadow. It represents not just what we might refuse to admit about ourselves, but also what we refuse or are reluctant to use, or what we use unproductively.[40] If our psyche is out of alignment, we need to look at our misused centre to understand how we might begin to restore ourselves to balance. It cannot be emphasized strongly enough that all the centres are necessary and vital. Ultimately, our goal is to bring all three into a balanced relationship so that we can regain our wholeness and live with energy, insight, and happiness. If we confine our knowledge of ourselves to understanding just one "space" on the Enneagram, we lose the search for that precious balance which integrates all the energies and constitutes stability and holiness.

Throughout this book, the goal is to encourage a sense of the totality of our personhood rather than to compartmentalize ourselves, which can readily inhibit our psychic growth and transformative work. Merely coming to greater understanding about ourselves is not enough; the Enneagram is about movement, not stasis, and it helps show us how to begin our turning away from the egocentric self and moving towards our divine centre.

The Hornevian Groups

The psychiatrist Karen Horney (1885-1952) did much useful work on neuroses and how they oppose healthy growth. She outlined three dominant categories of the human psyche which can inhibit our self-realization: she referred to persons who were either self-effacing, expansive, or resigned personality types.[41] While Horney's discussion of these types is mainly in terms of neurotic behaviours, she does focus on movement into healthy resolution of neuroses; her terms connote the shadow or undercurrents of the human psyche. Using her groupings to help us understand the misused centres in the Enneagram enables us to see more clearly how people prefer to interact with others: some will be "moving toward" people (self-effacing), others will be ready to interact with them in either positive or negative confrontations ("moving against" or expansive), while a third group is happiest when observing or standing back from people ("moving from" or resigned). Understanding when each social dynamic is at work in ourselves as well as in others is one of the basic observations useful in personal transformation and growth.

Enneagram teachers Kathy Hurley and Theodorre Donson refer to these groups as the Repressed Centres and they have been instrumental in applying this knowledge to expand our understanding of the Enneagram's dynamic.[42] Don Richard Riso and Russ Hudson refer to them as Hornevian triads.[43] In this book, we have chosen to translate Horney's terms somewhat differently while continuing to rely on much of her descriptions. We refer to them as compliant (Horney's "self-effacing"), assertive (Horney's "expansive"), and withdrawing (Horney's "resigned"). The terms also suggest the application of the Law of Three insofar as they indicate balance in the psyche. Assertive energy moves outwards, withdrawing energy pulls back, and compliant energy holds the tension in between.[44]

Together, the nine types give us a complete picture of the human self. In our moving towards others (compliance), our moving against others (assertiveness), and our pulling back from others (withdrawing), we experience the full range of possibilities through which we can be transformed. Whatever type-space we "prefer", all need to work together in an harmonious balance to call forth more fully the Divine image in each person.

Each misused centre contains three of the nine types. These three consist of one from each of the Thinking, Feeling, and Doing centres.

FIGURE 5

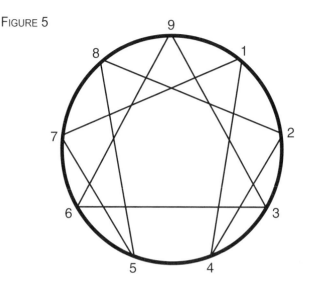

Compliants, Self-Effacing, Moving Towards: 1, 2, 6
• Ones comply to their inner critic
• Twos comply to their need to give
• Sixes comply to an outer authority

Assertives, Expansive, Moving Against: 3, 7, 8
• Threes assert their need to achieve
• Sevens assert their need to be free of pain
• Eights assert their need to determine their course of action

Withdrawing, Resigned, Moving From: 4, 5, 9
• Fours withdraw to their deepest feelings
• Fives withdraw to their thoughts
• Nines withdraw to a place of inaction

Hence by studying the misused centres, we are at the same time looking at all three aspects of Thinking, Feeling, and Doing. No matter what a person's type may be, therefore, he or she will find some aspect of it is better understood through looking at any one of the misused centres.

In terms of the Enneagram, we can restate this typology by saying that types One, Two, and Six fall together as the compliant aspects of the self; types Seven, Eight and Three form our assertive tendencies; and types Four, Five and Nine are the energies of our personalities which demonstrate resignation. This categorization is useful because it plays down the necessity of locating ourselves exclusively within one space and invites us to examine those general tendencies which may be obvious to us about ourselves as well as the "shadow" aspects which we might otherwise ignore.

Body, Mind, and Heart

"God forbid that I should part what he has joined,
the body and spirit.
For God wants to be served with body and soul,
both together."

– *Cloud of Unknowing*, ch. 48

When we apply the principles of the Enneagram to our understanding of the various biblical characters presented here, we find that their stories are illuminated in ways which invite a new form of reflection. We perceive their choices and conflicts through our understanding of the movements people in all times make towards integration or disintegration. For the biblical characters under consideration, it is useful to try to discover for each what their basic energy is. When we go on to consider what their needs are and how they do or do not get them met, we move on to examining their misused centre. Most importantly, we are shown examples of how God works within each unique self to help bring that person to healing, growth, and union with the divine. The action of God is not limited to one particular form. In the nine types represented on the Enneagram, we find that each encounters the divine in its own way. If a centre is misused, God knows how to engage it and show how to bring it to growth and fullness. We are not limited by our own type in learning the multiplicity of God's kindnesses to humanity. Even though we "prefer" one type, we move within all nine energies, and none is immune from access to the Divine.

The notion of conversion in response to the divine call runs like a leitmotif throughout the Hebrew and Christian traditions. It begins with the story of Adam and Eve in the Book of Genesis who are shown to us in their original state of union and rightness with themselves, with one other, with nature, and with God. But this state of oneness is soon disrupted as our first parents choose to discover good and evil for themselves through disobeying the divine command not to eat of the forbidden tree. In this they are of course like all of us, who early in life choose to layer over our innocence by responding to the commands of our ego. Like Adam and Eve, we then try to hide from God, who calls out to Adam, and to us, "Where are you?" (Genesis 3:9). Like us, Adam and Eve also hide from each other when they notice their vulnerability, the nakedness which now reveals too much of themselves, and they feel fear and shame. They cover themselves up with fig leaves which God mercifully replaces with animal skins. This is the story of each one of us as we move from the innocence and simplicity of childhood into the difficulties and problems of adult life. Very early in our lives we, too, reach for fig leaves to cover up who we really are, and we lose a clear sense of our location in this universe. Yet God continues to replace our poor attempts at covering ourselves with a generous reaching towards our plight. The nine Faces of God are also the nine ways in which God meets us and effects our transformation.

The work of the Enneagram is to recover our original unity. We cannot return to the Garden of Eden but we can move forward into the world of our cities and villages always seeking and welcoming the encounter with the Divine which will restore us to wholeness. The work of the Enneagram brings us a message of liberation from the compulsions which we formed very early in our lives. It shows us how to undergo a conscious movement towards arriving at our Essence, the self that is hiding under the fig leaf. In its movement from level to level, from one space, energy or type to another, it shows us the soul aspiring to self-knowledge. We learn that we can move consciously from a place of darkness to one of light, from a conditioned force of habit to a new energy of freedom. The Enneagram shows us one way to begin this movement of unveiling, of turning away from the egocentric self and towards our divine centre, and helps us determine which is the direction that will lead to our personal and planetary transformation.

'Transformation', then, does not refer to the small bumps of the ups and downs of ordinary life, in which movement in one direction is often countered very soon with contrary movement. Such vacillations are not necessarily, or even usually, indicative of genuine transformation. While we are still in a state of vacillation, we are often aware of a sense that we are a divided self: we act out of one set of beliefs while holding in our awareness a idea of what for us are merely "pious wishes" which never really take root. Rather, as William James explained, genuine transformation refers not to such waverings but to a change of attitude, belief, or behaviour which "grows so stable as to expel definitively its previous rivals from the individual's life."[45]

We are often excited at the beginning of a process of change or conversion, yet its implementation may soon become difficult and be delayed because of our own internal confusion. In this we are certainly in good company: "For I do not do the good I want, but the evil I do not want is what I do", wrote St. Paul to the Romans. (Romans 7:19). St. Augustine also writes of this dilemma memorably in his *Confessions*, in which he laments how he postponed his response to God by saying "give me just a little while," and that his "little while" proceeded to go on for a very long time.[46] Yet at the same time he is able to pray, "Let it be now, let it be now."[47] We live in this state of tension between our urge for a "long time" and our desire to "let it be now." The inner work is about letting the process be *now*.

About This Book

> "But in this work, cast discretion to the wind!
> I want you never to give this work up all the
> while you live."

> *– Cloud of Unknowing*, ch. 41

We hope that readers of this book will read it from beginning to end. It may therefore seem odd to include a short section here on *how* to read it. The intention of doing so is to underscore that everything written here is meaningless until it takes root and awakens in the life of the reader. Like the starving man in the restaurant to whom everything on the menu sounded so delicious that he proceeded to eat the menu itself, no benefit will be had simply by reading about the work of transformation. It requires experiencing it in body, mind, and heart. Books, tapes, lectures, and workshops all have their place in helping us on our way, but they remain little more than junk food for the mind if they are not activated in our own lives. We hope the stories in this book will come to life in the lives of its readers and inspire further meditation on the Bible and integration of its words into daily practice, always remembering that it is God who brings it to life in us.

While the book's sections on the nine Enneagram types could be read in any order, the ideal is to read them all in the order in which they are presented. Since each misused centre contains Head, Heart, and Body types, the reader will continue to encounter familiar types throughout the text. The three components of personality, while they may be treated separately, are never totally disconnected, and it is generally not helpful to our inner work to focus solely on the one with which we feel most at home. Discussion of each of the nine types will therefore highlight their complementary as well as their distinguishing features. The Enneagram's spirituality is very concrete, and can readily be perceived within our own selves. The scriptural characters are given as examples which embody everyone's personal experience, show us concrete examples drawn from ordinary life, and yet retain their mythical or archetypal significance.

For each of the Enneagram's nine spaces, readers will discover two portraits of scriptural characters who represent that particular space. Eighteen characters are explored in terms of their misused centres, their direction of integration, and particularly how God meets them wherever they are and invites them to conversion or transformation. A delightful synchronicity is also discovered when we realize that, in the Hebrew alphabet, letters are also used to represent numbers, and in choosing 18 characters for our discussion and analysis, the number corresponds to the Hebrew letter for the numeral 18. This letter is transliterated as *chai*, and it is also in the Hebrew language the letter that begins the word for "life." Thus these 18 characters, representing the nine spaces of the Enneagram, suggest the richness and the totality of human life both in its brokenness and in its transformation to wholeness. The divine image exists in all persons and in many forms, and discovering it within creation and within ourselves is a process that unfolds and deepens over a lifetime.

A further reminder of what may seem obvious: biblical characters come to us through a long oral tradition. Their stories have been historically conditioned and interpreted by diverse cultures. With few exceptions (such as the apostle Peter), we have only sparse historical details. These characters are therefore not treated necessarily as real or historical persons. Even as powerful archetypes or stylized symbolic personages and mentors, they can help us learn more about ourselves.

Each character discussed illustrates the lively interplay between the Enneagram and the Bible. His or her story can be useful to all of us in avoiding needless pitfalls and in guiding us towards sound spiritual growth. As the author of the Letter to the Hebrews puts it: "Indeed, the word of God is living and active, sharper than any two-edged sword, piercing until it divides soul from spirit, joints from marrow; it is able to judge the thoughts and intentions of the heart" (Hebrews 4:12). This should be recalled constantly as each character's story unfolds: it is told not for entertainment but to pierce us to the bone and to awaken an awareness of the intentions of our own hearts.

The stories of each of these characters spin their variations on the endless theme of the divine indwelling in every person, and the possibility of uncovering it in ourselves. The motifs and themes begun in Genesis, of creation and work, of a journey and a promised land, of liberation and justice, and of the sabbath, present us with the archetypes of our own movement from original and inner chaos to meaning and revelation. As the story tells us, the Spirit of God which hovered over the waters at the beginning of our story brings order out of chaos and awakens creation into life. The movement is initially an individual one, but soon manifests itself as a drive to create relationships among individuals and with the universe.

At the end of each character's story, there is a psalm which can reflect the energy of that particular character and Enneagram type. These psalms may simply be read, or they may be pondered and contemplated from within the energy of that particular space. They are there to help us promote the unification between our head as we read them, our heart as we feel them, and our body as we sense them and make them a part of our daily life. No psalm is unique to just one Enneagram type, so they can all be read for insight and inspiration no matter where we find ourselves in terms of our personal energy.

Each section on a particular type concludes with a summary of the positive points of the type, an invitation for the reader to begin to develop the particular gifts found in each biblical character, and some general suggestions of how to make this happen in our own lives. Unlike the starving man in the restaurant, we are encouraged to satisfy ourselves with more than the text in front of us.

This book is intended to inspire practical implementation towards a path of personal growth, integration, and fulfilment in whatever ways these may occur.

Each biblical character presented as a mentor to us provides much fuel for our imaginations, our thoughts, and our actions. The following four questions could be asked of each one:

1. What characteristics of this particular type does this mentor display?
2. What can be learned about myself through this character?
3. How does this mentor provide assistance to me in experiencing meaning in my own life?
4. What element of Essence in this character speaks to me?

These 18 different facets of the human experience all reside within our individual psyches no matter what Enneagram space we believe we are in. In each story, God offers them, and us, a way of transformation. This book seeks to encourage the exploration of the many ways the spiritual life unfolds in each person, and the many transformative occasions which life presents. It does not try to provide pat solutions according to the Enneagram; rather, it attempts to open hearts and souls and minds to the indwelling divine energy, conveyed through the stories in the Bible, but always and ever alive in our own stories and lives, and calling us to pursue the work of conversion and growth towards human perfection.

Group 1: The Compliant Types

Ones, Twos, and Sixes

"For my thoughts are not your thoughts,
nor are your ways my ways, says the LORD."

– Isaiah 55:8.

The triad belonging to the compliant types are the Ones, Twos, and Sixes. Commonly accepted names given to persons associated with these three spaces on the Enneagram are the reformer or perfectionist (One), the helper or giver (Two), and the guardian or loyalist (Six). These are of course very general categories and, as with all the types on the Enneagram, there are many variations and shadings within each. What they share as the compliant types is a misused (sometimes referred to as repressed) Thinking centre. Misusing the Thinking centre does not mean that these types do not know how to think, or that their intelligence is weak or perhaps used only rarely. In fact, these types may often be prone to over-thinking or being overly analytical. However, we say that their Thinking is misused because their intelligence, while active, is often unproductive. For these three types, their thought processes can analyze very well, but because the vastness of a situation often makes the information surrounding it seem overwhelming, clear decision-making becomes difficult for them. These types get stuck trying to form decisions based on a clear assessment of the big picture. Alternatively, they may become hyper-critical. Often it feels as if they are just spinning their wheels and unable to move forward.

Overcoming this difficulty and achieving clarity of thought for the compliant types may be hindered in a number of ways. Each type has its own particular hurdle to overcome. For the Ones, who tend to be perfectionists and idealists, clarity of thought is obscured by their overwhelming need to do what is right. Of several possible options before them, they will analyze and judge them all in the desire to find the perfect solution. Until the right answer is indisputably clear to them, they feel unable to act.

For Twos, the caregivers and nurturers, their thinking becomes misused and complicated. Their need to be loved is translated into their need to be helpful, which can be so great that a sense of their own self gets lost in the process. In being concerned predominantly with the needs of others, they overlook or are not aware of their own needs. In their thinking they have not learned to clearly incorporate themselves into the picture.

For Sixes, who are loyalists, their thinking is often misused because it can complicate their decision making, offering too many options which might destabilize their need for security. Unlike the Ones, whose main preoccupation is to come up with the right answer or attitude, Sixes hesitate in their thinking because of their allegiance to a group and whether they are conforming to the assumed norms or rules. Even though they sit at the midpoint of the Thinking triad (Fives, Sixes, and Sevens), and their Thinking centre is also their preferred centre, their desire for information and the need to make good decisions is hijacked by its own hesitations.

All three of these types, then, find that their thinking, while often prolonged and anguished, is generally unhelpful or unproductive, hence misused. This is what makes them "compliant" in the psychological sense. While in its ordinary usage the word may connote people who are passive and wait to receive and accept whatever crosses their paths, compliance can also be a bending to an inner authority, whether we call it conscience, a sense of what is "right", an idea of how we should act toward others, or obedience to a learned set of rules and values. Compliant types do not live with a "doormat" approach to the world, but they do pay close attention to what others are saying and doing. In their relationships to other people, they are best characterized as moving towards them, but in a non-confrontational way.

There is in fact a wide variety of patterns in how those who are compliant types seek to do the "right" thing, either by listening to an inner or an outer authority. Ones will be concerned with the justice and rightness of their actions. Twos will be aware of how they can best serve the needs of others. Sixes will want to make their communities into better places for all. The word also connotes how we react to a situation: thus the One will comply to the inner critic, the Two will comply to the perceived need, and the Six to whatever constitutes the authority.

The vulnerability of these types usually begins early in life, arising from the tension that exists between their desire to rebel and their deep need for affection. While to some degree this is true for all people, the compliant types feel it more keenly than others. Their need for affection triumphs over their rebellious urges and, as a result, they become compliant, spending enormous amounts of energy trying to gain approval and win over others.[48] If they begin the process of personal transformation, they will have to unravel their false start. This will mean having to give up their tendency to embrace suffering and perhaps a sense of failure or helplessness, learned in the name of pleasing others at the cost of their own integrity. Those who are Ones will move towards greater self-confidence and grow in wisdom; Twos will learn a healthy love of themselves and grow in understanding; and Sixes will amaze themselves with new fearlessness and will grow in both inner and outer endurance.

There are thus different qualities of compliance. True compliance, in its healthiest form, enables us to seek to do the right thing even when we feel fear or hesitation. In its less helpful form, however, it may instead *prevent* us from doing that very thing. False compliance occurs when there is a silencing of our own inner authority because we are looking to the letter of the law rather than to its spirit. If we show allegiance to our legalistic sense of things, we are looking outside ourselves hoping to find something which will undertake our transformation for us. It cannot be done: no matter how much we may know or even how deeply we believe, until our knowledge and faith are integrated into our innermost being, we are still living out of the false sense that because we know a lot about transformation we are actually transformed persons. The genuine transformation of our compliant self is accomplished when we learn to rely predominantly on our inner spiritual authority rather than solely on an external knowledge of "what the rules are." In touch with our divine centre, we will act out of love and compassion, and "against such there is no law" (Galatians 5:23).

When we apply these aspects of compliance to scripture, we probably find that we do not think of the most memorable characters in the Bible as being either self-effacing or compliant. Images of greatness and strength accompany our impressions of the biblical figures we may have heard about since our youth. Most people might find it difficult to come up with even a single character who might be called "compliant". And to be self-effacing (Horney's term) in our world often connotes a person who conveys little sense of personal energy or power, hardly someone we might wish to imitate.

However, when we understand compliance, we see it as a virtue which enables some of the greatest biblical heroes and heroines to turn from their preoccupations with their ego-based sense of who they are and be confronted by the divine presence calling them to realign themselves with their holy essence. At first glance, the biblical characters chosen to represent these types might appear to have little in common: how can we place the forthrightness and zeal of John the Baptist next to the gentle loyalty of Ruth, or the wavering complexities and loyalties of Peter beside the straightforwardness and clarity of Paul? Does Ruth's kind and honest kinsman Boaz really have anything much in common with the mother in the Book of Maccabees who watches her seven sons put to death one by one? The answer is that, despite their superficial differences, these six persons share deeper personality traits that may not immediately be apparent to one who has only read their stories as literal narratives, that is, as sequences of events that are mainly interested in describing "what comes next" in the episode. Using the Enneagram as an entrance into their stories invites us to explore them from a different angle. Like facets in a diamond, they will be given further clarity and brilliance when illuminated by the insights and wisdom of the Enneagram.

As we have seen, the compliant types often act out of a sense of fairness if they are Ones, out of a deep feeling of wanting to help if they are Twos, or impetuously out of loyalty or fear if they are Sixes. When we turn to the biblical models of each of these types, we can notice how God's presence or sudden intervention in their lives is the impetus which enables them to begin the process of transformation from their earlier outer-directedness to a newly aligned inner focus. This new stance looks very different from ego-centricity. Heightened awareness and inner focus identifies them with the divine centre within themselves, and it is from this source that they derive their sense of justice, of love, of faith and of loyalty. They are able to bring forth and develop the misused Thinking part of themselves so that it assists them in identifying the work that is needed: John the Baptist comes to understand his intimate and united relationship to Jesus; Paul is able to reverse his destructive and angry thinking and become a missionary in the new Christian faith; Ruth learns, with the help of Boaz, that love of others united with love of self brings new life to all and to future generations; Peter understands that loss of nerve need not mean loss of faith; and the Maccabean mother finally attains a bitter-sweet triumph in overcoming fear for the body and attaining life for the soul. All these biblical mentors learn to be compassionate towards themselves. They understand that their salvation comes not from without, from doing what is acceptable to others, but from within, from learning to let the ego-self die so that they are free to be truly and lovingly compliant to the clear and gentle prompt-ings of the Spirit.

Type One: John the Baptist and Paul

> "What does the LORD require of you, but to do justice,
> and to love kindness, and to walk humbly with your God?"
>
> – Micah 6:8

The Ones are the reformers and the perfectionists in our world. Situated in the Body centre of the Enneagram, their basic desire is to be virtuous and do what is right. Therefore they also fear being less than perfect.[49] The virtue of the One is serenity, and their sin is resentful anger.[50] Their ideal is to live for a higher purpose, and their true nature is to be wise and discerning.

The two reformers presented here, John the Baptist and Paul, represent the tendency to be a perfectionist. They are motivated by knowing or finding out what is "right," and seeking to make the world fit their definition of this. When the world, or a part of it, rejects them, they are prone to fall into resentment and even anger, wondering why others do not recognize what to them is so obvi-ously right, just, and wise. When we find ourselves in our One space, we can remember that our strength is our inner wisdom, which derives not from the ego but from spiritual awareness, and our weakness is our resentment of those who do not see or agree with it.

One might find it strange that such figures as John the Baptist and Paul are "compliant" types, since we perceive them as strong, even dominating, persons who might even have seemed somewhat argumentative, determined to succeed in getting their way. They are perceived as bold, outspoken, and fervent for what they believe. They preach to public crowds and both suffer physi-cally for what they proclaim, even to the point of giving their lives. Being compliant does not mean being a pushover. In terms of the

Enneagram types, transformed compliant characters are ones who have learned how to listen to their inner authority. They have awakened to their confusion about what obedience means and come to a new awareness based on the law of love.

Along with the other compliant types (the Twos and the Sixes), Ones share a misused or repressed Thinking centre. Their preferred centre is their Doing centre, and it is supported by the Feeling centre. Ones are therefore people of action and movement, and their actions are often determined by their passionate feelings of being right or of wanting to establish justice in a situation. Because Thinking is often misused, the Ones' desire for saintliness and perfection often prevents them from having any conscious feeling of pride, since pride would not fit with the desired self-image.[51] Movement into self-awareness might therefore mean that the One can acknowledge his or her helplessness or smallness without losing the connection with the divine essence. When Paul experiences his conversion, his change of name reflects this new self-knowledge. His previous name, "Saul," was the name of Israel's first king, an important name for an important man. After his conversion, Saul is known as Paul, a name which means "little one." Paul joyfully adopts this new name, a sign of the melting down of his ego-self. Similarly, John the Baptist, speaking of Jesus, says that "He must increase, but I must decrease" (John 3:30). Both are therefore mentors for us in learning how to shed our false identities and live out of our true divine centre.

Both John the Baptist and Paul were movers and shakers, reformers and outspoken critics and prophets of the people of their own time and, by extrapolation, of the people of any time. They both show the compliant's ability to move towards people and engage with them. Both of them were also able to adapt as the situation changed, and both of them gave their lives over to the ideals they envisioned. The abilities to become a genuine reformer, a person who is sensitive to issues of injustice, and a champion of the

call to conversion, are all manifested in these scriptural Ones —
John the Baptist and Paul.

John the Baptist

> "There was a man sent from God, whose name was John.
> He came as a witness to testify to the light, so that all might
> believe through him."

> – John 1:6-7

John the Baptist, one of the few characters who is present in
all four gospels (a sign of an indisputable tradition), brought to his
ministry some of the predominant characteristics of those who are
in the Body space. We know that he fasted, spent time alone in the
desert preparing for and exercising his ministry. He seemed to live
out of the knowledge that if the body is open and also disciplined,
the Spirit will be free and freely exercised.

In all four gospels, John is placed at the beginning as a tran-
sitional character who functions as a prophetic bridge between the
Hebrew scriptures and the teachings of Jesus. In this role (which
is functional and literary as well as spiritual), he embodies the
work of the One who "knows" that something new and "right" has
been added and is in a privileged position to be able to announce it.
He shows the One's longing for perfection and completion, and
accepts his responsibility in bringing about the emergence of the
kingdom. He also manifests the impatience of the One who wants
others to see what he sees and can be intolerant when they are
slow to cooperate with the vision.

John the Baptist's story presents us with a good example of
a liminal or "threshold" experience in which we cross over from
the old life into new territory. This stepping across signals an
initial waking up to one's inner life, the beginning of the journey
into transformation. Literally, this is depicted by baptism, the
immersion into the Jordan River after repenting of one's sins, and

emergence as a cleansed soul who is now prepared to begin walking on a new path.

All four gospel writers are careful to subordinate John's ministry to that of Jesus. John represents the summary and conclusion of the prophetic history of the Hebrew people, standing on the threshold and looking both backwards and forwards. Jesus, however, looks not to the past but to the present and the future. John's ministry closes off an era, and Jesus opens the door to a new way of life: John proclaims of Jesus that "this is he of whom I said, 'After me comes a man who ranks ahead of me because he was before me'" (John 1:30). Already we see John's ability to combat the One's tendency towards resentment. None is present here, just a sense of acknowledgment and willingness to allow Jesus to dominate the scene.

This is a difficult position for a One to be in. Ones want to know that they are right; to know that another is coming who is greater and who will in effect bring his role to its conclusion might have raised difficulties for John. When Jesus submits to him for baptism, and a voice from heaven proclaims Jesus to be the beloved Son in whom God is "well pleased" (Luke 3:22), we might not be surprised to hear John at that point exclaim, "But what about me? I've been busy telling people about this very moment and done all the hard work, exhorting them to reform their lives and prepare the way. Are you not pleased with me also?" Potential resentment and anger hang over this moment, yet John displays neither. Here is a model for the One in us to look towards when we face our own swelling resentments at not being recognized for all that we have done. John's character teaches us what the fruits of transformational work look like in the life of the One.

Jesus knows how to meet the One where he is. He affirms John's quest for the right by insisting that John baptize him with the baptism of repentance in the waters of the Jordan. In doing so, Jesus stands in solidarity with the Chosen People, his own people, who are also being called to metanoia, to turning around and changing one's mind about how life should be lived. Humanly speaking, John is the prophet who helps Jesus grow in his understanding of his earthly mission. So John does indeed perform a major task, greater than that of all the previous prophets, in announcing the presence of the Messiah and baptizing him with water.

John and Jesus had grown up knowing each other: their mothers had a kinship as cousins and a close friendship before their births. Their children were born only six months apart (Luke 1:26). We recognize the closeness of the family when we learn that Mary, herself newly pregnant, goes to visit Elizabeth "in the hill country" and stays with her cousin for three months, until the birth of John (Luke 1:39, 56). Mary's entrance into the house of Elizabeth and Zechariah causes Elizabeth's unborn child, John, to leap for joy (Luke 1:44), the first indication of John's unresentful response, even while both are still in the womb, to Jesus. It would be hard to imagine the women not raising their sons together, as far as distance and opportunity would allow, but it does not appear that their kinship caused any difficulties for the young boys.

John's own birth had been a result of divine intervention. Elizabeth was barren and both she and her husband Zechariah were getting old (Luke 1:7). The angel Gabriel appeared to Zechariah and told him that they would have a son who would be "great in the sight of the Lord" (Luke 1:15). Did Elizabeth and Zechariah ever tell John the story of his birth narrative? Did Zechariah ever sing to him the song he sang when the Holy Spirit filled him and inspired him to call John "the prophet of the Most High" who would "go before the Lord to prepare his ways, to give knowledge of salvation to his people by the forgiveness of their sins?" (Luke 1:76-77).

If we presume that they did, then John's work began in his childhood when he first learned of these things. He was able to nurture his vision of a perfect world, with himself as its announcer, knowing that it had divine sanction: "the child grew and became strong in spirit, and he was in the wilderness until the day he appeared publicly to Israel" (Luke 1:80). His growth and his strengthening spirit are here connected, indicating that his growth was not just physical but was also accompanied by progress in his own inner work. He lives in the "wilderness," a place of waiting and expectation, just as the Hebrews journeyed in the wilderness for 40 years in hope of reaching the Promised Land, and as Jesus himself was to spend 40 days in the wilderness before beginning his public life and ministry.

The wilderness is also a place in which we encounter temptation and wild beasts, and, if we meet them directly and openly, we finally receive the ministry of angels (Mark 1:13). It is a psychic as well as a physical place, a time in which we confront our obsessions and fears. For John, who lived in the wilderness until the appearance of Jesus, it fosters his self-control, self-knowledge and discernment, all positive qualities of the One. His wilderness experience must have assisted him in avoiding the pitfalls which could have accompanied his life's work. For him, as well as for us, the danger lies in assuming that we are chosen for such work because there is something *in us* that is unique, something which we have achieved and for which we can take credit. This is a swelling of the ego that can readily lead to pride and subsequent resentment.

The gift of the One that can lead beyond this is the recognition of a Perfection which does not originate in our own desire to be right but is already found in the Rightness of what is. When we read that John "became strong in spirit," we are not to assume that his own sense of self-importance and determination was strengthened, but rather that he allowed the divine Spirit to mould and transform him into a prophetic voice of God. Being a prophet means leaving the concerns of the ego behind. It is frustrating and often humiliating. Moses tried very hard to get out of his calling to go to Pharaoh by presenting God with numerous arguments rising out of his ego concerns: that he was a nobody, that no one would believe him, and that he could not speak well (Exodus 3:11-17). John the Baptist might also have had similar concerns, but none of the Gospels even raises this possibility. All four of them depict him as a voice crying out in the wilderness to prepare a way for God (Matthew 3:3). Only out of the wilderness experience and its purification of the ego can one become a road for the divine. Preparing a way for God entails that the prophet must say what *is*. He or she can only know what *is* as the result of a deep and real encounter with the divine, with the One whose very name is "I Am" (Exodus 3:14).

John's preparation for his prophetic work enabled him to recognize the presence of the Messiah when he appeared. Even so, there is some indication that John was not entirely certain right at the beginning of his public ministry what Jesus' mission represented. Jesus is hope-filled and optimistic, proclaiming the good news to the poor, release to the captives, and the time of God's favour (Luke 4:18-19). John, on the other hand, lashes out more pessimistically, calling the crowds who come to him a "brood of vipers" and warning them of "the wrath to come" (Luke 3:7). John allows the judgmental attitude of the One and the rigidity which goes with it to dominate. He comes "neither eating nor drinking" in contrast to Jesus, who was called "a glutton and a drunkard" (Matthew 11:18-19) by his detractors because of his enjoyment of food and friends, and his notorious association with people considered public sinners. John limits his diet to locusts and wild honey (Matthew 10:41), while Jesus multiplies bread and wine and fish, and provides food in abundance for those who are hungry.

The gospels, however, do record a movement of John towards fuller understanding of his role and into greater self-knowledge. Self-questioning and self-observation, undertaken honestly, lead to greater self-knowledge, and this is indicated in John's questions once he has been imprisoned. His arrest is perfectly consistent with John's character: he was imprisoned because he was so outspoken when he saw behaviour that was not right:

> For Herod himself had sent men who arrested John, bound him, and put him in prison on account of Herodias, his brother Philip's wife, because Herod had married her. For John had been telling Herod, "It is not lawful for you to have your brother's wife."

– Mark 6:17-18

In prison, John appears to have entered once again into his personal wilderness and wrestled with questions about the wisdom of his teachings and his actions. In fact, we might even ask if John was having serious doubts concerning whether he was right about who Jesus was. It is very difficult for a One to face the possibility that his beliefs or actions may not have been perfectly right, or that he may have not completely understood what Jesus was about. The people who to John had seemed a "brood of vipers", the tax collectors and soldiers, were not castigated but welcomed by Jesus. Perhaps John had been mistaken, an awful thought for a One to dwell on.

We see at least a hint of this when the imprisoned John hears reports of what Jesus has been teaching. Having been told by his father that he was to be the "prophet of the Most High," John receives word that Jesus has taught, "Whoever welcomes a prophet in the name of a prophet will receive a prophet's reward" (Matthew 10:41). Yet there is John, languishing in prison. He may be wondering if Jesus even knows he is there, and what sort of "prophet's reward" this represents. Does Jesus consider him a prophet, or is he being judged? Once again, John must face the One's tendency to fall into anger and resentment, and to pronounce judgment on all situations. In unhealthy Ones, there can even be an increasingly inverse ratio between how much they have actually succeeded and their own inner security.[52] The greater their success, the less secure they feel, not out of false humility but out of a harsh critical judgment on themselves. This is how easily a One can misuse the Thinking centre and spiral down into self-pity.

We see John confronting this dilemma and attempting to resolve it by looking not to his own sense of achievement but by sending a message to Jesus, poignantly asking him, "Are you the one who is to come, or are we to wait for another?" (Matthew 11:2). In other words, have John's life and his imminent death been a witness to the truth, or has he been living a delusion based on an egocentric self-righteousness? John needed to adapt to new circumstances, to his own apparent abandonment, and to a new turn of events as the one whom he had early proclaimed as the Messiah seemed to be getting into controversy and pushing the edges of what were acceptable beliefs. John had proclaimed that "He must increase, but I must decrease" (John 3:30), but the reality of this truth was painful. The "increase" does not just refer to the growing popularity of Jesus, but on a spiritual level it indicates the necessary decrease of the ego as the divine centre or essence of a person grows and expands to fill one's entire being. John's spiritual "decrease" is symbolized by his physical imprisonment as his ego becomes lessened so that his true self may be experienced.

For a One, the knowing of what is right and true is crucial. John needs to know if he has been right. If he has been, then his baptisms and the reforms he began and to which he called others would continue, and social change might result. He had called many to repentance and conversion. If, however, he had been wrong, his misery would have swamped him into melancholy and a sense of self-delusion and deep resentment. As a One, he harboured a great potential for such anger and resentment, traits which could be used zealously to call people to conversion, but which could also be turned inwards into self-recrimination and regret. John's position as a compliant type would make it possible for him to move in either direction. The positive movement towards growth, however, would only occur if he became compliant with the call to personal transformation and not to destruction.

John the Baptist stands as an exemplar of righteousness and rightness, one who lived his life as a preparation for "the way of the Lord," making paths straight, setting crooked things right, striving for perfection even in this imperfect world. Some depictions of John show him as angry, rigid and judgmental, as someone of whom we would likely be afraid were we to encounter him by the side of the Jordan. This type of personality is often present in Ones, who have to work very hard not to be impatient with the sluggishness and imperfection of others, and at the same time be aware of their own limitations. Ones can see clearly the pressing needs which have to be addressed. They want reform and conversion, and they want it now. This is why John's question from prison is so moving. John, the righteous perfectionist, is able to ask whether he did indeed get it right, whether Jesus is in fact "the one who is to come, or are we to wait for another?" We must assume that John is ready to hear the answer, whatever it may be, and that his compliancy will enable him to accept what he hears.

Jesus hastens to reply to John in a way that a One would understand and treasure: he tells him that the blind are receiving their sight, the deaf are hearing, the unclean are being cleansed, and the poor are hearing good news, and then he says, "And blessed is anyone who takes no offence at me" (Matthew 11:6). First addressing John's concern for the social and spiritual ills of the day, Jesus assures him that justice is being done, that his vision has not been lost. Then Jesus gently asks John to persevere in his belief and to take no offence at what Jesus says and does, to relax his self-judgment and be open to his blessedness. This response to John's wanting to be right both affirms and encourages him as he realizes that justice and righteousness are indeed being carried out, and that they will continue even without his active participation. His job is completed. His ego can let go of his need to see the conclusion of his mission. Just as Moses died before he could enter the Promised Land, so John's subsequent martyrdom is undergone not as a powerless victim but as a champion of what is right. He does not live to see the fulfilment of the reign of God but his death to self brings him to new birth and new life.

The role of the reformer is to help others wake up, and perhaps to help them soften their hardened hearts when they face discouragement or despair in confronting the evils of the day. We see in John the Baptist the gift of the One, which lies in the ability to see what is wrong and needs to be changed, to move past the status quo into transformational behaviours, to exercise, in other words, the gift of prophecy. As prophet, the One is able to detect flaws in a situation or a system, and envision the wholeness that can arise from them. In its purest form, the call to repent and reform arises not from a condemning judgment, but from a passionate desire to see justice carried out and life perfected and whole.

Jesus' characterization of John could not be more to the point here: he says that John was not "a reed shaken in the wind" or "someone dressed in soft robes" (Matthew 11:7-8), images of pliability and accommodation but very different from the compliancy to the inner truth which John has learned to understand. John is strong and sure, and has learned to let his ego decrease for the increasing of the spirit within him. Jesus declares that John is "more than a prophet," more than a mouthpiece of God, for he has achieved his own inner transformation. Jesus proclaims John is the one who was foretold as the messenger of God, that is, the one who can bear God into the world. His proclamation of John as the transformed One, able to see past his anger to the Wisdom of the truth, would be music to the ears of a One: "Truly I tell you, among those born of women no one has arisen greater than John the

Baptist" (Matthew 11:11). God meets the Ones in their desire for perfection and justice, and assures them that these qualities are already present in their divine core, ready to be manifested in the world not by what the One does out of his or her own ego, but out of compliance with the workings of the divine spirit within.

Prayer in the Spirit of John the Baptist
Psalm 1

Happy are those
   who do not follow the advice of the wicked,
or take the path that sinners tread,
   or sit in the seat of scoffers;
but their delight is in the law of the LORD,
   and on God's law they meditate day and night.
They are like trees
   planted by streams of water,
which yield their fruit in its season,
   and their leaves do not wither.
In all that they do, they prosper.

The wicked are not so,
   but are like chaff that the wind drives away.
Therefore the wicked will not stand in the judgment,
   nor sinners in the congregation of the righteous;
for the LORD watches over the way of the righteous,
   but the way of the wicked will perish.

Paul

"We have not ceased praying for you and asking that you may be filled with the knowledge of God's will in all spiritual wisdom and understanding."

– (Colossians 1:9)

The works of justice often call for radical changes, not just in society but also, and especially, in the individual. Probably the most dramatic reversal in all of scripture is recorded in the story of the conversion of Paul. Paul's story embodies the strengths and the weaknesses of the One in a way which humanizes him and yet has often caused him to be vilified as well. He has perhaps gotten more bad press than any other character in scripture, chiefly for some of his comments addressed to local communities about such things as the role of women in the churches and the relationships between husbands and wives. To excerpt some of his writings and present them in a modern context is often upsetting and even offensive to many. Often his strength of character and his charismatic qualities are discarded and his writings dismissed because of a few difficult passages. Yet in his writings, his eloquence and profound sense of the divine have given us some of the most beautiful and insightful portions of the Christian scriptures. Paul very clearly embodies the strengths, and the weak points, of the One.

Here is one of his accounts of his own conversion:

> [Christ] appeared to Cephas, then to the twelve. Then he appeared to more than five hundred brothers and sisters at one time, most of whom are still alive, though some have died. Then he appeared to James, then to all the apostles. Last of all, as to one untimely born, he appeared also to me. For I am the least of the apostles, unfit to be called an apostle, because I persecuted the church of God. But by the grace of God I am what I am, and his grace toward me has not been in vain. On the contrary, I worked harder than any of them – though it was not I, but the grace of God that is with me.

– 1 Corinthians 15:5-10

In this description we see the kernel of the transformation of the One: from a sense of rightness, even one of righteous anger, to a lot of very hard and not always rewarding work, ultimately leading to a humbling of the ego and a compliance not with the outer but with the inner grace-filled authority. Paul's true greatness lies in his willingness to let his ego-driven concerns drop away and to admit that he had been wrong, perhaps the hardest thing for a One to do.

Often such an admission tempts a One into self-pity, even self-contempt, and wallowing in regrets for past mistakes. The hard work of transformation requires a *metanoia* or turning around from this unhealthy response towards a more expansive mode of being. The perfectly realized ideals of the transformed compliant type can be seen in Paul's description of the results of the loss of ego and contact with one's essence, which he calls the fruits of the Spirit: "love, joy, peace, patience, kindness, generosity, faithfulness, gentleness, and self-control" (Galatians 5:22). It is also true that for a One, helplessness and suffering may also be seen as positive fruits, but only if they are not focused on how much the poor ego has undergone but instead on how they are merely incidental and to-be-expected side effects of living a genuine life.[53] Again we find evidence of this attitude in Paul's own writings:

> Three times I was beaten with rods. Once I received a stoning. Three times I was shipwrecked; for a night and a day I was adrift at sea; on frequent journeys, in danger from rivers, danger from bandits, danger from my own people, danger from Gentiles, danger in the city, danger in the wilderness, danger at sea, danger from false brothers and sisters; in toil and hardship, through many a sleepless night, hungry and thirsty, often without food, cold and naked.
>
> – 2 Corinthians 11:25-27

Paul does not use this list to indulge in self-pity or resentment. He goes on to show us how he has used these events to help him move to the transformative expansive energy which extends beyond his ego self to embrace all humanity: "Who is weak, and I am not weak? Who is made to stumble, and I am not indignant?" (2 Corinthians 11:29). His list of sufferings makes him reach out towards others in an empathic way and his attitude towards his own situation is thereby lightened and dissipated.

As Saul, before his conversion, he busied himself with "ravaging the church" by dragging men and women off to prison (Acts 8:3). His moving towards others was destructive rather than helpful. He truly believed he was being righteous in his indignation against the followers of the Way, as the early Christians called themselves (Acts 9:2). He was a Pharisee, a teacher and upholder of the Law of Moses, and he could not tolerate those who appeared to be watering down the strict law which he had studied and practiced all his life. At that time in his life, he showed his compliant nature by being enslaved to the external law. His inner authority was totally one with the outer code. He fulfilled in his own mind the One's desire to be "perfect" by his adherence to all the statutes of the law of Moses, to the 613 commandments and to the tradition, and his zeal drove him to despise anything that countered that way of life. He later wrote that he was "as to the law, a Pharisee; as to zeal, a persecutor of the church; as to righteousness under the law, blameless" (Philippians 3:5-6). Zeal, righteousness, and blamelessness are all ideals for the One, but they need to be maintained not for gratification of the ideals of the ego-self but out of their reflection of the divine nature. Saul was unable to see past his own desire to have things his way. The new sect of Jews who were followers of Jesus was a threat to the order of his world view. They clearly did not get things right, and misunderstood what they had been taught about the law and the prophets. Arresting them was the right thing to do to ensure that justice would be accomplished. His solution to the problem they created for him was to try to force other people to change.

But these followers of the Way were reluctant to change, even to the point of being willing to die. Saul himself presided over and witnessed the first recorded martyrdom in the Christian scriptures, the stoning of Stephen. Presumably, Saul had also heard Stephen's lengthy speech just before he was stoned, in which he argued that Jesus had been the Righteous One whom Moses had foretold. He would have heard Stephen's dying words claiming as he breathed his last that he saw Jesus glorified at God's right hand (Acts 7:52-58). Immediately after Stephen's death Saul began his persecution of the scattered church, "ravaging" it in house after house (Acts 8:3).

Anger is often a result of a person's fighting reality which will not bend to the person's wishes. Saul's burning anger drove him on to Damascus to extend his arrests to the Christians there. He was full of self-righteous zeal, "breathing threats and murder against the disciples" (Acts 9:1). In this angry state, the One finds disintegration rising from an anger and a deep resentment which shake the entire body. It arises from the righteousness of the ego sealed off from the greater righteousness of God.

But as a man of God, Saul also had a deep integrity and genuine love for God which led his zeal and anger to suddenly give birth to a blinding flash of insight that allowed him to ask himself the question, *what if I am wrong?* As has already been pointed out, for a One, being wrong is one of the most terrifying realizations, the equivalent of being knocked off a horse. And that is exactly what happens to Saul. He falls off his horse and loses his sight, an indication that he can no longer "see" things as he used to. He has a vision of the risen Jesus asking him why he is persecuting him. Saul is tossed into a new reality. He must learn to see anew and to re-examine what his desire for righteousness means. At the moment of his conversion, the truth of the moment is printed indelibly on his mind. He sees himself more clearly and more objectively, and in this state of clarity Ones become open and non-reactive. They are able to drop their judgments of themselves and others and their need to defend the truth, and they allow their souls to relax and revelation to enter.

Some people have claimed that Saul may have fallen into a trance, or achieved what we might today call an altered state of consciousness, which has a dissociative character about it but which also confirms and reinforces what was already present.[54] In other words, Saul, now Paul, opened himself to confirming what he had already come to know in his unconscious as true, namely, that Stephen's words were accurate. This openness and acceptance is the greatest confirmation we have that Paul genuinely desired to know the truth. As William James has pointed out, such a sudden conversion is often connected with someone who has an active subliminal self which can cause such 'uprushes' from deep within.[55] Acting out of a lively subliminal self does not diminish its significance, for the changes are real and the fruits are lasting. When Paul allowed the Holy Spirit to 'uprush' from within and fill him, he reported that "something like scales fell from his eyes, and his sight was restored" (Acts 9:18). The scales of his self-righteous ego perceptions through which he had judged the world had to fall away so that he could finally see with new eyes the wider reality of the righteousness of God.

All the characteristics of the One fit Paul to perfection. He has been vividly described as "God's own CEO, a motivator, an organizer, a hands-on manager, a tireless leader-by-example, a 'Take-Charge Guy' with his eye on the Big Picture."[56] He is rational, idealistic, principled, orderly, perfectionist, and self-righteous. Yet as he grows in his new conviction that the people he has been persecuting are after all right, he needs to adjust his earlier sense of what constitutes 'right' in the eyes of God. In his profound change of mind and heart, he can now say that he wishes to "gain Christ and be found in him, not having a righteousness of my own that comes from the law, but one that comes through faith in Christ, the righteousness from God based on faith" (Philippians 3:8-9). This is the true strength of a compliant type: a willingness to change if necessary, even if it is painful, in order to listen to a new voice of authority growing from within, and not imposed from without. This new voice is the voice of the Spirit. The more Paul "gains Christ," the more his ego is liberated, enabling him to see the seamless beauty of all existence.

Conversion does not mean perfection, but at least it sets one on the road towards it. Judging from his own writings, we can also determine that even after his conversion Paul could still manifest the tendency of the One to be self-righteous, intolerant, and inflexible. We see this when he attacks those who were insisting that the new Christians should submit to the Law of Moses and be circumcised: Paul writes that he wishes "those who unsettle you would castrate themselves!" (Galatians 5:12). He continues to be frustrated with his own lack of perfection: "For I do not do the good I want, but the evil I do not want is what I do" (Romans 7:19). He is impatient with the quarrels within the new church communities: "Has Christ been divided? Was Paul crucified for you? Or were you baptized in the name of Paul?" (1 Corinthians 1:13). And he clearly retained a shadow of his resentment when he refused to take John Mark with him because of a previous desertion (Acts 15:38).

Paul's impatience has a positive side to it as well, when it is directed not to the desires arising from his ego-self but to his yearning for complete union with Christ and the perfection of all creation. He writes that he longingly awaits the new creation as we "groan inwardly while we wait for adoption, the redemption of our bodies" (Romans 8:23), and he is himself eager to "depart and be with Christ, for that is far better, but to remain in the flesh is more necessary for you" (Philippians 1:23-24).

We see clearly Paul's healthy connection with the Body space in the seemingly limitless energy which drives him undeterred in his missionary activity: "For this is the will of God, your sanctification... that each one of you know how to control your own body in holiness and honour" (1 Thessalonians 4:3-4). In the One, the Body space is supported by the Feeling centre, so that feelings strongly influence what one does. Paul provides us with an excellent example of how this works when he disagrees profoundly with Peter over whether Christians needed to observe the Law of Moses. Paul's strong feelings enable him to act clearly and decisively. He reports that "When Cephas [i.e. Peter] came to Antioch, I opposed him to his face, because he stood self-condemned" (Galatians 2:11). As Riso and Hudson point out, "Ones in particular are powerfully motivated to be honest in all of their affairs."[57] In this example we see in Paul the clarity of the One when he believes he is in the right, for in his confrontational style he openly opposes Peter at Antioch face-to-face and not behind his back.

In writing to the Galatians, Paul clearly shows how he has dealt with one of the burdens of the One, namely, bearing one's own faults without attempting to rationalize or justify them. It is a burden which has to be borne by all, but Ones with their longing for perfection feel it the most keenly. Paul writes that when we see another's transgression, we should be very careful to "restore such a one in a spirit of gentleness" (Galatians 6:1) and take care that we are ourselves not tempted; that is, to be sure that we also observe ourselves well and not fall into judgmental attitudes. We are to "bear one another's burdens" (Galatians 6:2) which includes putting up with their failings and their unpleasant behaviours.[58] Paul goes on to say "all must test their own work" and "all must carry their own loads" (Galatians 6:4-5) as a safeguard against falling into a judgmental attitude towards others. Carrying our own loads means bearing the burden of our humanity, again without self-justification or bitterness.

Perhaps because Ones can never quite escape lamenting their imperfections of the past, they have the ability to convert these lapses into the seedbed of virtue so that their greatest weaknesses becomes their greatest allies. Paul illustrates this ability when he comments that "God... judged me faithful... even though I was formerly a blasphemer, a persecutor, a man of violence" (1 Timothy 4:11). He acknowledges his past failings, but also knows how God meets the One in that very space of self-righteousness and converts it into faithfulness. The harsh judgment of the One is redirected into a healthy ability to discern without having to invoke unhealthy emotional outbursts.[59] Paul's past actions become something of which he can boast, not because he is proud of them but because he has been redeemed from them.

The One's gift for leadership is enormous if he or she can accept a leadership role without getting sidetracked into having it feed the ego's need for perfection and acceptance, and so Paul can claim, "there is reserved for me the crown of righteousness, which the Lord, the righteous judge, will give me on that day" (2 Timothy 4:7-8). The tendency to judgment of self and of others is here transformed into allowing God alone to be the judge in a way which frees Paul from getting overly caught up in the outcome of his actions. He also recognizes that God is the one who awards the "crown," and not himself with his own sense of self-importance. Because the only true judge is God, the One can relax into letting things be: "Let us therefore no longer pass judgment on one another" (Romans 14:13). This is an enormous relief to a One, freed from the self-imposed burden of trying to make everyone perfect. Paul's deep joy in this knowledge leads him to plead, "I appeal to you, then, be imitators of me" (1 Corinthians 4:16). His call to perfection is not to be lorded over others, as in an unhealthy One, but to be shared with all who seek the truth. Paul knows that in imitating him, we are in fact imitating the divine essence within him which we all share.

Paul, thanks to his detailed confessions, provides us with wonderful insights into the conversion process of the One and the workings of the Divine moving along the One's lines of energy. While all personalities tend to react automatically in certain situations, thereby losing their objectivity and becoming trapped by their own judgments, phobias, or biases, Ones are the most burdened by this "reactivity", which is central to their personalities. Ones' biggest issue is self-criticism, a perception of self as deficient, and hence they yield to impatience, resentment, and their compulsion to correct things which are not as they 'should' be. They often endure a vicious circle of frustration caused by their never-ending, and inherently misguided, attempts to be 'perfect,' something that is by nature impossible.

Paul, the self-confessed rigid and perfectionist Pharisee, is eventually led to see and denounce the killing rigidity of the 'law.' Paul, the angry crusader, is turned around by a personal call to compassion from Jesus, who says that Paul is persecuting him by pursuing his followers. As Paul begins himself to suffer persecutions and hardships, he gradually mellows, becoming as tender as a nursing mother. The former holy crusader against the infidel, the relentless persecutor of the fledgling church, comes to perceive his own inner conflicts and contradictions. He is finally able to submit to a deeper Law, the law of the Spirit, without losing his intensity, but becoming serene and objective as he follows the call to greater persecutions and glories in suffering for the 'Name.'

Paul comes to embody the One's natural 'brilliance' or intelligence of the soul accessed when a person is truly present to reality, and the One's capacity to synthesize, which is a source of true wisdom realized when all elements coalesce to produce a whole within. He comes to contemplate the depths and height of God's plan and to become ecstatic over the beauty of this universal design. Eventually he becomes One with Christ, in whom he recognizes the perfection or true essence of the One, and identifies solely with him: "For to me, living is Christ and dying is gain" (Philippians 1:21).

Thus, Ones who study Paul can follow the path of their own call to transformation, and more readily accept being led by the Spirit towards their own essence. They can see their own anger blinding them to the truth of what 'is', their tendency to judge themselves and others by idealistic standards, and their occasional lapses into the very faults they condemn in others. They can discern how they are invited by divine grace to see their own inner gifts and perfection, not through the filters of their own subjective judgment, but as divine blessings bestowed upon them, made as they are in the image of God, and thus open and able to be 'perfected,' and not condemned.

Ones can let themselves be touched by everything that 'is', 'as it is,' and let the truth of created reality impact on them. They can let the perfection inherent in all of creation reveal its true self to them, unobscured by their inner judgments. Liberated from their compulsion for endless self-improvement, they can begin to experience self-compassion, and cease to compel themselves to become 'better.' Their experience of the mystery of suffering, which Paul himself knew intensely, will be accompanied by serenity.

The wisdom of the One can be found throughout Paul's writings. He prays that his readers will also "be filled with the knowledge of God's will in all spiritual wisdom and understanding" (Colossians 1:9). He knows that God's wisdom is unattainable by humans, yet does not react to this with resentment but with deep joy: "O the depth of the riches and wisdom and knowledge of God! How unsearchable are his judgments and how inscrutable his ways! 'For who has known the mind of the Lord'?"(Romans 11:33-34). The desire to know in order to be right has here been transformed into a thirst for an intimate knowledge of God who knows all and is in control of all. Paul does not have to do it himself anymore: "it is no longer I who live, but it is Christ who lives in me" (Galatians 2:20), a statement of unbelievable freedom for the One, who is now able to act not from the ego and its need to be right, but from the divine centre which is joyful, wise and open to growth.

Prayer in the Spirit of Paul
Psalm 17

Hear a just cause, O LORD; attend to my cry;
  give ear to my prayer from lips free of deceit.
From you let my vindication come;
  let your eyes see the right.

If you try my heart, if you visit me by night,
    if you test me, you will find no wickedness in me;
    my mouth does not transgress.
As for what others do, by the word of your lips
    I have avoided the ways of the violent.
My steps have held fast to your paths;
    my feet have not slipped.

I call upon you, for you will answer me, O God
    incline your ear to me, hear my words.
Wondrously show your steadfast love,
    O saviour of those who seek refuge
    from their adversaries at your right hand.

Guard me as the apple of the eye;
    hide me in the shadow of your wings,
from the wicked who despoil me,
    my deadly enemies who surround me.
They close their hearts to pity;
    with their mouths they speak arrogantly.
They track me down, now they surround me;
    they set their eyes to cast me to the ground.
They are like a lion eager to tear,
    like a young lion lurking in ambush.

Rise up O LORD, confront them, overthrow them!
    By your sword deliver my life from the wicked,
from mortals – by your hand, O LORD–
    from mortals whose portion in life is in this world.
May their bellies be filled with what you have stored up for
them;
    may their children have more than enough;
    may they leave something over to their little ones.
As for me, I shall behold your face in righteousness;
    when I awake I shall be satisfied, beholding your
    likeness.

Summary of the Ones:

His untimely death by decapitation does not permit us to see in John the Baptist the maturing process of the One unfolding itself fully. However, we can readily appreciate how even before his death he has already achieved a key goal for a One, that of making a difference and living for a higher purpose. Himself already a renowned public figure with many followers, John also clearly rejoices in the fact that he himself must decrease, whereas Jesus must increase. His true nature is also readily visible in his wisdom and quality of discernment.

In Paul's case, we watch the arrogant persecutor grow beyond his obsession with perfection, his fault finding and his projection onto others. His sudden conversion has borne abundant fruit. He has adjusted his ideas to a greater reality and his total being is now focused on the process of becoming, not on being, perfect. With serenity he accepts whatever will happen to him. The once impatient Paul now lives no longer for himself but for Christ. He is empathetic and supportive of the many communities he has founded and to which he is totally dedicated. He continues to work hard but is no longer as tense and relentlessly driven as he once was. Still aware of his imperfections, he is in no way paralyzed. But his vision has broadened well beyond his personal preoccupations. In the midst of a busy ministry, his teachings show him basking in the contemplation of God's unfolding purpose.

Type Two: Ruth and Boaz

> "If you then... know how to give good gifts to your children, how much more will your Father in heaven give good things to those who ask him!"
>
> – Matthew 7:11

Twos are known as the helpers or the givers of the world. They are one of the three types in the Heart centre, and they long most of all for love. For them, their ideal self nurtures itself as well as others, and their true nature is to be good to themselves. Compassionate and benevolent towards everyone, their chief virtue is humility, and their corresponding sin is its opposite, pride.

Like the One, the Two also has a misused Thinking centre. Unlike the One, however, the Two's preferred centre is the Feeling centre, while the Doing centre supports it. This means that the actions of a Two are often aimed at producing for themselves the feeling of being loved. In its unproductive form, their desire for love can become a fantasy of merging with another to produce the false belief that they have found the unity they seek. In fact, the desire for union is actually their unrealized desire not for another person but for the inner union which occurs when the soul knows it is one with the Divine. This is the inner marriage which is represented through many different images: the Lover and Beloved in the Song of Songs, the union of yin and yang, the marriage between Christ and his church, and the integration of animus and anima, to name just a few. Such a "marriage" is not only for Twos but for all who seek to be united with their divine centre, out of which is born love and compassion for the self and for others.

There is a dual movement in the Two, of out and in, giving to get, love and war. The untransformed Two appears to be giving a benevolent gift but in reality demands recognition and appreciation. Twos want to be needed while at the same time they want to be independent of others. They do not want to recognize any laws or authority which might inhibit their giving. Their care-giving tendency, their consistent reaching out and even imposing, is indicative of the Twos' need to be needed. As one of the compliant types, Twos truly believe that their value hinges upon how much and how often they give to others. When this is the reason for giving, it becomes its own reward, a good feeling, a false charity which is really self-interest that masquerades under the form of altruism.[60] This is the real trap for the Twos. They easily get caught in self-deception, false generosity, and self-aggrandizement of their own self-image in the form of self-flattery. Jesus' parable of the separation of the sheep and the goats in Matthew's gospel is an illustration of this false masquerade. In that story, the truly loving souls will not know that they have been givers: "Lord," they ask, "when was it that we saw you hungry and gave you food, or thirsty and gave you something to drink?" (Matthew 25:37). They simply did what they needed to do, with no awareness of being unusually good or giving, or the reward of going home with the glow of having done an act of charity. It was just something that happened: done and forgotten.

The transformed Twos reflect this quality of unattached giving, freely pouring out of their abundance which comes not from the ego-self but from the divine fountain endlessly surging up from within. They are able to give not out of the pleasure they will derive for themselves but out of the divine understanding and compassion which they allow to flow through them. Then it truly becomes not their own egos doing the giving but the Divine Giver bestowing gifts on creation through the openness and availability of those who are dwelling in the healthy Two space. The results of their inner work will radiate an energy that is bigger than the individual through self-surrender. In describing the experience of such conversion, William James wrote that "when the new centre of personal energy has been subconsciously incubated so long as to be just ready to open into flower, 'hands off' is the only word for us, it must burst forth unaided!"[61]

We see this "bursting forth" in the biblical characters of Ruth and Boaz, whose beautiful giving and receiving has long been held up as a model for behaviour. They exhibit the true compliant self of the Two as Ruth accepts her place among a new people and grows in love for them, and Boaz fulfils his legal obligations not from an automatic reaction but out of genuine love and admiration for Ruth and her family. Looking at the Two means looking at relationships, and so it is useful to examine two characters whose stories are not separate but woven together into a narrative that shows its readers how a loving and a covenantal relationship between two people can mirror the inner state of the individual soul when it aspires to union with its essence.

Ruth and Boaz

> "Where you go, I will go; Where you lodge, I will lodge;
> your people shall be my people, and your God my God."

> – Ruth 2:16

The entire Book of Ruth can be opened up through the insights offered by the nature of the Two. Its themes of covenant, marriage, and the giving of oneself readily lend themselves to issues surrounding the Two. Its structure supports the movement of the Two from a fragmented to an integrated state. Its four chapters outline the path from weeping and broken hearts, through hard work, to waiting and pondering, and finally to marriage and the sealing of a covenant.

The Book of Ruth explores the nature of divine providence in providing help to widows and strangers and caring for the outcast, and a sense that this divine providence is moving towards a happy resolution of apparently unsolvable human problems. The characters are all in their own ways both givers and receivers of help and care within their society. Both Ruth and Boaz are willing to take a risk and make a commitment in order to bring a good resolution out of bad times, a theme which resonates throughout the Bible as an aspect of God's love for humanity.

The Book of Ruth provides us with not one but two characters who manifest the traits of the Two. They show this compliant type's ability to "go with the flow," to find and utilize the good in every situation. Their compliancy is a flexibility that opens up for them and for those in their immediate circle unforeseen possibilities for growth and change. Their compliancy also accommodates itself to the perceived needs of others. At best, Twos are deeply unselfish, humble, altruistic, and joyful. As givers, they put the needs of others first, generally to the exclusion of their own, and can sometimes be known as the "people pleasers."[62] As helpers they are caring and nurturing, though their people-pleasing tendency sometimes makes them overly expressive in their feelings and effusive in their friendships.

In Ruth herself, we find the common need of the Two to be a "special friend" who has a privileged place in the life of another.[63] When Ruth's husband, the son of Naomi, dies, her clinging to her mother-in-law assures her of this status of favourite daughter. It is doubly assured when her counterpart, Orpah, also a widow of one of Naomi's sons, decides *not* to stay with Naomi but to return to her own people. No blame is attached to Orpah's decision to return, but she serves the dramatic function of highlighting Ruth's contrary decision to remain. Orpah's leaving shows clearly that Ruth did have a choice and could have done the same thing.

Boaz is the other Two in this narrative. He is a near kinsman of Naomi, and he embodies the Two's characteristic of wanting not just to be involved in any important decision but also to be seen to be in that position by others.[64] He does both admirably in the story, as he steps in to assist Naomi and Ruth when they return, and makes certain that he publicly announces what he intends to do for them. Because the stories of Ruth and Boaz are intertwined, it is helpful to look at them together.

In the eyes of many, Ruth is often held up as a model of loyalty, but it appears from the story that her loyalty is based more on her desire to remain with her mother-in-law Naomi than on an attraction to the Hebrew tribe and its way of life. Naomi may well also represent to Ruth an authority figure, one to whom she looks to bend her will accordingly, something the Two is adept at. The two women are widowed, and Ruth's decision to go back with Naomi, rather than return to her own people, the Moabites, perhaps comes from her basic needing to belong and to be loved more than it does from the inherent attractiveness of the God of Naomi's people, although this, too, is clearly part of the pledge she makes: "your people shall be my people, and your God my God" (Ruth 1:16). While this really does sound like a selfless oath of loyalty, it also has a touch of the Two's desire to merge totally with another. Merging with another is often a substitute for engaging in the inner work which will result in the merging of our self with our divine essence.

We are not given the sort of information about Ruth that we would demand from a modern story-teller. We do not know if her reluctance to return to her own people comes from experiences with them that she wishes to put behind her, or indicates a lack of familial ties which would recall her. Her request to accompany Naomi instead is phrased in such a way that it could, to a modern sensibility, even suggest an almost unhealthy clinging to Naomi rather than establishing her own identity as a person.

Such concepts are not a part of the Hebrew story, but through the Enneagram's understanding of the character of Ruth we can see manifested in her the potential of the Two to be unconsciously manipulative, a tendency which may also be perceived as just plain meddlesome. She will not take no for an answer, but emphatically and impulsively says to Naomi, "Do not press me to leave you or to turn back from following you!" (Ruth 1:15). Ruth is asserting herself, demanding a privilege regardless of what the established values of another people might allow. She easily and readily crosses the boundary between two peoples without pausing to consider if there might be any consequences. The desire for human company is often a sign of a Two's feeling lost when alone. Being alone might be taken as proof of being unwanted and unliked, and because it is felt as a disgrace, it is also kept secret. Feeling alone creates a need for others to supply the meaning and add "zest" to whatever one is doing.[65]

Naomi is then given a lengthy (considering the brevity of the entire story) speech lamenting her widowhood, her age, and the fact that even if she were to remarry and have more sons, Ruth could not possibly be expected to wait for them to be grown. In her melancholy, Naomi speaks as a Four (discussed below), dramatically putting forth her feelings and calling attention to her inner state of unhappiness. Perhaps the attraction Ruth feels towards her mother-in-law at this point represents an intuitive knowledge that as a Two her growth lies in learning how to take care of herself and her own feelings as well as always looking out for the needs of others. Twos can thereby learn how to attain the deep satisfaction which can only come from an authentic experience, not a manipulated one. Discovering her own neediness becomes an avenue to such an experience of the integrated wholeness between outer and inner realities. Naomi knows how to do this; Ruth must learn it, and she can if she stays with her mother-in-law.

The story's motif of a setting of barrenness moving into a time of fruitfulness parallels a similar growth in Ruth's character. The women had left Bethlehem because of a famine; they now return to Bethlehem at the time of the barley harvest and discover there is food to be had. The name of the town, Beth-lehem, means "house of bread", which itself reinforces the theme of abundance to which the story turns. This movement from hunger to fulfilment underscores the turning point for Ruth, who, in her determination to help Naomi, finds herself gathering ears of grain for them both. The Two must discover that she can best give to others when she also gives generously to herself, a compliancy that not all Twos learn easily.

Ruth sets to work gleaning in the field "without resting even for a moment" (Ruth 2:7). This incessant movement is common to a Two undergoing stress: a kind of aggressive attentiveness to one's basic needs takes over. Ruth must be aware that the workers in the field have noticed how she has been working non-stop since dawn, and this extra attention feeds her sense of worthiness. Twos normally have a low tolerance for routine, but the extra attention and the knowledge that she is doing something pleasing to Naomi soften her potential boredom.

Boaz, a near kinsman of Elimelech, Naomi's deceased husband, enters the story at this point in the narrative. He is portrayed as a wealthy and kindly figure whose generosity rescues both Ruth and Naomi from poverty and hunger. He allows and even encourages Ruth to continue gathering food from his field. His helpfulness is behind the scenes, for Ruth does not know (though the reader does) that he has instructed his reapers to deliberately let a bit more grain than usual fall from their bundles; in fact, they are to deliberately pull some out and let it drop to the ground so that she may have all that she needs.

Boaz is a healthy Two who is unselfish, altruistic, and genuinely charitable. He is able to be a giver without calling attention to himself. In allowing Ruth to work in his field, he also admonishes her to stay close to the women in the field, and assures her that the young men will not bother her. When she questions his kindness, he replies that it is because he has heard of her goodness to his kinswoman Naomi, again displacing self-congratulation with a practical reply. He manifests empathetic caring and supportive giving, two traits which characterize the healthy Two.[66]

When a Two meets a Two, there can sometimes be a clash of effusiveness. If neither Two wants to be outdone in giving, not only will their behaviour degenerate into meaningless one-upmanship, but they will also lose sight entirely of the necessity of remaining grounded in their own neediness. In the story of Ruth, however, this dynamic does not materialize, suggesting that both Ruth and Boaz are ultimately able to be in touch with their own needs as well as with those of others. Boaz is happy to assist this young woman, and Ruth is able to receive his help.

Often, the Two's own need for help becomes a kind of dependency which in its extreme or unhealthy form believes that others should take over and do their work for them, and even give meaning to their life so that they can live vicariously through others.[67] Ruth does not go to this extreme but it is worth noting that the potential for such reliance on Boaz is latent here. However, she resists moving in this direction, an indication of her own healthy knowledge that she, too, has needs which must be met.

Boaz welcomes Ruth into Israel, praises her for all she has done for her mother-in-law, and prays that God will reward her for her deeds. Ruth's acceptance of his praise is a healthy sign for a Two, and she allows her feelings to surface and become aware of herself as she really is.[68] She says to Boaz, "you have comforted me and spoken kindly to your servant, even though I am not one of your servants" (Ruth 2:13). She is attached yet detached here, receiving assurance from Boaz without merging herself into his identity. It is a difficult balance for a Two to achieve.

Boaz helps her further by offering her bread and wine among his own reapers, showing his generosity and also his respect for her own needs. He cares for her without suffocating her with his kindness. Presumably, it is out of her hearing that he told his workers to throw a few extra handfuls of grain her way. In doing this he demonstrates the Two's basic virtue of doing unselfish good to another. Later, he comes to have a more personal interest in Ruth, but at this point his goodness at least appears to be disinterested.

Naomi seems less further along in her own growth. As a Four, when she experiences stress, she would commonly move out of her typical melancholy and begin to worry about her relationships and try to find some ways to get closer to the people she likes.[69] This tendency may underlie Naomi's suggestion that Ruth try to find "some security" (Ruth 3:1) by presenting herself to Boaz with the intention of having him marry her according to the levirate law, which obligated the next-of-kin to provide children for his relative's widow (Deuteronomy 25:5-6). Naomi is of course concerned about the future of herself as well as of Ruth, but what she suggests is presented solely as helping Ruth: "so that it may be well with you" (Ruth 3:1). A Four's fear of abandonment may sometimes cause her to disguise her nervousness by acting as if helping another is her sole motivation, yet she really hopes to keep the other near to her for her own sense of security. By the end of the narrative, Naomi does move forward in her own growth: as a Four who has undergone a transformation, she moves into a full and loving participation in her community once Ruth's child has been born. Naomi becomes the child's nurse and is blessed by the women, who assure her that indeed she has not been abandoned, and that God "shall be to you a restorer of life and a nourisher of your old age" (Ruth 4:15). She comes to know that her fear of having no identity of her own has been absorbed in God's unwavering regard for her. Her sense of being an isolated self has broadened into an awareness that she is not an intruder but an integral part of a community and of a family.

When Naomi explains to Ruth that it is Boaz's duty to father Ruth's child, her directions to Ruth contain no hint of salaciousness or impropriety in their narrative description. Naomi is concerned with providing a legal heir for her deceased husband and also for her daughter-in-law. Following Naomi's instructions, Ruth waits until Boaz has eaten and drunk and is "in a contented mood" and then proceeds to "stealthily" lie down beside him (Ruth 3:11).

Boaz is startled awake at midnight when he finds Ruth next to him. His reaction indicates that he is among the healthiest of Twos, for he is appreciative of her offer of herself, yet also disinterestedly aware of what she is asking of him. He does not instantly seize her, nor does he evidence glee at the prospect of doing so at a later time. Striking in its omission is the frequent formula of biblical narrative that "he went in to her" or "he knew her."[70] In this case, Ruth "goes in" to Boaz and he regards her act as an act of loyalty, not one of seduction. He declares her a "worthy woman,"(Ruth 3:11) thereby connecting her with the *eshet hayil*, or the woman of valour described in the lovely wisdom poem which concludes the Book of Proverbs (Proverbs 31). The poem traditionally praises the virtues of all the noble women in the Hebrew tradition, and Ruth is clearly one of them, even though she is not a Hebrew by birth.

Altruistically, Boaz recalls another kinsman who is in fact a closer relative of Ruth than he is, and who must therefore be approached first as having the prior claim. The narrative suggests quite strongly that Ruth and Boaz spend the night together with no sexual encounter (they "got up before one person could recognize another" [Ruth 3:14]), even though she, a beautiful young woman, has clearly offered herself to him. Boaz evidences the extent to which the generosity of the Two can go when he puts his kinsman ahead of himself in the matter. When he sends Ruth back to Naomi, he generously gives her six measures of barley so that she will not return empty-handed, another indication of his desire to give gifts and to take care of her.

The way Boaz goes about securing the claim for himself is an interesting example of how a Two can appear to be well-meaning and yet also have a hidden ulterior motive. Sometimes their giving is for selfish reasons. While he is indeed capable of disinterested charity, Boaz is also able to use this characteristic to satisfy his own sometimes unacknowledged need for acceptance and love.[71] He cleverly manipulates the bargaining with the other kinsman by introducing the matter only partially. He tells the kinsman first that Naomi's land is for sale, and the kinsman declares his interest in buying it. Boaz then adds the important bit of missing information, that in buying the land, the man is also acquiring Ruth and must keep the inheritance in the name of her house.

The kinsman objects to this, since it would endanger his own inheritance, and Boaz is now free to acquire both land and Ruth for himself, and he is quick to move into the vacant position. The cost of the land never becomes an issue, and this is consistent with the compliant type's need to feel accepted and to measure personal value not through money but through love, by how much they are liked or needed.[72] While a Two can sometimes be patronizing, this does not appear to be Boaz's attitude here, as he is genuinely moved by Ruth's claim on behalf of Naomi's family, and he has also settled a business transaction which benefits himself.

While the Two's compulsion is pride, as the Two grows into genuine humility, the Heart and the Head come together in mutual giving and receiving. The Twos of Ruth and Boaz recognize the blessings they have received from God and from one another. Their moving towards each other reflects in its love the moving of God towards all humanity. While God is not an active character in this story, it is clear that Ruth's attraction to Israel and Boaz's attraction to Ruth symbolize the way in which God works to transform the Two through relationships.

Ruth, previously a foreigner, is accepted into his household and the elders liken her to Rachel and Leah, the mothers of the 12 sons of Jacob "who together built up the house of Israel" (Ruth 4:11). She is further compared to Tamar, another widowed woman whose cleverness and persistence ensured the birth of an heir to the house of Judah when Judah, in stark contrast to Boaz, failed to provide for his widowed daughter-in-law.[73] The context here makes it quite clear that Ruth is numbered among the matriarchs of Israel. Obed, the son conceived by her and Boaz, and given to the household of Naomi, becomes the father of Jesse, who is the father of David. Ruth is therefore the great-grandmother of David, who was to become the greatest king of the house of Judah. The moral ending of this story seems to underscore that without Ruth's untiring efforts, her determined loyalty, her abundant willingness to give and, finally, to receive, there would have been no messianic line established in the house of David.

The story of Ruth reads a lot like a parable or fairy-tale, and these are often the stories in which archetypes are most clearly seen and perceived at both conscious and unconscious levels. As a moral tale, the Book of Ruth's emphasis is anti-exclusionist and even its concept of God is presented in terms of the Two: it reinforces the idea that the God of the Hebrews is also the God of the non-Hebrews, a giver who is not limited, who is effusive and full of abundance, and that even foreigners can partake of this generosity and fulfil essential roles in the development of sacred history. As an archetypal story, it gives us the character of the outsider who becomes the key person in establishing a new order in the community. It is kin to the rags-to-riches stories that everyone loves, because we all feel at some level that we, too, have only "rags" and need to be assured of our "riches." The Two that is in everyone needs to be aware of its own neediness and its desire to be loved, even as it wishes to give to others fully and selflessly. In the marriage of Ruth and Boaz we see an image of the integrated soul, a metaphorical depiction of the giving and receiving within the self which, in its proper balance, produces new life and gives it to the world.

The love of Ruth, first for Naomi, then for Boaz, is the love that embraces you and that saves your life.[74] It is no accident that this love turns out to be the love that grows out of the transformed inner self. The birth of Obed announces that what is created by this inner harmony is the beginning of a new order which will continue through subsequent generations. The giving and the receiving are seen to go on within ourselves but must inevitably pour out into our world in an abundance of life and growth.

Prayer in the Spirit of Ruth and Boaz
Psalm 66

Make a joyful noise to God, all the earth;
    sing the glory of God's name;
    give to God glorious praise.
Say to God, "How awesome are your deeds!
    Because of your great power, your enemies cringe
    before you.
All the earth worships you;
    they sing praises to you,
    sing praises to your name."

Come and see what God has done:
    God is awesome in deeds among mortals.
God turned the sea into dry land;
    they passed through the river on foot.
There we rejoiced in God,
    who rules by might forever,
whose eyes keep watch on the nations –
    let the rebellious not exalt themselves.

Bless our God, O peoples,
    let the sound of God's praise be heard,
who has kept us among the living,
    and has not let our feet slip.
For you, O God, have tested us;
    you have tried us as silver is tried.
You brought us into the net;
    you laid burdens on our backs;
you let people ride over our heads;
    we went through fire and through water;
yet you have brought us out to a spacious place.

I will come into your house with burnt offerings;
    I will pay you my vows,
those that my lips uttered

and my mouth promised when I was in trouble.
I will offer to you burnt offerings of fatlings,
    with the smoke of the sacrifice of rams;
I will make an offering of bulls and goats.

Come and hear, all you who fear God,
    and I will tell what God has done for me.
I cried aloud to God,
    and God was extolled with my tongue.
If I had cherished iniquity in my heart,
    the LORD would not have listened.
But truly God has listened;
    God has given heed to the words of my prayer.

Blessed be God,
    who has not rejected my prayer
    or removed God's steadfast love from me.

Summary of the Twos

In both Ruth and Boaz we see many of the issues facing the Two: the fear of being rejected, the strong desire to be loved unconditionally, the search for intimacy and the need to be nurturing and giving. Ruth manifests the positive elements of the Two in her abandonment to a higher purpose, and her accepting the love of Naomi and Boaz as unconditional.

Boaz, like Ruth, is a hard worker, sensing the needs of others and responding to them selflessly. Both Ruth and Boaz mirror the beauties of true friendship and easy relationships. They are both givers and helpers who genuinely care for each other's well-being. Empathetic and sensitive, they are also altruistic and loyal. Both of them reap the rewards of their willingness to take a risk on behalf of others – Ruth by remaining with Naomi, and Boaz by taking Ruth as his wife. By the story's end, all the characters know that they are loved by others, and as a result they also have learned how to love themselves.

Type Six: Peter and the Maccabean Mother

Cast all your anxiety on God, because God cares for you.

– 1 Peter 5:7

The Sixes are the loyalists and the guardians. The ideal for the Six is to trust the self and trust in the goodness of creation and life. Sixes are dedicated and faithful, dependable and endearing. Their true nature is to be courageous and competent in any and all circumstances of life. Their virtue is courage, and their corresponding sin is cowardice or fear. While fear is not usually considered a sin or vice, it is in fact the direct opposite of love in John's epistle: "There is no fear in love, but perfect love casts out fear; for fear has to do with punishment, and whoever fears has not reached perfection in love" (1 John 4:18). Sixes long to be secure, and fear arises in them when they feel that they do not have support and cannot survive on their own.

The Sixes are the third type of the compliant or dependent group. Like the Ones and the Twos, they too have a misused Thinking centre. For the Sixes, Thinking is misused because their insecurity makes them look to others for support and to rules and structures for guidance rather than thinking clearly for themselves.[75] At the same time, the Sixes are located right in the middle of the Thinking triad (Fives, Sixes, and Sevens) on the Enneagram. Thus the Thinking centre is also their preferred centre, but works against them because even when they receive whatever information they may need, they still proceed to question its reliability.[76] This makes it difficult for Sixes to come to any decisions, yet at the same time they think that decision-making is an important activity. While they have highly developed thinking skills, their vivid imaginations often cause them to get caught up in the potential harm or threat in a situation.

The virtue of the Six is courage, often achieved with enormous difficulty because courageousness can involve decision-making during times of stress, and Sixes do not make decisions quickly or easily. Demonstrating such difficult courage can lead the Six into a position of leadership, and this role will often be accompanied by devotion to the community or an organization being led. On the other hand, Sixes may just as likely go the other direction and become defiant of any authority and even appear to be manifestly incompetent. Their movement is a back and forth shifting, while they weigh and consider all the information they have. They do not act on a good idea as readily as they might because doing so depends upon another's opinions and suggestions. This wavering can paralyze their ability to act. Faced with a need to do something, Sixes often hesitate, doubting their own abilities, and are good at procrastinating and becoming anxious because they are undecided. They may replace action with further analysis of the relative benefits of doing or not doing something. For them, the potential pitfalls are more real than the possible achievement. Their thinking constantly wonders, doubts, and questions. Thoughts in the head of a Six may sound like a committee meeting, constantly coming up with diverse opinions for and against whatever is going on.

For this reason, Sixes will often distract themselves and take on another action unrelated to the matter at hand. Peter's decision to go back to his fishing after the crucifixion of Jesus is a good example of this response. Going fishing helps him avoid dealing with his questions, hesitations, and possible risks in what the future may hold.

Sixes require something to believe in and they desire security in their lives. Often they look to others to provide them with the security they cannot find within themselves. This can take the form of loyalty to a leader or group so that their decisions can be made by someone else. They search for an authority, but they also distrust authority. The work of transformation for the Sixes consists of taking back the unquestioning allegiance they have given to an outside authority and putting it back into themselves. Jesus' encounter with Peter after the resurrection does this for Peter. By questioning Peter about his love, Jesus helps Peter to look within himself and discover the love within him that is not offered solely in reaction to what is expected of him. Sixes who turn to their inner strength learn to act out of compliance to what they know from within rather than what they have been told by an external authority. This aligns them with the other two compliant types, the Ones and the Twos, but for the Sixes, their practice of endurance more than of wisdom or understanding is the form in which their gift becomes manifest. After his encounter with Jesus, Peter is able to continue his discipleship out of his newly-found courage and love, even to the point of ultimately suffering martyrdom.

A Six may react to a stressful situation either by running away from it, or actually running directly towards it in order to dispel it. These two different reactions are illustrated in the two examples below, in Peter, who flees when Jesus is arrested, and in the Maccabean mother, who drives herself and her seven sons headlong into their martyrs' deaths. Both characters are deeply affected by their sense of duty: Peter is miserable when he realizes he has run away from Jesus, and the mother uses her strong sense of duty and obligation to her faith to enable her to confront the unthinkable, the deaths of all her sons, without wavering. Their endurance through suffering to freedom marks the path of transformation for the Six.

Peter

> "Lord, you know everything; you know that I love you."

> – John 21:17

The naming of Peter as a Six, and hence as a compliant type, might seem contrary to the popular perception of him as a stubborn or headstrong man. But compliant types can indeed be stubborn if their compliance is to a strongly held belief or personality trait. This may at times be true for Peter, yet there is a side to him which is also eager to please and to be liked, as well as a need to develop his trusting side and allow his latent courage to overcome his fear. His is a constant struggle to remain courageous and at peace despite original deep inner doubt as to his own strength and capabilities. His story provides us with clear evidence of his willingness to "bend" and to shift his compliance from stubbornness, as is seen in his well-known triple denial that he knows Jesus, into affirmation when he encounters the risen Christ and is able to express his love and fidelity.

In Jesus, Peter had finally found an authority on whom he could depend, and with whom he felt safe and secure. He may have had some initial doubts about his being called into membership in the small band of people who followed Jesus and tried to learn what his message signified, but these were overcome by a vision of what this leader might accomplish. Peter became their leader as they lived the vision step by step, so its demands were not too overwhelming or fearful. A strong faith, the gift of the Six, made Peter able to trust himself in the moment and not allow personal fears to dominate. Only when he thought he might himself be harmed did he let his fears take over and he fled at the moment of Jesus' arrest and trial.

Peter manifests the Six's characteristics of duty, loyalty, respect for tradition, and working relentlessly for a cause he knew could affect the entire community. It is fitting that the long line of popes, who claim succession to Peter, has become identified with those same characteristics, representing leadership and loyalty and fidelity to a faith and to an institution, a compliance with a code and with a history. Peter's iconography consists of a set of keys, signifying the "keys of the kingdom," a good symbol for the Six of authority, security, and belonging. In his first epistle, we see that Peter himself encourages respect for authority when he admonishes his audience, "for the Lord's sake accept the authority of every human institution, whether of the emperor as supreme, or of governors, as sent by him to punish those who do wrong and to praise those who do right" (1 Peter 2:23).

A Six is often identified with a particular group and can appreciate and enjoy its intensity and purpose. The Bible frequently mentions the trio of Peter, James and John in the gospels, indicating that this 'group' was probably a sort of inner circle of the larger group of disciples gathered around Jesus. Peter seems to enjoy pre-eminence not only in this smaller group but in the larger group of disciples as well. All four gospels testify to his leadership, one of the few details which all of them share. They all contain a version of his profession of faith, presumably speaking on behalf of them all, that Jesus is the Christ, the Son of God, the Messiah who was to come.[77] The stories and events in the Bible arose out of an oral tradition which sought to preserve them. The ones which are repeated over the years or centuries are the ones which reflect the basic convictions or assumptions of their tellers. The role of Peter was obviously regarded as central to the telling of the story of the life of Jesus.

Peter's importance is emphasized again when we see him assume a strong leadership role among the disciples after the resurrection. In the Acts of the Apostles, he addresses with confidence crowds of 3,000 people (Acts 2:14 ff). He speaks persuasively but not heavy-handedly, and convinces many in the crowd to receive baptism. When the crowd responds to the teachings of the apostles and asks what they should do, Peter is acknowledged as their authority when he replies in the name of all, "Repent and be baptized every one of you in the name of Jesus Christ so that your sins may be forgiven; and you will receive the gift of the Holy Spirit" (Acts 2:28). We can recognize in the sequence of accounts which include Peter how the work of a Six can lead to the acceptance of a leadership role which is not designed to feed the ego. Peter is focused on the good of the people and what they need to hear and accept. His own instinct towards self-protection might even have alerted him to a potential danger when he spoke so boldly to the crowd, yet he knew the message he delivered was even more important than his own life.

There are many leaders who assume their positions, whether over 12 or over 3,000 people, who rely on an external code, like a constitution, or Robert's *Rules of Order*, to govern their actions. Sixes who are leaders often appeal to some form of external authority to bolster their roles and to which they can appeal in times of uncertainty. This form of support carries with it a corresponding danger. Looking mainly to an outer authority can cause a leader to solidify and justify his or her own opinions and refuse to bend to the real needs of the group. For Peter, the danger was less that of becoming a dictator than it was of forgetting where his real authority lay, which was not in an external system but in his inner conversion and his acceptance of Jesus' law of love and service.

When Peter loses sight of his focus on Jesus, and is distracted by his fears, he flounders. This is played out literally in the account of his walking on the water of the lake towards Jesus during a storm, a literalizing of the compliant's moving out towards other people (Matthew 14:28 ff). Peter sees Jesus walking towards his boat, and instead of trusting his inner knowledge that this was indeed Jesus, he demands that Jesus prove himself, saying, "Lord, if it is you, command me to come to you on the water" (Matthew 14:28). Peter is looking for an outer confirmation so that he can comply with it rather than with his own inner sense of the truth.

Jesus knows with whom he is dealing here, and what Peter needs to be encouraged. Meeting the Six's need for support and security, he issues the order, "Come." At this stage, Peter requires an external order to call forth a demonstration of his belief, and Jesus willingly provides it. But Peter falters. He steps out of the boat with confidence, but starts to pay attention to the strong wind, the outer turbulence which destroys his inner security, and he becomes afraid. What began as an assuring call to him has turned into his loss of self-confidence. As a Six, he has complied not to an order from within but to one from without, the call of the storm which warns him that it is impossible to walk on water. The internal debate overpowered him as he realized he was walking on water, and also knew that he could not in fact do so.

And so he begins to sink. Jesus reaches out his hand and catches Peter, which tells us that they must not have been very far apart when Peter started to go under. Peter was in fact almost where he wanted to be, but at the last minute he wavered. The wavering Six has to find a way to get back up on his feet and find his true security. Jesus pulls Peter towards him and to safety, and helps him to see that his anxiety and his uncertainty are what threatened to pull him under, saying, "You of little faith, why did you doubt?" (Matthew 14:31). Immediate help was close at hand all along, and Peter learned to trust that he would never be allowed to drown. This movement from anxiety to security, trust, and peace is basic to a Six's growth, and Jesus encourages this movement in Peter.

Despite their closeness and Peter's understanding of who Jesus is, when the tension becomes dangerous and Peter's own security is threatened, he denies any association with Jesus. His denial is perhaps the best-known event in Peter's life. Its familiarity signals that it resonates with the experience of many people who know what it is like to brag that you will never give up on someone or something, and then when put to the test, that is exactly what you do.

This well-known episode is also shared by all four gospels (Matthew 26:33ff.; Mark 14:26ff.; Luke 22:31ff.; John 13:36ff). The importance of it is as great as the earlier importance of Peter's profession of faith in Jesus as the Messiah. Both are recorded in the oral and then written traditions which remember the things that speak to people over time and space. Together, the two events beautifully illustrate the Six's difficulty in finding balance and commitment, and both are commemorated in the gospels as turning points in Peter's life.

We may wonder how Peter could do such a thing as deny his friendship with Jesus. Such a betrayal may have even been a harsher one than that of Judas Iscariot, who turned Jesus over to the authorities but who never denied that he was a member of his group of followers. Peter's denial is a stark contrast to his earlier bold assertion that he would be willing to lay down his life for Jesus (John 13:37). The wavering of the Six is at its extreme here, as Peter swings from unqualified loyalty to stark terror.

The Six's desire to be liked means that he might say or do anything in order to obtain the friendship or approval of another. Together with the Six's fear of being left alone, this desire might help in part to explain Peter's behaviour. His earlier display of bravado might mask a deeper fear that is reacting unhappily to Jesus' saying "Where I am going, you cannot follow me now" (John 13:36.). Peter needs human contact, especially that of Jesus, and easily feels lost without it. Without Jesus and the group of disciples that has gathered around him, Peter knew he would feel cut off from life.[78]

The very thought of losing his master, of being abandoned, must have terrified Peter more than the thought of death itself. Though he claimed he would be willing to die with Jesus, Peter is at heart still the indecisive Six, not sure he could actually face it if the moment were to arrive. Waiting to see what others will do, whether to run or to stay, is typical of a Six. A confused and anxious Six may even lash out violently when he does not know what to do. This helps us understand Peter's aggressive and useless action when he cuts of the ear of the High Priest's servant who comes to arrest Jesus in the garden of Gethsemane (John 18:10).

The type on the Enneagram with which we most identify represents not our predestined lot in life but describes our most familiar and habitual way of responding to the world. Like homing pigeons, we circle back to it and we fly home to it when we could have the whole sky to explore. Our transformational work will lead us to new parts of the sky even while we are conscious of our 'home.' Peter's actions during the arrest of Jesus show us that he has returned 'home' to his familiar pattern as a Six, one which looks for security and wavers between faith and courage. He sits outside in the courtyard, waiting for news of Jesus' trial which is going on inside. He has been with the light of the world for three years, warming his soul. Now he tries to warm his body at a charcoal fire (John 18:18). He is near to where Jesus is, but cannot bridge the distance. Unlike his attempt at walking on the water, this time there is no Jesus there to rescue him.

A relative of the man whose ear Peter cut off recognizes him, but Peter cannot face that moment of self-recognition either, and denies that he knows Jesus (John 18:26). After his third denial, the crowing of the cock brings Peter to his lowest point. The cockcrow becomes his 'wake-up' call, telling him that it is time to face his fear and his faith without the physical presence of Jesus to guide him. He must have gone away to do so, for in John's gospel, Peter disappears from the narrative at this point, and does not return again until he and John run to look into the empty tomb on Easter morning. We do not know how Peter spent the time between the trial and the empty tomb.

We can imagine that during that time Peter must have wrestled with self-doubt, wanting to believe that Jesus could be trusted, but afraid to face the possibility that Jesus had failed. Keenest of all must have been the remorse and guilt he felt at having abandoned his friend. Sixes need to look hard at their beliefs and determine whether they come from an inner or an outer authority. In so doing, they may become aware that the internal voices which are noisily arguing both for and against any decision they face are actually fearful aspects of their own imagination. Realizing this will help them to quiet their mind and be able to find the right answer.[79] Perhaps Peter was later able to write, "discipline yourselves, keep alert" (1 Peter 5:8) as a result of what he came to learn about himself during those long hours of sorrow.

The Epilogue to John's gospel (John 21) shows us what Peter is like after his experience of self-doubt. He has returned to what he knows best, his fishing. Jesus meets him right there. Peter and the others have caught nothing, and Jesus calls to them to trust him once again, to cast their nets one more time, and when they do their nets are overflowing. Jesus is preparing Peter for his commission as a fisher of souls, teaching him that things are not necessarily as they appear, and that complete trust will yield a rich return.

Jesus also calls him by his old name, Simon. It is as if he has to go back to the beginning to recall his earlier trust and faith and learn to rely on it, to show compliance to what he knew then and which is being strengthened now. When he sees Jesus across the sea and Jesus calls out to the disciples, Peter jumps into the water under his own authority, acting out of faith and trust. There is no hint that he is afraid. This time Jesus does not call him as he did on the lake in the storm, and Peter arrives on the shore without needing Jesus to rescue him. Peter had been embarrassed to have Jesus wash his feet at the Last Supper, uncertain if Jesus was servant or Lord, but now, when Jesus feeds the disciples breakfast, Peter raises no objection to being served by his master. We can see in these shifts in Peter how Sixes can do the work of transformation. They, like Peter, can learn to move from uncertainty about others, and a tendency to react out of anxiety, to a stable, receptive, and trusting way of being.[80]

After they have been fed, Jesus questions Peter three times, asking him, "Do you love me?" He knows how to help Peter strengthen his faith. Jesus' question is not meant to raise an emotional dynamic. He is not asking Peter to describe his feelings. Jesus is appealing to Peter's faith in God, knowing, as Peter knows, that the first and greatest commandment is to love God with all one's heart, soul, and mind. So Jesus is asking Peter, "Do you love me with all your heart, soul, and mind? Is your faith renewed and strong? Have you overcome your doubt and fear which led to you to forgetfulness and denial?"

Jesus is giving Peter an opportunity to remedy his earlier triple denial, but he is also understanding the concern of the Six not to be afraid in making a decision or declaring his faith. The English translation does not tell us that the word Jesus uses for 'love' is initially the Greek word *agape*, a love that is self-sacrificing and total, the love of God and the love of Christians for one another. Peter does not respond with the same word but instead uses the word *philio*, the love one has for a friend. He is still uncertain of his own faith and love of God, but he knows he wants to have Jesus' friendship back.

The same words are repeated by Jesus and Peter. Then, the third time, Jesus does not use the word *agape*. Instead, he uses the word *philio*, and asks Peter if he loves him with the affection of a friend. Peter is hurt by this because, for a Six, this would appear to be a movement away from loyalty, demoting his love from love of God to simple human love. Yet Jesus does not rebuke him, but instead commissions him to "feed my sheep" (John 21:17), calling attention to the body as well as to the soul. Jesus knows the fear and anxiety of the Six, and meets Peter where he is, gently drawing him back to strengthened faith and great courage. His repeated words give Peter authority to look after the community, to feed the faithful. In telling Peter to do this Jesus is showing his own trust in Peter, and it calls forth Peter's trust in Jesus. He is helping Peter to establish a strong inner authority which will not be fearful or egocentric but faithful and Christocentric. Peter grows to become a strong and courageous leader. His doubts are gone and his faith is renewed. The vision which Jesus had embodied becomes Peter's vision, now internalized as his own.

We sometimes do not consider the pastoral side of Peter. He appears in the gospels, and especially in the Acts of the Apostles, as a man who is committed, who knows cooperation, and who is able to put aside his own interests and accept the direction the spirit seems to be leading him and for the fledgling Christian community. Paul's account in Galatians (Galatians 2:11 ff) recounts how he disputed with Peter over the necessity for new Christians to first accept the Law of Moses, including its demand for male circumcision. Apparently, Peter had been influenced by the conservative element of Jewish Christians, and as a compliant type, had been ready to be persuaded of the correctness of their stand. He argued against Paul that new converts had first to submit to the Law of Moses before they could be baptized, while Paul asserted that Gentiles could enter the Christian community without having first to undergo circumcision. We see in this debate no sign of Peter's previous wavering. Although he lost the argument to Paul, Peter's stand was decisive and strong.

Many people find it very hard to bend at all in this sort of disagreement, and this particular one was of major significance for the early church, as well as for the church today. However, Peter's chief critic, the apostle Paul, was also a compliant type, a One. The early church was therefore led by two men who were both compliant types who had undertaken their own work of transformation and who were eager to see the work of the Holy Spirit carried out, ready to obey, and awake to the divine authority which resided in their own souls.

Before meeting Paul to discuss their dilemma at the Council of Jerusalem in 70 C.E., Peter had allowed the work of the Spirit to teach him that "God shows no partiality, but in every nation anyone who fears [God] and does what is right is acceptable to [God]"

(Acts 10:34). When the leaders of the early church met to deal with the issue which threatened to create a schism, Peter was able to yield to Paul's arguments that new converts did not first need to become Jews before being baptized into the Christian community. Once he recognized the direction the Spirit was leading, Peter was able to trust it and remain faithful. The compliance of both Peter and Paul became manifest in their obedience to the Spirit and not to their own egos.

Peter also demonstrates that a Six operates out of a respect for authority and can even become appropriately authoritative when someone's loyalty to the community is called into question. We find this illustrated in his blunt condemnation of Ananias and his wife Sapphira, for their betrayal of the community (Acts 5:1-11). They had sold property for the community, but kept some of the money back for themselves. Peter knows instantly what they have done. He challenges them directly, asking, "How is it that you have contrived this deed in your heart? You did not lie to us but to God!" (Acts 5:4). Peter's accusation of the dishonest couple causes Ananias, and later Sapphira, to fall down and die. His sense of outrage may not be directed at any perceived offence to his own authority but he is angry on account of the lie which undermines the unity of the community. His newly acquired authority has become not his own but God's.

Having allowed himself to be purged to become a vehicle for God's action in the world, Peter is able to bring God's healing just as Jesus had done. The sick lie on their mats in his path so that his shadow might fall on them and cure them (Acts 5:15). It is not Peter's 'self' which cures them, but his shadow, the part of him which is manifest when he stands in the light. That light, of course, is the light of the world, who now warms and inspires Peter not for Peter's own pleasure but for the healing of the world.

Peter as a Six can serve as a model for anyone's personal

growth. He is a much loved apostle, for many people see in him an aspect of themselves which wants to be loyal and strong, yet often fails at the moment it counts. The Peter in each of us can be stubborn and spontaneous, but when it lovingly encounters God, it can also learn to be fearless and faithful. Peter's words in his second epistle encapsulate beautifully the movement of the Six towards integration. Peter writes that faith, which is of great importance to a Six, must not act on its own but has to be supported by goodness and love:

> You must make every effort to support your faith with goodness, and goodness with knowledge, and knowledge with self-control, and self-control with endurance, and endurance with godliness, and godliness with mutual affection, and mutual affection with love. For if these things are yours and are increasing among you, they keep you from being ineffective and unfruitful in the knowledge of our Lord Jesus Christ.

> – 2 Peter 1:5-8

The inner and outer authorities coincide in a life which, like Peter's, is rooted in love and produces the fruits of the Spirit. Like Peter, we too can experience transformation of consciousness as Peter did on the Mount of Transfiguration, when he saw reality with new eyes (Matthew 17:1-5). We can then descend from that awakening back into our communities which need so much healing and feeding. Our inner Peter is the part of ourselves which can admit failure and not be beaten by it, rising to new courage as we experience and enact the call to feed others.

Prayer in the Spirit of Peter
Psalm 25

To you, O LORD, I lift up my soul.
O my God, in you I trust;
    do not let me be put to shame,
    do not let my enemies exult over me.
Do not let those who wait for you be put to shame;
    let them be ashamed who are wantonly treacherous.

Make me to know your ways, O LORD;
    teach me your paths
Lead me in your truth, and teach me,
    for you are the God of my salvation;
    for you I wait all day long.

Be mindful of your mercy, O LORD, and of your steadfast love,
    for they have been from of old.
Do not remember the sins of my youth or my transgressions;
    according to your steadfast love remember me,
    or your goodness' sake, O LORD!

Good and upright is the LORD;
    therefore he instructs sinners in the way.
He leads the humble in what is right,
    and teaches the humble his way.
All the paths of the LORD are steadfast love and faithfulness,
    for those who keep his covenant and his decrees.

For your name's sake, O LORD,
    pardon my guilt, for it is great.
Who are they that fear the LORD?
    He will teach them the way that they should choose.
They will abide in prosperity,
    and their children shall possess the land.
The friendship of the LORD is for those who fear him,
    and he makes his covenant known to them.

My eyes are ever toward the LORD,
  for he will pluck my feet out of the net.

Turn to me and be gracious to me,
  for I am lonely and afflicted.
Relieve the troubles of my heart,
  and bring me out of my distress.
Consider my affliction and my trouble,
  and forgive all my sins.

Consider how many are my foes,
  and with what violent hatred they hate me.
O guard my life, and deliver me;
  do not let me be put to shame, for I take refuge in you.
May integrity and uprightness preserve me,
  for I wait for you.

Redeem Israel, O God,
  out of all its troubles.

The Maccabean Mother

"O mother of the nation, vindicator of the law and champion of religion, who carried away the prize of the contest in your heart!"

– 4 Maccabees 15:29

As we have seen, the virtue associated with the Six is courage, and the corresponding basic fear is that one will have no support. Sixes can relate to authority and authority figures either by becoming fiercely loyal or else anti-authoritarian. The Mother of the seven sons in the Book of Maccabees took authority into her own hands as she expressed her opposition to the oppressors of the Hebrews. She embraced their cause and their beliefs, and was heroically able to sacrifice herself and motivate her entire family to do the same thing.

We see in this remarkable woman a picture of how a Six's loyalty and faith may cause her not to run away in fear but instead to run headlong into the face of danger. While this may seem to go directly against our instinct for self-preservation, for Sixes, embracing their fear and confronting it directly, while difficult, can be the result of having entered their transformative work. They are able to anchor themselves in the present moment and use its strength and the strength of the divine to combat what they most fear by facing it and staring it down. This does not mean that they will always avoid pain or loss, but that they will be able to meet life's events with a sense of detachment and balance that keeps them centred in their true self.

The Mother in the story of Maccabees who prefers to witness the death of her seven sons over seeing them betray their religion and commit the sin of idolatry can be a mentor for us in learning how to face danger and live out of our faith.[81] Her story is one of the most appealing and also one of the most heart-rending in the scriptures.[82] The narrative is connected to the story of Judas Maccabeus, and recalls the courage and valour of those Jewish people who chose to abide by their religious beliefs and laws in defiance of civil law. It arose during the time when Antiochus IV, known as Epiphanes ("god manifest") had become king (175-164 BCE), a period when the Jews were trying to live in the Greek world yet retain their own faith and devotion to the God of Israel and the Torah. Antiochus was neither reasonable nor rational (his opponents nicknamed him Epimanes, or "madman"), and he forced the Jews to forsake their laws under threat of death. He polluted the temple in Jerusalem, renaming it the temple of Zeus, and it became a place of outrageous sacrileges.[83] He began arresting Jews and forcing them to eat unlawful foods, killing them if they refused.

Among the persons arrested were a mother and her seven sons. In her refusal to obey the demands of the tyrant Antiochus, this Mother, through her civil disobedience, nonetheless shows the

Six's characteristics of obedience and loyalty in her devotion to God and God's laws. When Sixes are secure in their beliefs, they can be tenacious in their behaviour, embodying their faith in all that they say and do. One characteristic often assigned to a Six is the role of 'devil's advocate,' and surely this is how the Maccabean mother must have appeared to her persecutors. The Mother willingly and strongly resists the foreign authority when it demands she be disloyal to her own. Her sense of her inner and outer authorities is the same: to obey the law of God is also to follow her own desire. In the horrifying account of her fate, all of her seven sons are tortured and killed in their mother's presence before she in turn is put to death. The several versions vary in details, but the substance of the story is the same.

As we saw with John the Baptist, for the compliant types, there can sometimes be an inverse ratio between their success and their sense of inner security. The more successful they are, the less stable and more nervous they feel within.[84] Flipping this ratio over suggests the possibility that the less they succeed outwardly, the stronger they feel within. This certainly appears to be true in the story of the Maccabean Mother, for her defiance and that of her sons strengthens and encourages her so that she finally faces her own death without wavering. We see in her no evidence of the Six's inability to decide what to do. She is clear right from the outset that death is a small price to pay for fidelity, and her courage shows no tinge of fear.

The Mother holds in balance her deep love for her sons and her undying love for God and fidelity to the Law. The Jewish Law is founded on the conviction that there is only one God and that no other gods are to be worshipped or obeyed. God is her security, and on God she depends totally. False gods, which here include any hostile worldly authorities, are to be rejected. The Law is of utmost importance to a Six, and the Mother in this account performs a typical balancing act, which a Six can do almost spontaneously. She must balance her love for her children with her sense of duty to the law of her God. Her maternal instincts are sacrificed as she reaches an agonizing decision in favor of the Law, even though it will lead to the death of her sons. Her legendary heroism has become a model for generations of people who have endured opposition and resistance to their beliefs. It does not represent willingness to die for a cause but fidelity to God. If that faith leads to death, then so be it. Death is not sought but it may well be the outcome.

Many elements of the Six are manifested in this story. We see the Mother as both self-affirming and engaging, and a committed loyalist to God and to God's law. While some Sixes express their obedience through developing a passive-aggressive stance, even a tough attitude, this Mother is clear and firm without being aggressive. If she were a Six who had not entered into her work of transformation, she could under her unusual circumstances have easily become hysterical or even masochistic. But her sons do not perceive her this way, and neither does the reader. She elicits a strong, supportive response from her sons. She must have effectively taught them and loved them so that her family became wholly dedicated to the Jewish faith. She and her sons are strong and reliable in the midst of their persecution. They are willing to sacrifice themselves and to support one another in their trials.

A lengthy interpolation of the gruesome details of their deaths is given in 4 Maccabees. The story spares nothing in its graphic description of how the sons were beaten, tortured, flayed, dislocated, and roasted. One of the brothers willingly flings himself into the brazier, a striking image of a Six rushing headlong into danger. The brothers' strong belief in their inner security, and their unshakeable faith in God, are expressed through their true courage and collaborative leadership, despite the horrible end of the story. Their mother is praised for urging them on to death for the sake of their faith: "Take courage, therefore, O holy-minded mother, maintaining firm an enduring hope in God."[85]

An average Six might be willing to invest time and energy in what is credible and safe. One who is actively engaged in living out of a transformed space, however, will imitate the behaviour of the remarkable Maccabean Mother. When strong alliances are formed with people of a similar belief, as the Mother does with her sons, the Six can become courageously angry in relations with those who might disagree. In this story, we can hear the tone of this family's language of defiance addressed to the tyrant Antiochus. They call him an "accursed wretch," tell him that "for you there will be no resurrection to life," and proclaim that God's "mighty power will torture you and your descendents!"[86]

The sons and their mother are partisan and defensive, unwilling to negotiate. This is a story of popular heroes and they are naturally depicted in their best light, and their character as Sixes is lauded and held up for emulation. While their behaviour could be interpreted as a sort of fanaticism, its origins do not come from a desire to satisfy the ego but from loyalty to God and a desire to glorify God's name. It is people like the Maccabean Mother that William James must have had in mind when he said that "our final judgment of the worth of such a life as this will depend largely on our conception of God, and of the sort of conduct he is best pleased with in his creatures."[87]

While she is committed, engaging, responsible, and defensive, her story also warns us that an unintegrated Six could readily disintegrate into paranoia. In an unhealthy Six, zealousness for the law could so overwhelm genuine human love that the deaths of one's family or friends would feed one's sense of righteousness. The story of the Maccabean Mother, like the story of the Akedah (the binding of Isaac by his father Abraham), has sometimes been used in this way to sustain people in times of persecution, but also encouraging them to believe that their deaths are pleasing to God, whom they desire to obey.

Yet there is something horrifying when the story is interpreted in this way. Like the story in Genesis, in which Abraham believes he will have to sacrifice his son Isaac to show his love and loyalty to God, this narrative can also make us uneasy. How, we wonder, could any parent watch (or in the case of Abraham, be willing to cause) the death of his or her own child? And how could that parent give glory to God for such an event? How is our inner Maccabean Mother responding to this situation?

What Abraham learns when he is about to sacrifice his son Isaac is key here: the sudden flash of inspiration or insight which he receives at just the critical moment tells him that God does not desire human sacrifice, that God does not take pleasure in the taking of a human life.[88] In his zeal to serve God he was prepared to take the life of his son, and God had to intervene to tell him not to do so.

This is perhaps one of the greatest transformations which the Six in us can undergo: to let go of our false gods, the voices which we are so certain are right and which must be obeyed, and to listen humbly for the voice of the true God telling us not to commit violence against each other. Sometimes death results from fidelity to God and refusal to serve false idols, but surely God is not pleased with the murder of anyone, whether in the name of God or anything else.

Thus, if there is virtue in the devotion a Six can practice, there is also a danger that the Six's loyalty could lead to fanaticism. William James states that when devotion is unbalanced, one of its manifestations may be fanaticism, which is another way of explaining loyalty that is carried to an extreme:

> an immediate consequence of this condition of mind is jealousy for the deity's honour. How can the devotee show his loyalty better than by sensitiveness in this regard? The slightest affront or neglect must be resented, the deity's enemies must be put to shame.[89]

To see the Maccabean Mother as a model of transformation for the Six requires us to focus on her willingness to overcome her natural fear or aversion to what she must witness and experience. She must know that perfect love can cast out her fear. Love of her sons is not opposed to her love of God. The love she experiences includes both, and is passed on to her sons so that they, too, can place their total trust in God and die confident and secure. Her encouragement of them only ceases with her own death. She is not spared what she encourages her sons to undergo, and in her death she is set free from the limitations of the oppressive law, which cannot follow her there. While many today will not be faced with a literal death for their beliefs (though, unfortunately, many indeed will), the loyalty of the Six in all of us helps us understand the potential we have for courageously persisting in a right course of action.

Prayer in the Spirit of the Maccabbean Mother
Psalm 127

Unless the Lord builds the house,
    those who build it labour in vain.
Unless the Lord guards the city,
    the guard keeps watch in vain.
It is in vain that you rise up early and go late to rest,
    eating the bread of anxious toil;
for he gives sleep to his beloved.

Sons are indeed a heritage from the Lord,
    the fruit of the womb a reward.
Like arrows in the hand of a warrior
    are the sons of one's youth.
Happy is the man who has his quiver full of them.
He shall not be put to shame when he speaks with his
    enemies in the gate.

Summary of the Sixes

The story of Peter offers us an excellent model of growth and transformation. He moves beyond his initial concern with personal security and becomes centred on Christ and his mission to humanity. The bold and impetuous leader who claimed he would never abandon Jesus, even if everyone else did so, has reflected at great length on his betrayal and has come to a deeper and more genuine self-knowledge. His stubborn arrogance and judgmental comparisons of others whom he regarded as less faithful are transformed into the humility of someone who can honestly say to Jesus, "Go away from me, Lord, for I am a sinful man!" (Luke 5:8).

The cock crowing after his triple denial of Jesus has indeed been for Peter a wake-up call. He responds to Jesus' triple invitation to affirm his love by simply and humbly replying, "Lord, you know everything; you know that I love you" Later, he can himself encourage others to "keep alert" (1 Peter 5:8). His experience of the unchanging love Jesus offers him transforms his shaky faith into rock-like security.

The man "of little faith" (Matthew 14:31) no longer needs an outside authority to direct him but can speak from his own inner convictions based on his own experience of the fidelity of Jesus to him. Peter's compliance is not longer directed by outside circumstances but emerges from his own heart. He can now take initiatives as a leader without hesitation, jumping into the water on his own, not needing to be told by Jesus to do so. He is ready for anything, including martyrdom.

The Maccabean Mother as an archetypal figure teaches us that there is a greater freedom beyond all human successes and achievements. She illustrates the deeper gift of spiritual maternity, the life-giving power of one who can go beyond instinctual maternal claims into the realms of the spirit. She proves that we have the capacity in our own hearts for courage, fidelity, and determination in the pursuit of what we know to be just and right. This

Mother is a model of the faithfulness and love which can overcome fear and anguish of heart. She is able to face the madman tyrant who believes he has absolute power over life and death, and proves that he is only able to kill the body but not the spirit. Against natural compliance to the tyrannical human law, she balances her compliance to the greater divine law, convinced that there an be no negotiation between the two of them. The Maccabean Mother invites us to look within ourselves to the deeper law inscribed on our own hearts and discover in our essence the source of all true security for all that we undertake in a spirit of faithfulness and love.

Group 2: The Assertive Types

Sevens, Eights, and Threes

Keep your heart with all vigilance,
for from it flow the springs of life.

– Proverbs 4:23

The assertive types on the Enneagram are the Sevens, Eights, and Threes. The most common designations given to these are the dreamer or enthusiast (Seven), the confronter or challenger (Eight), and the achiever or performer (Three). As the assertive triad, they share a misused (or repressed) Feeling centre. Of course these types have feelings, but their feelings are not able to provide them with useful information about themselves or about the world. They may express their emotions only indirectly and prefer instead to use their Thinking or Doing centres in their interactions with others. In contrast to the compliant types, who are characterized by their moving towards others, the assertive types in their relationships are best characterized as moving *against* others, not avoiding confrontations and challenges.

Each of the three types in this group manifests these tendencies in different ways. The Sevens, who are the enthusiasts, keep busy and productive, and usually spend a lot of time in social situations but their busy-ness is often a way to avoid engaging with their deep feelings of pain or sadness. Their feelings may get lost in their dreaming of possibilities which avoid being present in the moment, which is where the feeling lies.

For the Eights, the confronters, feelings get swept aside in favour of action, and they may find that they prefer relationships which allow them to avoid dealing with sensitive or emotional issues. Feelings can interfere with their sense of self-assertiveness and independence and are therefore threatening. They have little time to worry about the feelings of others since they do not place a high importance on information received through the emotions.

The Threes are the performers who love most of all to have everything look good and successful. Their feeling centre is misused because they are most concerned with the impression they are making, and this is done through their words and their actions. How they feel about something is less important to them than how things appear to others. They often have difficulty finding an emotional link to someone else because they are so used to performing and achieving that their relationships may be tinged with deceit without their being aware of it.

Sharing a misused Feeling centre, these three types are referred to as the assertive triad. This does not mean they are necessarily pushy or that they always have to have their own way. They are assertive because their movements tend to go up against people rather than moving away from them. They often act without feeling for what others might consider or wish, and may tend to choose the best for themselves: a Three might choose the best place to be seen, an Eight might take over the best chair, and a Seven may choose the best wine or biggest piece of cake. All the types, of course, have some degree of assertive energy, and we can recognize it in ourselves in the times in which we tend to move outwards, whether to other people, projects, or causes. During these moments of our lives, much of our energy is directed not to the present, and certainly not to the past, but almost exclusively to the future.

The assertive types are like this most of the time. They want to make the world live up to their image of it, and are able to bring an excitement and energy to the opportunities any given situation offers. Transformation for the assertive types often consists of consciously working to develop a movement which is contrary to their natural desire to move outwards and away. They will learn to deliberately focus themselves on an opposing rhythm of pulling back and slowing down to get a good look at themselves. Constant practice will teach them the necessary balance in which the inner Spirit, rather than the ego, will be the motivator of the astounding amount of energy these types often possess. They will learn to use their feelings to bring depth (for the Seven), tenderness (for the Eight), and honesty (for the Three) to their relationships and to their lives.

When they are not engaged in their inner work, the assertive types are easily misunderstood by those around them. Because their impact is so often on the world 'out there,' their inner world is often a mystery to themselves and a complete cipher even to close friends who think they know them well. The assertive types may, intentionally or not, deflect attention from their souls' pre-occupations and point it outwards towards their projects, their dreams, or their social issues. These are areas in which they are extremely talented, and so their outer work tends to get reinforced by the outside world, delaying them from devoting more attention to their inner work of transformation.

When they begin to focus on their feeling centre, and learn to use it effectively, the assertive types often discover they are developing a counter-movement to their usual way of being. They quickly find that they are experiencing themselves as two or more 'selves' along the way. Their outer self is spirited, outgoing, and successful, and has an almost heroic aura to it. At the same time, their inner self is cut off from its feelings. They are aware that their feelings exist but are unable to access them usefully, and may feel a certain degree of self-contempt arising as a result. This double awareness competes with itself time after time, creating confusion over who is the real 'me' at any given moment.

Of course, everyone experiences the same thing, more than once and at different stages in life, but for the assertive types these two different layers of awareness do not go away. Their responses to living with this tension often cause them conflict and thus they learn to live with contradiction probably better than anyone else does. Their desire to achieve mastery over their situation gives life its zest for them.[90] They believe that every obstacle life places in their way can be overcome, whether in the realm of the social, the intellectual or the personal. Thus the assertive types are in marked contrast to the compliant types, who are ready to be accommodating in all the challenges life presents, while the assertives desire mastery of them.

We see these three things – the desire for mastery, the tendency to move outwards 'against' others and the conflict between one's different 'selves' – operating in the biblical characters chosen for this section. Solomon believes he can use his wisdom to master all, and indeed it appears to him that God has assured him of the truth of that belief. He knows many things and has many possessions. He also has many influential wives and can answer 'hard questions' but needs to find meaning in the moment.

The energetic and engaging Woman at the Well is not intimidated by her meeting with Jesus, and even tries to get the 'mastery' over him in their conversation. His dealing with her honours her outgoing nature and also challenges her to understand that true mastery is self-mastery, even while she tries to defend and hold on to contradictory images of herself.

The Canaanite woman found in the gospels likewise believes she can master the situation when Jesus is reluctant to acknowledge her right to appeal to him for help. In fact, she does achieve mastery. Her strong movement outwards 'against' Jesus results in her getting what she wants. In her debate with him, she helps him arrive at her own conviction that there can be no distinction made between Jews and Gentiles when it comes to showing God's mercy.

Martha of Bethany lives with her 'contradictory half,' her sister Mary, and is ready to confront Jesus for his tardiness in arriving at their home after their brother Lazarus has died. She wants Jesus to fulfil her wish for mastery over the situation. He does so, but in a way which shows the path to wholeness and peace.

Saul begins his reign as first king of Israel with an apparent mastery in his divinely chosen role but he is ultimately not able to control either the armies of Israel or his own sense of self-importance. Of all the characters presented here, he is the only one to have a tragic ending and we can trace his misery to a conflicted and divided inner self which he is never able to resolve.

In contrast, Saul's successor David shows great mastery in his musical talents, in his loyalty as a subject to King Saul, in his remarkable military skills, and in his role as King of Israel. Even so, he is divided within himself over his desire to obtain Bathsheba while her husband is still alive. The difference between Saul and David lies chiefly in how they respond and are open to the divine presence in their lives.

For all these assertive types the misused centre is their Feeling centre, and they all prefer to avoid direct confrontation with their feelings or emotions and just get down to the business at hand. When they do come up against their emotions (as David does when the prophet Nathan confronts him and reveals his sin to him), they are presented with a possibility of transformation. They are given the opportunity to acknowledge what they have been avoiding and to grow into more integrated and holy people.

The art of mastery and the desire for it are not limited to these three assertive types but it is to them we most readily look for its clearest models. Certainly members of all the types wish to excel at what they do: for example, the Ones have the drive for perfection, and the Fives demonstrate the desire to know everything possible. With the assertive types, however, there is a difficulty in using their feelings to assist them. They experience an inner contradiction between what they deeply desire and what they actually find themselves doing. As St. Paul, Augustine, and many others have pointed out, it often seems like there are two forces within us, pulling us in opposite directions. The one which is in control tries to silence the other one, which is telling us the direction we need to go for our soul's health.

For members of the assertive triad, their path of transformation lies in learning to integrate their feelings into their lives. When they do so, they discover compassion for others, they are able to join in the joy and creativity of life, and they learn generosity of spirit. The fruits of personal growth for the assertive types will be evident in their newly realized virtues of temperance and balance (Sevens), generosity (Eights), and truth (Threes).

Type Seven: Solomon and the Woman at the Well

> Be filled with the Spirit, as you sing psalms and
> hymns and spiritual songs among yourselves,
> singing and making melody to God in your hearts.
>
> – Ephesians 5:18-19

The Sevens are the dreamers and the enthusiasts. Their true nature is to be happy and to enrich the lives of everyone they encounter. The virtue to which they most aspire is temperance or moderation, for their natural tendency is to want too much of everything, not just material things but ideas, plans, and dreams as well. Sevens are part of the Thinking triad of the Enneagram. They are always planning and thinking ahead, and find it difficult to stay centred in the present moment. Their inner work leads them to try to find balance in using their energy so that they can joyously celebrate all of creation, express their gratitude, and spread happiness in all their encounters.

Because of their apparently endless energy and quick thinking, Sevens are often described as being busy, fun-loving and the kind of people you definitely want to have at a party. However, they can also become excessively manic, for they have an immense need to be happy and to avoid pain at any cost. This urgent need to fill up the moment is the less visible side of the Seven, and its root is their underlying sadness. As long as they keep busy, they will not be forced to confront the emotions they have not learned to use well. The party-loving, outgoing energy they display to those around them, and which makes them so easy to like, often serves to mask a deeper pain. Sevens are always subtly aware of its existence just below the surface of their behaviour, and to keep it from breaking through, they make every effort they can to cover it up and push it away from their immediate concerns. This makes them constantly future-oriented and they find it difficult to stay focused on the 'now.'

Thus the aspect of the Sevens which is outwardly perceived as always being busy and making plans has usually been constructed by themselves as a means of avoiding any direct confrontation with their inner wounds. They are thereby able to protect themselves, at least for a while, from any further pain as they skilfully deflect their attention and that of others onto their current projects and preoccupations. This is their particular manifestation of the assertive triad's preference for moving outwards against other people as their way of encountering the world.

Because of the talent Sevens have for planning and looking forwards, the 'Holy Idea' associated with the Seven is Holy Work, Holy Wisdom or Holy Plan.[91] In undertaking their inner work, the dreaming and planning which Sevens had used as an escape or an anesthetic become transformed into Holy Work which is connected to the biblical understanding of Wisdom as a creative agent of God.

We often think of wisdom as something associated with the head, with thinking wise thoughts. Sevens do have a dominant Thinking centre, but biblical wisdom is not primarily about thinking but about creation. In the scriptures, especially in the Book of Proverbs and the Book of Wisdom, Wisdom is intimately connected to creation and the works of creation. In Proverbs, Wisdom is personified as an active, creative aspect of God, who is not God herself (for in both Hebrew and Greek the word for wisdom is a feminine noun[92]) but created by God at the beginning of creation.

She says, "The LORD created me at the beginning of his work, the first of his acts of long ago" (Proverbs 8:22). She describes how she was an agent of God in shaping the earth, the mountains, the heavens, and the deep (Proverbs 8:23-31). Thus God's work in the world, seen in all of creation, is also the Wisdom of God. She is a manifestation of the divine, as she herself tells us in Proverbs:

> When [God] marked out the foundations of the earth,
>   then I was beside him, like a master worker,
> and I was daily his delight, rejoicing before him always,
>   rejoicing in his inhabited world and delighting in the
> human race.

– Proverbs 8:29-31

She is at work in the material and natural world, hovering over its activities and holding it together.

When we talk of the Sevens and Holy Work, therefore, we are going well beyond the ordinary sense of work as what one does to make ends meet. Holy Work occurs when we are able to take our place in creation and see in ourselves a replication of the ongoing work of God in the world.[93] When we choose to make our home with Wisdom, as the Book of Proverbs enjoins us to do, it is Wisdom herself who acts and not our own ego:

> In every generation she passes into holy souls
> and makes them friends of God, and prophets;
> for God loves nothing so much as the person who
> lives with wisdom.

– Wisdom 7:27-28

The desire for mastery, which is a characteristic of the assertive types, expresses itself on the egocentric level as a desire for control and power. It has a kind of childishness about it. When it aligns itself with Wisdom, however, it becomes a channel for the work of God to be carried out in the world. "Lay aside immaturity," says Wisdom, "and live, and walk in the way of insight" (Proverbs 9:6).

Immaturity is egocentric while insight lays aside the desires of the ego and sees into the truth of things.

We see this contrast in the two characters chosen to represent the Seven space. Both Solomon and the Woman at the Well who meets Jesus demonstrate busy-ness and preoccupation with many issues. They attempt to divert themselves from pursuing their innermost desires but finally allow them to be brought to the surface and discerned. They begin with their plans and thoughts that they use to try to distract themselves but they also have a hidden thirst for Wisdom, though their desire to make their home with her takes two quite different forms. In both of their stories, God touches them with insight that arouses their feelings and shows them the true nature of Holy Work.

Solomon

> "With you is Wisdom, she who knows your works
> and was present when you made the world."

> – Wisdom 9:9

Solomon succeeded his father David as King of Israel (see Threes, below). His father had been a popular and good king, who served God and the people. Now Solomon had the difficult task of assuming the throne to which his father has named him (for there were other contenders). On his deathbed, David had charged Solomon to walk in God's ways and keep God's commandments so that he would prosper as king and would himself have a successor (1 Kings 2:2-4). Solomon loved God (1 Kings 3:3), and wanted to serve God well but felt that he did not know how to do so.

As a Seven, Solomon would have been accustomed to using his Thinking centre to solve his problems and help him figure out how to be a good king. He decided to go to Gibeon, the highest of the high places, and, demonstrating the exuberant excess of the Seven, he offered an extravagant sacrifice to God of a thousand burnt offerings (1 Kings 3:5). This is not what God has required of Solomon, but rather than discussing Solomon's misplaced extravagance with him, God chooses to confront Solomon in a dream. While Sevens are dreamers, their dreams are in their conscious minds, in plans they hope to achieve. But Solomon cannot control this dream from God, and it appeals to the deep emotions which can surface when our conscious mind is sleeping. In the dream, God does not talk about Solomon's offering, but instead invites him to, "Ask what I should give you" (1 Kings 3:5). There is almost a fairy-tale element in this offer, reminiscent of genies in lamps and strange elves met in the woods who offer a traveller the granting of a wish for having lent a helping hand. God's invitation is for Solomon to use his Seven's gift of imagination to ask for whatever he wants and to do so while both his body and his conscious mind are asleep. This leaves nothing but the Feeling centre for Solomon to look to for his answer.

With his usual preferred ways of knowing closed off, Solomon is able to quickly access his feelings. His reply to God comes not from the head but from the heart. He speaks of God's love for his father David and how God has kept this love for David by allowing his son to sit on the throne. Solomon acknowledges that he is "only a little child; I do not know how to go out or come in" (1 Kings 3:7). He cannot mean this literally, for he is a grown man but when the Feeling centre is working, he speaks of relationships, of dependence on God, and of his own need to connect emotionally with God as his father and with himself as a little child.

Having opened this access, Solomon discovers the freedom of a little child, and without hesitation asks for "an understanding mind" in governing the people. Solomon knows how to think but he now asks to add the gift of understanding to his thinking, so that he can incorporate the emotions in order to see the bigger picture, and readily "discern between good and evil" (1 Kings 3:9). God is pleased with his request and, in response to it, grants him the gift of "a wise and discerning mind" (1 Kings 3:12) such as no one before or after him has had.

God's gift of Holy Wisdom to Solomon is the gift of the transformed Seven. He also gives him long life, riches, and honour, for when we are in touch with our Essence, everything falls into place. While Solomon received all these things literally, we can also see in God's gifts the spiritual gifts of inner riches and godly honour, and life that is abundant and eternal. His prayer shows us that prayer is not intended to change the divine plan but to open us up to become a channel through which God can give us what we need to have.

Immediately after Solomon receives the gift of Holy Wisdom, we see how he uses it to solve the dilemma of the disputed child (1 Kings 3:16-28). Two women claim the same baby as their own and Solomon decides their relative claims by asking for a sword so that he can cut the child in half. Immediately the true mother, filled with compassion for her son, rushes forward and says the other woman can have him. The other woman, however, says that neither shall have him and he should be divided in half. Solomon instantly knows the first woman to be the true mother. And how does he know this? Through his newly awakened and enlivened Feeling centre. He did not ask the women to debate the matter, but appealed instead to their feelings, and the mother's compassion gave him the answer he sought.

These initial incidents in Solomon's life establish him as a wise king, touched by God where he needed to be awakened and using his wisdom for the good of the people. One of his busiest activities was the construction of the First Temple. In the fourth year of his reign (c. 960 B.C.E.), Solomon went about formulating elaborate plans for building a temple to God. 1 Kings recounts the many details of its size, the stones used in building it, the wood used to line the walls, the details of the sanctuary, the carvings, the entrance to the nave, the windows, the pillars, the basins and the lamps. It took seven years to build. It was a huge project, involving 550 overseers (1 Kings 9:23), and it lasted as the focus of ritual worship for Israel until its destruction by the Babylonians in 586 B.C.E. In its details and planning we can see the jumping forward of the Seven who is future-oriented, and the ability of the Seven to plan and to dream.

In building the temple and in other plans, Solomon's reign came to be marked by the exuberance of the Seven, who as an epicure can never have too much of something good and is always thinking ahead to the next project. Before he began building the temple, he kept himself busy learning about the natural world which, we have seen, is one manifestation of divine wisdom in the world. He knew all about trees, animals, birds, reptiles and fish, he wrote proverbs and songs, and he dispensed wisdom to people who came to him from all nations (1 Kings 4:32-34).

Among these people was the Queen of Sheba who tested him with her "hard questions" and marvelled at his ability to answer them (1 Kings 10:4-6). The Seven's desire for mastery led him to display his knowledge and exploits to her, certain that there was nothing he could not do and no one he could not win over.[94] People who encounter Sevens are often amazed at their high energy, their enthusiasm, and their ability to keep several projects or ideas going all at once. The Queen seemed to feel this way about Solomon. Her response to his energy was breathlessness: she was overwhelmed with his wisdom, his house, the food he served, the seating arrangements, his servants and what they wore, and his burnt offerings (1 Kings 10:4-6). She tried to respond to his abundance and his energy by giving him gifts that included more spices than had ever been seen before or since (1 Kings 10:10). But it is hard even for a Queen to keep up with a Seven. She returns to her own country, having had her desires satisfied. The Seven in Solomon has achieved its purpose of impressing her and receiving her admiration but their relationship was based not on emotional intimacy but on plans and activity.

It took 20 years to build both the temple and Solomon's own palace (1 Kings 9:10). While Solomon, we are told, was operating on instructions from God to build God a temple, there is still a driven-ness in his effort which might also illustrate the Seven's desire to be distracted from other affairs. Our own inner Solomon knows very well how easy or attractive it is to keep extremely busy not only to get the job done but also to avoid the pain of dealing with other, perhaps more pressing, concerns.

Solomon had many projects undertaken during his reign – he "excelled all the kings of the earth in riches and in wisdom" (1 Kings 10:23) – and his goal seems to have been to build up Israel as a power worthy of notice by the surrounding nations. Again we see in his activities the lack of temperance which characterizes a Seven. He built a fleet of ships which brought gold from foreign territory (1 Kings 9:26-28). He imported 12,000 horses from Egypt and maintained 14,000 chariots (1 Kings 10:26). Most notorious in his reign was his excessiveness when it came to wives: although he had made a political marriage with the daughter of the Egyptian Pharaoh, he also "loved many foreign women," roughly 1,000 of them (1 Kings 3:1, 11:1, 3).

Such overindulgence proved to be his downfall, for we are told that when he grew older, his wives lured him away from God and he built shrines for foreign gods. The writer of Deuteronomy, writing well after the reign of Solomon, reflected on his excessiveness when he wrote that when Israel would have a king, he must not acquire many horses or wives for himself, "or else his heart will turn away; also silver and gold he must not acquire in great quantity for himself" (Deuteronomy 17:17).

This desire for excess, as has been noted, often results from an inner emptiness. In his constant desire for more, Solomon's restlessness sought to satisfy itself in outer rather than inner solutions. At the beginning of his reign, this does not appear to have been the case. When God told him to ask for whatever he wished,

Solomon asked for the wisdom to be a good king. As a youth beginning to reign over Israel, he was aware of his own inadequacy and
his need for divine assistance. What, then, drove him to such outward excesses?

To understand the Seven's inner state, it helps to consider that
Solomon's glorification of God through building the temple might
well have been a projection of his attempt to gratify himself. By
desiring to master life through using their Thinking centre, Sevens
may cling to a self-portrait which is idealized and hence unrealistic.
In speaking of his many exploits and successes, Solomon can
impress people (like the Queen of Sheba) without actually having to
engage them at an emotional level, and will receive their admiration but not their love. Identifying with one's idealized self is a kind
of narcissism and, in the case of the Sevens, it enables them to stay
unaware of their deep feelings of self-doubt.[95]

Solomon's building of the temple may have given him a sense
of importance and a false belief that all would go well and conform
to his wishes. After all, even God went along with him and granted his wish for wisdom. While on the surface of life things might
appear to be going well for a Seven, there may yet be an underlying refusal to notice any area which has not been mastered, especially in the area of feelings.

The misused Feeling centre of the assertive types is often seen
in their failed or shallow relationships. After Solomon's death we
read that his servant Jeroboam complained to the new King
Rehoboam, Solomon's son, that "your father made our yoke heavy"
(1 Kings 12:4). Solomon may well have believed that the work of
building the temple and his palace was more important than the
workers who built them. We have already seen that Sevens do not
treat emotions and relationships as if they have any great importance. Perhaps Solomon's proliferation of wives was also a way of
avoiding the deeper feelings that would come from having just a
few intimate relationships.

Sevens accumulate details in their lives to continue their illusion of mastery, but they do so at the expense of having deep relationships with other people as well as with the divine. Their excessiveness may lead them completely away from the divine encounter. Solomon's love of foreign women, who had their foreign gods and who thus brought with them idolatry, finally led Solomon away from God when he was an old king (1 Kings 11:9). God still did not break the relationship he had established with Solomon years earlier when he had called to him in his dream as a young king. He knew that Solomon needed to have his heart touched and would not punish him for his emotional difficulties. However, at Solomon's death, his kingdom was divided, a fitting emblem of a king who was himself divided from his feelings for much of his life.

Some may think that Solomon, despite his apparent mastery of many things during his life, failed in his most important duty of remaining faithful to God. Certainly the writer of 1 Kings seemed to believe this. The biblical histories, however, are written after their events and account for historical occurrences with the benefit of hindsight. The kingdom was indeed divided after Solomon's death and, from a standpoint of divine retributive justice, this could only mean that Israel was being punished for its sins, personified in its leader Solomon.

But we can also find other indications that perhaps Solomon did not die rejected by God but was able, finally, to accomplish the work of transformation required by the Seven. To examine this possibility, we need to look at the biblical book attributed to the older Solomon, Ecclesiastes. While it is generally accepted that the historical Solomon did not write Ecclesiastes, nevertheless, as a character or 'type' of him, the persona of the Teacher (some translations call him the "preacher") speaks in the voice of the disillusioned king for whom pleasure ultimately does not endure. The 'moving against' of the assertive types is seen through Solomon as a moving against many of the conventional ways of thinking of people of his time. Ecclesiastes gives us a portrayal of Solomon later in life, the voice of an older and more experienced king who has seen much of life and now has added to his infused wisdom from God the wisdom he has learned from looking at the world. The persona is convincing in his teaching since, if the king who had it all is prepared to conclude that all is vanity and emptiness, then we cannot simply blame his conclusion on a case of sour grapes. If the wisest of the wise is complaining, then there must indeed be something serious in his complaint. The author of Ecclesiastes reflected on the world as it was and placed these thoughts into the mouth of Solomon, the wisest of all people, so that we would listen to them.

Solomon says that he has tried many pleasures to distract himself, which is what Sevens do readily to avoid facing life's pain. What he finally learned, despite his attempts to hold on to pleasure, was the fleeting nature of everything in this life. He tells us that in his planning and dreaming, he built himself a palace and planted vineyards and gardens and parks. He amassed silver and gold. He employed musical and sensual delights. After he had done all this, he ultimately learned that none of them could provide him with the answer to the immense question of our purpose here, and why it includes pain and sadness as an inevitable part of life's path (Ecclesiastes 2). In his searching we see the pattern of the Seven who wants to keep things moving and find enjoyment in all his forward-looking plans, while using these activities to blunt the pain and sadness of life.

The elderly Solomon whom we hear through the voice of Ecclesiastes speaks as a Seven who has undergone the work of transformation. Instead of the exuberance and bravado of the younger king, the voice of this older Solomon acknowledges the poignant sadness he has felt in his life. The Solomon presented here is finally able to stop planning for the future and has learned how to be rooted in the present moment. He lives in the real world, and is reflective and full of the insights of true wisdom. There is a calmness and an equanimity in his realization that God "has made everything suitable for its own time; moreover he has put a sense of past and future into their minds, yet they cannot find out what God has done from the beginning to the end" (Ecclesiastes 3:11).

Gone is the urgency to plan for more and better things. If we cannot even know what is happening "under the sun" (Ecclesiastes 8:17), there is no point in making many plans or living in the future. There is also no point in worrying about any of it: "Go, eat your bread with enjoyment, and drink your wine with a merry heart; for God has long ago approved what you do" (Ecclesiastes 9:7). There is a simple beauty in these words which do not avoid the feeling realm but encourage the experience of deep and pleasurable human emotions.

Solomon is also able to face the pain which mortality brings. He has finally looked directly at the troubles and inconsistencies of life over which there can finally be no mastery. It is not an occasion for despair but simply an acceptance of what is. Inherent in Solomon's account of his discovery that all is emptiness and a chasing after the wind, and that all things are wearisome, lies the acceptance of life's sorrows and defeats as part of the cyclical nature of time. This is the great insight which Sevens come to know. Instead of the excesses which consume them, they find the reality of the present:

> For everything there is a season, and a time for every
> > matter under heaven:
> a time to be born, and a time to die;
> a time to plant, and a time to pluck up what is planted;
> a time to kill, and a time to heal;
> a time to break down, and a time to build up;
> a time to weep, and a time to laugh;
> a time to mourn, and a time to dance;
> a time to throw away stones, and a time to gather stones together.

– Ecclesiastes 3:1-5

In acknowledging that there are opposites to his early career of building, planting, and gathering stones, Solomon has discovered that there are corresponding times of deconstructing, uprooting and reducing. He has learned that weeping is as necessary as laughing and that his feelings can support and not undermine his work.

Ecclesiastes concludes with an acknowledgment of death as the end of life's pleasures, when "the dust returns to the earth as it was, and the breath returns to God who gave it" (Ecclesiastes 12:7). The sadness of the Seven may be connected with the knowledge of mortality which gives an urgency to life and makes swift living appear to be a necessity, even though he knows that "the race is not to the swift, nor the battle to the strong, nor bread to the wise, nor riches to the intelligent, nor favour to the skilful; but time and chance happen to them all" (Ecclesiastes 9:11). Solomon has learned to slow down and to acknowledge life's pains as well as its pleasures. "Better," he says, "is a poor but wise youth than an old but foolish king" (Ecclesiastes 4:13), perhaps reflecting on his own life which began with the fervour and wisdom of his youth and in the end left him with his folly.

Solomon has learned that returning to God means ceasing his life of distraction: "See, this alone I found, that God made human beings straightforward, but they have devised many schemes" (Ecclesiastes 7:29). He has seen that the return to the direct simplicity of our divine origin means to abandon the life of complexity and distraction and find a home with Wisdom, the divine creative agent. God sends her freely to those who seek and desire her, and she did not abandon Solomon in his old age. Transformation can begin at any time of life, and the wisdom and balance of the older Solomon show that he has indeed done his work. He knows that, for all our planning and building, we cannot compete with the true creativity which is our origin and our end: "Just as you do not know how the breath comes to the bones in the mother's womb, so you do not know the work of God, who makes everything" (Ecclesiastes 11:5). Solomon's elaborate dreaming and making have finally yielded to the nurturing creativity of God who, we must fervently hope, welcomed Solomon with much merriment into the celestial city not made with living hands, and in which there is no temple, not even Solomon's, to be found.

Prayer in the Spirit of Solomon
Psalm 49

Hear this, all you peoples;
    give ear, all inhabitants of the world,
both low and high,
    rich and poor together.
My mouth shall speak wisdom;
    the meditation of my heart shall be understanding.
I will incline my ear to a proverb;
    I will solve my riddle to the music of the harp.

Why should I fear in times of trouble,
    when the iniquity of my persecutors surrounds me,
those who trust in their wealth
    and boast of the abundance of their riches?
Truly, no ransom avails for one's life,
    there is no price one can give to God for it.
For the ransom of life is costly,
    and can never suffice
that one should live on forever
    and never see the grave.

When we look at the wise, they die;
    fool and dolt perish together
    and leave their wealth to others.
Their graves are their homes forever,
    their dwelling places to all generations,
    though they named lands their own.

Mortals cannot abide in their pomp;
>they are like the animals that perish.

Such is the fate of the foolhardy,
>the end of those who are pleased with their lot.
Like sheep they are appointed for Sheol;
>Death shall be their shepherd;
straight to the grave they descend,
>and their form shall waste away;
>Sheol shall be their home.
But God will ransom my soul from the power of Sheol,
>for he will receive me.

Do not be afraid when some become rich,
>when the wealth of their houses increases.
For when they die they will carry nothing away;
>their wealth will not go down after them.
Though in their lifetime they count themselves happy
>– for you are praised when you do well for yourself –
they will go to the company of their ancestors,
>who will never again see the light.
Mortals cannot abide in their pomp;
>they are like the animals that perish.

The Woman at the Well

With joy you will draw water
from the wells of salvation.

– Isaiah 12:3

The Woman at the Well in chapter 4 of John's gospel gives us another view of the Seven. She is not wealthy like Solomon, nor does she have his status in society. In fact, she is quite the opposite of him. She is an outsider as far as the Jews are concerned, for she is a Samaritan, a group shunned by the Jews. She is also a woman, which also confers on her marginalized status in the patriarchal world of the first century.

We know far less about her than we do about Solomon. We do not even know her name. However, in John's gospel, the unnamed characters generally signify archetypal roles. They are anonymous because they represent the universal believer at any time and in any place. John has told us at the end of his gospel that all the stories he has included are recorded so that we might come to have faith in Jesus, and in finding that faith we will find eternal life (John 20:31). So we already have the key for unlocking the meaning of the episodes John includes in his narrative.

The Woman at the Well joins the list of other unnamed persons in the gospel of John who are also exemplars of what it means to come to believe in Jesus: the servants at the wedding at Cana (John 2:9), the Man born blind (John 9), the lame Man at the pool (see Nines, below), and the Beloved Disciple (John 13:23, and elsewhere). In different ways, all of these are models of the possible stages of conversion people may pass through when they come into contact with the Divine, and how their lives are transformed as a result of the encounter.

The Woman who meets Jesus at the well stands for all those who want to quench their spiritual thirst. She is a Seven and therefore one of the assertive types. She is energetic and engaging, and her thoughts dance around with rapidity and ease. Like Solomon, the Woman at the Well demonstrates what appears to be a practiced skill at distracting attention from her innermost self. Whereas Solomon built a temple and palaces, the woman's more humble position has required her to learn other, simpler ways to avoid feeling pain.

One way she has learned to do this is to come to the well alone at noon, a time when others would have already left and she could avoid their direct ostracizing of her. John adds the detail about the time of day to highlight the moment when the day pivots between morning and evening. It is to be a turning point in both the inner and the outer worlds for the woman.

Tradition also holds that the fall in Eden occurred at noon, and John suggests an interesting parallel between the Woman and Eve. The Woman at the Well comes for water, and Eve comes to the Tree of Knowledge to eat of its fruit. Both are filled but Eve is filled with pain while the Woman's pain, covered over by her Seven-ness, is about to be released. It is also the hour at which the crucifixion would take place, and this event at the well is linked to it as well as to Eve's 'fall' in the garden. What all three liminal moments suggest is a cataclysmic moment of radical change between how things were before and how they will be after the hour of noon. The simple addition by John of the time of day invites us to read the entire story of the encounter as representing a major event in the life of the believer.

As a Samaritan, the Woman is an outsider as far as the Jews are concerned. Jesus had come to the well before she arrived. He was tired and thirsty, and he sat there at noontime to rest (John 4:6). In these few details, John gives us a wealth of information. He tells us that the well is called Jacob's well and lies in the land which Jacob had given to his favourite son Joseph. It represents the history of Israel and the covenant God made with them and in which he met them.

In the Hebrew scriptures, wells were often meeting places where betrothals occurred. Jacob's mother Rebekah had been betrothed to his father Isaac at a well, and Moses later was to meet his wife Zipporah at a well. Thus the type-scene of the prophet encountering the woman at a well had already been established as a sign and precursor of a marriage. If this scene in John's gospel followed the model, it would naturally have been expected to culminate with a betrothal between Jesus and the woman. Literally, of course, this does not occur. However, John always invites us to see behind the literal story he is telling to uncover the spiritual significance of what is happening. By the end of Jesus' encounter with the Woman at the Well, typologically a spiritual marriage does take place and the woman is transformed by it.

In this highly symbolic story, then, we initially meet an unhealthy Seven who is in flight from herself. As an assertive type, she is moving against her society and, internally, against herself. She is experienced in the world's ways, coming to the well at a safe hour of the day. The pain involved in her solitude and rejection as an outsider causes her to avoid occasions which would evoke further pain. In her desire to escape from encountering these feelings, she goes to the well alone. However, Jesus is already sitting there, wordlessly presenting her with an image of stasis and rest, something a Seven needs to learn to do.

This is an important detail, for Jesus does not arrive to intrude on her solitude. Instead, John is showing us one of the basic truths of our encounter with the Divine Presence, namely, that wherever we go, God has gotten there first. There is no escaping. But there is also no need to be afraid.

The Woman must have been surprised to find that she was not alone at the well. She may have tried to ignore Jesus, not out of fear of a male stranger but out of the Seven's fear of finding herself having to confront her feelings or even her pain. However, Jesus is the one who starts the conversation. This in itself is astounding to her. He does not seem to mind that she is a woman and a Samaritan.

As a Seven, the Woman is probably hurrying to draw her water and return home, thinking ahead and planning the rest of her day. To begin the work of transformation, a Seven needs to slow down and become less distracted and more focused. Jesus opens his encounter with her by focusing clearly on a simple fact: he tells her that he is thirsty. This draws the attention away from her and onto him, dispelling any fears she might have had that this man might immediately begin to berate her. Jesus' supreme courtesy in dealing with her is veiled as a request. This disarms her and places her in the position of doing something for him.

Asking a Seven for help invites her out of the pattern of accumulating and desiring more (seen so clearly in Solomon's planning and building) and encourages her to give. The request also grounds her in the present moment, not the future where Sevens prefer to live. Jesus also does not intrude on her feelings at this moment but relates to her in a way with which Sevens are comfortable, as a social encounter with a simple transaction as its topic.

Her response, however, is not a direct reply to Jesus' request for water. Instead, unable to stay in the moment, she changes the subject to ask him why as a Jew he is asking her, a Samaritan, for water. Perhaps her reply contains a hidden taunt, suggesting the possibility that she will not give him what he needs and that their relationship will never be anything more than a business encounter.

Instead of forcing her back to the moment and insisting that she give him drink, Jesus meets her question with a cryptic reply that invites her to think outside of the literal meaning of his request. He alludes to something called "living water" (John 4:10), which she could have from him were she to ask. This puts her in an odd position. She can cease the discussion, give Jesus a drink, and go home, or she can engage him further to find out what he is talking about. As a Seven, her curiosity about learning something new, and perhaps interesting and exciting, gets the better of her. On the other hand, Sevens are wary of relationships which might uncover any of their well-guarded emotions.

She avoids Jesus' offer. Instead of asking directly for the "living water," she once more digresses, pointing out that Jesus has no bucket (John 4:11). The Seven in her is able to keep several things going at once in her mind, and at this point she is still unwilling to slow down and focus on one thing at a time. She does not wait for Jesus to respond about his lack of a bucket but adds yet another question to their conversation, asking him if he is greater than Jacob who gave them the well.

The woman's mental agility and inability to focus on one thing at a time do not arise because she takes things literally but because, as a Seven, she wishes to hold onto many options, keeping them all going at once: thirst, buckets, living water, Jacob and his sons, and a Jew in conversation with a Samaritan woman. Of the many responses Jesus might have given her, he chooses the one which will bring a Seven back to the present. Paradoxically, he recalls her to the moment by talking about the future. He knows that is where she prefers to function, and so that is where her work of transformation can begin. He also raises her curiosity, knowing she will respond quite naturally to another option he offers. He does both these things by telling her that those who drink the living water he offers will never be thirsty, and the water will become in them "a spring of water gushing up to eternal life" (John 4:14). To a Seven, this could sound like an unlimited source of possibility, excitement, and the best of waters. She is intrigued enough to ask him to give her some of that water.

As an assertive type, the Woman at the Well is not shy, though at first she is wary of entering into a conversation with a Jewish rabbi. She engages in it more and more deeply, questioning him and challenging him, eroding any social conventions of patriarchy in the moment. While it is clear that she respects Jesus, calling him "Sir" or "Rabbi" (John 4:15), she is not intimidated by his authority or by his knowledge. While her dominant thinking centre continues to multiply the possibilities and ideas of their conversation, Jesus remains centred and is not sidetracked by her attempts at intellectual manipulation.

When she asks directly for a drink of his living water, she finds herself instead in a direct confrontation with someone who appears to know everything about her and her past. In reply to her request, Jesus meets her directly in her Seven space, and changes the subject! At least he appears to, for he suddenly says to her, "Go, call your husband, and come back" (John 4:16). For the first time in their conversation, the Woman appears to be caught off guard. She answers directly that in fact she has no husband.

Why does Jesus do this to her? Why does he not continue the

discussion of the living water, which is surely more important than her marital status? Perhaps he knows that as a Seven she does not like to stay on one subject too long. Perhaps he wants her to think beyond the water which quenches physical thirst. Or perhaps he needs to direct their conversation away from the literal so that they can talk about her relationship to God.

Her reply that she has no husband is an equivocation. A Seven needs to learn to get to the heart of the matter, so when Jesus tells her that he knows she is right in saying that she has no husband, she may have felt that she had neatly gotten past that matter, until he adds that he knows in fact that she has had not one but five husbands (John 2:1-11). He affirms the truth of what she had said (that she had no husband) and then circles back to the very issue she was hoping to dodge.

The woman's five "husbands" may be a subtle allusion allegorically to the five books of the Law of Moses, the Torah, which in John's narrative is consistently presented as having failed to provide redemption and fullness of life. Also relevant to this context, her "five husbands" might also allude to the five different peoples who displaced the Jews and settled in Samaria under the king of Assyria.[96] These people worshipped the God of Israel but also worshipped their own gods, and placed their shrines on the high places of Samaria.

The marriage motif has been running through John's gospel since the beginning of Jesus' public ministry at the wedding feast at Cana (John 2:1-11). Just before Jesus meets the Woman at the Well, he had been depicted by John the Baptist as the divine bridegroom (John 3:29). It has already been pointed out that the typescene of a betrothal at a well is also being invoked in the meeting between Jesus and the Woman. Thus, when Jesus asks her about her 'husband,' he is also and primarily asking her about the state of her spiritual marriage to God.

This is not an unusual or new idea in the Bible. The motif

runs through much of Hebrew literature, in which Israel is portrayed as the bride who is 'married' to God:

> For your Maker is your husband, the LORD of hosts is his
> name;
> the Holy One of Israel is your Redeemer,
> the God of the whole earth he is called.
> For the LORD has called you
> like a wife forsaken and grieved in spirit,
> like the wife of a man's youth when she is cast off,
> says your God.

– Isaiah 54:5-6

Sometimes Israel is not faithful to her divine Spouse and is led astray and seduced by foreign gods but God always takes her back.

Like Israel, the Woman at the well has also been spiritually unfaithful. She has had five husbands but none of them is truly her husband, for the Law of Moses and the foreign gods of the Samaritans cannot bring about a mystical marriage with the Divine Spouse. Faced with her lack of a true marriage, both literal and spiritual, and probably taken aback, the Seven in her tries once more to avoid the painful inner conflict and she changes the subject, exclaiming to Jesus, "Sir, I see that you are a prophet" (John 4:19). Not pausing to linger on this insight, which might get dangerously close to unleashing a response from her feeling centre, she instead launches into a digression about the site of authentic worship, and about whether God is to be worshipped on that mountain or in Jerusalem (John 4:20). Because the assertive type must keep up a self-image of which she can be proud,[97] the Woman at the Well tries to give Jesus a good picture of herself both by acclaiming him a prophet and displaying her knowledge about where to worship God.

Jesus is not pulled into her distractions. He again attempts to ground her back in the present reality, quite literally and directly, by saying that "the hour is coming, and *is now here*, when the true worshippers will worship the Father in spirit and truth" (John 4:23). The moment is now, yet she cannot or will not absorb this reality, and again she tries to look to the future, replying, "I know that Messiah *is coming*. . . and *will proclaim* all things to us" (John 4:25). Her anticipation of what *will* come prevents her from seeing what *is* actually in front of her at the very moment, the very Messiah whom she awaits!

Jesus then speaks to her the words which finally succeed in bringing her back to live in the present moment. He announces to her that "I AM he, the one who is speaking to you" (John 4:26). As when God announced the Divine Name I AM to Moses (Exodus 3:14), so now the same Divine Name has pierced the ordinary and all the expectations of things to come, and announced its presence as the 'Eternal Now', constantly in motion yet ever unchanging. Finally, she has no reply. The Divine Name, speaking itself moment by moment into the present, removes her concerns for the future and leaves her in silence. The only reply to the Divine Name is to enact it in herself, to take that I AM into her entire being, head, heart, and body, and to rush off to tell others. Her impulsive nature as a Seven has been transformed into knowing what it means to be present in her heart as well as in her head. She runs off to tell her people about her encounter with the Messiah. In doing so, she leaves her water bucket behind, a wonderful detail which John provides to illustrate that she knows she cannot store up the living water for the future: it is for now, and to be shared with others.

As a Seven, the woman had bounced from one topic to another until she was finally able to grasp what Jesus was offering her. When she realized he was not about to lecture her or condemn her, or demand the emotional encounter which a Seven resists, she was able to hear about the living water which always flows in the eternal present. Her enthusiasm and excitement quite literally carry her away, racing back to her people to tell them what she has found. The Seven cannot be held back when something new and wonderful is presented; she will head off quickly in that direction, and want to include others in its discovery. Her hurrying off, however, is no longer a distraction, a running away from her reality or pain. It is now a transformative running towards others, forgetful of herself and filled with joy, demonstrating a transformed self which can give rather than take. In doing so, she receives for herself the living water which can never be exhausted.

The meeting with Jesus ends with a revelation to her about who Jesus is and also about who *she* is. She is not a rejected and cast off daughter of God, but is in fact the beloved who is being called to experience the mystical marriage within her own soul. No wonder she runs off joyfully, abandoning any thought of the water which makes one thirsty again to share instead the living water welling up within her and giving her a new life. The pain of the Seven does not disappear by being covered up and denied, but by being seen, accepted, and not judged. By revealing her past, present and future in the presence of the Messiah, she is transformed. This unnamed Woman is a model of what it means to become a disciple and to rely on the living water of the moment. The Seven in us which she represents can learn from her to slow down, to acknowledge the pain of our past, to resist our distractions, and to allow the healing transformation of an encounter with the Divine Name to occur within our own souls.

Prayer in the Spirit of the Woman at the Well
Psalm 63

O God, you are my God, I seek you
 my soul thirsts for you;
my flesh faints for you,
 as in a dry and weary land where there is no water.
So I have looked upon you in the sanctuary,
 beholding your power and glory.
Because your steadfast love is better than life,
 my lips will praise you.
So I will bless you as long as I live;
 I will lift up my hands and call on your name.

My soul is satisfied as with a rich feast,
 and my mouth praises you with joyful lips
when I think of you on my bed,
 and meditate on you in the watches of the night;
for you have been my help,
 and in the shadow of your wings I sing for you.
My soul clings to you;
 your right hand upholds me.

But those who seek to destroy my life
 shall go down into the depths of the earth;
they shall be given over to the power of the sword,
 they shall be prey for jackals.
But the king shall rejoice in God;
 all who swear by him shall exult,
 for the mouths of liars will be stopped.

Summary of the Sevens

 Early in his life, Solomon's insight and wisdom become a vessel through which he realizes the Seven's gift of Holy Work. As a young king, he is caught up in the busy-ness and distraction which characterize the Seven. He does not yet have silence and stillness of heart. While he appears to remain distracted for most of his life, the voice of the old king presented in the Book of Ecclesiastes shows the fruits of the transformation of the Seven. Solomon has learned to face the pains of life and no longer focuses on future goals and dreams. He knows that all things have their time, and acknowledges that weeping is as natural as laughing.

In touching the sadness of life he finds joy in the ordinary things of the present, in eating and drinking and doing one's work with joy. He has slowed down enough to realize the pains and pleasures of the human condition, and knows that true creativity comes not from racing around and building temples but from letting his true essence be raised into conscious awareness of the bittersweet joy of each moment.

The Woman at the Well is also called to face the reality of the present through her encounter with Jesus. She learns how to dialogue with her Divine Spouse, the Beloved whom her heart seeks. She had learned to live with multiple options and apparent contradictions to keep her busy and distracted, but Jesus called her to stop avoiding her pain and look to her abandoned heart.

She finds her Beloved is not outside her, to be pursued in all directions at once, but lives within her, like living water which endlessly wells up to give her nourishment and rest. She knows her heart will never be unsatisfied again, and she is eager to rush off not into distractions but into the present to bring this good news of living water to the world.

Type Eight: Martha and The Canaanite Woman

> "We who are strong ought to bear the failings of
> the weak, and not to please ourselves."
>
> – Romans 15:1

Eights are the confronters and challengers. They are the most powerful of the three assertive types. They are self-confident, decisive, and strong. It is important for them to feel that they are strong and in control, hence the thought of being controlled by others makes them very fearful. They are located in the Body triad of the Enneagram, and their moving against others is often accomplished literally through their physical presence and confrontational style. Their energy often fills a room and they are inclined to take command when they enter it, or else they check out where the power resides among those present. Their virtue is innocence and simplicity, while their characteristic vice is lust or vengeance. It is their nature to lead and they are capable of affecting the universe in powerful ways.

Eights are direct as they move in their Body or action space and they are intensely concerned with issues of justice, honesty and fairness. Their clarity in both their thinking and their talking supports this and they make good debaters. At their best, Eights can become heroes and heroines, leaders who are confident and inspire confidence in others. They are powerful workers and do not shrink from but welcome confrontation. If they are not healthy Eights, however, they can be bullies or power-hungry tyrants who rely on violence, ruthlessness and meanness.

With the other assertives, the Eights have a misused Feeling centre. In them, it takes the form of not appearing to care about feelings or seeming not to need others. They do not readily exhibit a gentle side and can even become hardened to mask their unspoken belief that they may themselves be unlovable.[98] Emotions get in the way for an Eight, who would prefer to develop relationships based on shared activities and ideas rather than sharing of feelings.[99]

Unlike the Seven, who attempts to achieve mastery through self-gratification, the Eight tries to master a situation by triumphing over it. In an unaware or untransformed Eight, this attempt can even turn into vindictiveness.[100] There is an intensity to the Eights and their power is quite noticeable when one is in their presence. Frequently, the response to an Eight's presence is to move away or distance oneself. In less aware Eights, there is often a competitiveness in their relationships and this can manifest itself as verbal sparring. If it is allowed to get out of check, it can turn into rage or even physical violence.

Keeping their strength is important to an Eight, but they also need to allow other people to retain their own as well. In their proneness to confrontation and their urgency to settle an issue, their inner work will help them learn to value the differing stances of others. Cooperation for the Eight means not always having to be the one with the power. When Eights move through the stages of transformation and use their strength to help others, there is no obstacle that they cannot confront and overcome. They can learn to move from a "we/they" confrontational consciousness to an awareness that there can be no division between persons or groups, and that all are united in the divine image they bear.

The two biblical characters which exemplify this space show the assertiveness of the Eight in their encounters with Jesus. Martha of Bethany and the Canaanite (or Syrophoenician) woman who debates with Jesus over whether she is eligible to receive the blessings promised to Israel both demonstrate the Eight's outward movement against others — in this case, Jesus — to put forward their demands for truth. They do not hesitate to engage Jesus in a debate and a confrontation. Neither one wants to talk about her feelings, yet both of them are motivated to address Jesus precisely because at the moment they are responding to deeply felt emotions. In the case of Martha, her brother Lazarus has just died, and she is sad and also angry that Jesus did not come in time to heal him. The Canaanite woman approaches Jesus because her daughter is ill, but she does not talk about her love for her daughter or fear for her life, but just asks Jesus to heal her.

Both these women exemplify the Eight's qualities of leadership and aggression, power, self-confidence and the willingness to confront. It is sometimes very difficult for a woman to be in the

Eight space because these very traits, which represent the Eight's strengths, often marginalize her and challenge some people's notions of what it means to be "feminine." Both Martha and the Canaanite woman are exemplars of what it means to have a strength which can redefine femininity so that it includes self-confidence, clarity, and the strength to speak one's mind. In each of their stories, Jesus both affirms and rewards them for their stance. He meets them in their power and helps them use it to heal others.

The Holy Idea of the Eight space is Holy Truth. Holy Truth reminds us that we cannot be partial. We cannot with integrity maintain that some manifestations of God are holy and others are not, or that some people are more chosen or special to God than others.[101] People who can only imagine a gentle, unchallenging God might want to dismiss the confrontational power of Eights as lesser channels of the Divine. The Eights, however, bring to our attention the strong, powerful and just side of the divine presence in our world. In so doing, they become clear manifestations of Holy Truth.

Martha learns that there is no separation in life or in death, and the Canaanite woman's encounter with Jesus shows us that indeed God has no favorites. Both women illustrate how coming into the presence of the Divine means giving up their personal control and allowing the Spirit to move freely and confer healing and life where they had not been before.

Martha

> "Yes, Lord, I believe that you are the Messiah,
> the Son of God, the one coming into the world."
>
> – John 11:27

That Martha of Bethany can be considered as an Eight might come as a surprise to people who only think of her as the woman in the kitchen, busy preparing a meal while her sister Mary sat and listened at the feet of Jesus. To them she might appear to be more like the Two, ready to serve and to give. However, in this story, and especially in the story of her meeting Jesus after her brother Lazarus dies, we can see in her a confronter and a challenger, someone who readily moves out against others. She operates from her Body centre, and has difficulty using her Feeling centre effectively in her encounters. For these reasons, she is discussed here as an Eight.

In the story in Luke (Luke 10:38-42), Jesus arrives at the house and Martha welcomes him into her home. Luke's account is very clear that it is *her* home, which she shares with her sister Mary. She is probably the older sister and is either entitled to or has assumed her role as being in charge of the household. In welcoming Jesus, Martha shows the Eight's characteristics of magnanimity and leadership. She must have been used to assuming all sorts of responsibilities and had acquired the virtues of being practical, efficient and hospitable.

There is also in Martha a hint of the Eight's negative trait of being domineering and rebellious. When Jesus arrives, probably bringing a group of his followers with him, Martha gets busy in the kitchen with her preparations for serving a meal. Eights enjoy entertaining others not because they are oriented towards serving them but because they find great joy in intense conversations, even arguments, about important things. So it must have irked Martha that she was missing out on all the lively or inspiring conversation that was going on in the other room while her sister Mary was right at the centre of it, and so she complains to Jesus about her sister's not helping her (Luke 10:38). It is interesting that she does not complain directly to Mary but prefers to make a public issue of it, and appeals to Jesus' authority, which an Eight would find particularly attractive in its strength and mastery.

The desire for mastery, a characteristic of all three of the assertive types, in the Eight can take the form of wanting to be the one to decide in a relationship how time together is to be spent. If refused, the Eight can become irritable or even sulking.[102] Maybe Martha had other ideas of how she would have preferred to show Jesus hospitality, perhaps offering him wine and joining in a discussion about justice and truth. Maybe she, too, would have sat at Jesus' feet if he and Mary had first offered to help her with her "many tasks." Instead, she finds herself overloaded with work in the kitchen and must have felt some rebellion against her role. Eights do not like to be controlled by others and, in this situation, Martha might have felt entirely dominated by the circumstances. Her Eight characteristics of perseverance and intensity arouse in her a passionate desire that justice be done.

Mary, on the other hand, simply sits at the feet of Jesus and listens to him. Many if not most interpretations of this story set up a hierarchy between Martha and her sister Mary in which Mary comes out holding "the better part" (Luke 10:42). While Martha is regarded as useful and even essential for the living of our ordinary lives, she is also often used to represent the active life which is assumed to be inferior to the contemplative. This assumption needs serious questioning, for it accepts the notion that the body is inferior to the mind and heart. The great spiritual teachings support the work of the Enneagram in asserting that body, mind and heart must form a balanced whole, and that if one of the three is out of alignment, the entire person will suffer. The anonymous author of the spiritual classic, *The Cloud of Unknowing*, has said of Martha that "What she said she said courteously and succinctly. We must hold her completely exonerated!"[103]

As an Eight, Martha brings the Body component into the story. Seeing Martha as an Eight sheds some important light on her character. In the last century, the value of an active and socially aware Christianity in issues concerning justice and service has been rediscovered and reclaimed with a new vigour as a necessary complement to the life of prayer. The role of Mary who only listens is not enough. We must acknowledge that Mary and Martha live together in the same house, complementary and equally essential.

Metaphorically, this tells us that Martha's challenge is to rest and listen, while Mary's is to get up and help out in the kitchen. Spiritually, the two sisters can represent two aspects of one person. Like the yin and the yang in Eastern practices of balance and wholeness, we aspire to have both live within us. The outer awareness of our Martha is to be balanced by the interiority of our Mary. And both of them need to be focused at all times on the presence of Jesus at the centre of their house, which is a metaphor for our very being. If the soul is centred in the Divine Presence, there is nothing that can come between it and God, for it is already united with God. In a transformed Eight, and indeed in all transformed types, action and contemplation become so integrated that one is never away from the presence of God.

This brief account of Martha and Mary in Luke's gospel also suggests to us an allegorical pattern of the disintegrated self. Jesus tells Martha that she is "worried and distracted by many things" (Luke 10:41). His statement cannot be minimized or ignored. Worry and distraction about anything are poison to the spiritual life. Worry for the Eights comes from their excessive activity and excessive anxiety. Some would even suggest that Eights thrive on anxiety and actually derive pleasure from it, enjoying its sheer intensity.[104] Perhaps Jesus knows this about Martha, and is inviting her to recognize her vulnerability and to let it go.

Jesus does not say that many tasks are bad, but that being distracted pulls a person away from the centre. Distraction implies being distracted *from* something, which indicates a separation in our perception. If our awareness is busy being pulled away from our centre, we are not where our souls need to be, in union with our divine core. Distraction and worry are affairs of the ego, and it is not just the Eights of the world who need to focus and perceive the non-dual nature of things, leaving behind the cares of the ego-self and welcoming the Divine Presence into their 'home.'

Jesus goes on to tell Martha that Mary has *chosen* the better part, not fallen into it. Mary is listening to what Jesus is saying. Without this attentiveness and focus, the outer tasks in which we engage are indeed distracting and worrisome. Martha, too, can choose the better part, and it need not mean she cannot continue her work in the kitchen. She can be as much at home with the divine amidst her pots and pans as when she is deeply rapt in silent prayer. The 'better part' will not, and cannot, be taken away from one who has chosen it because everything is then perceived as inseparable from the unity of God. There is no 'outside' to God and hence no way to be apart from or lose our 'better part.' Our inner Martha and Mary, if both are tuned in to the Divine Presence at the centre of their 'house,' go about their tasks of sitting, doing the dishes, pondering, or slicing the carrots, in a seamless awareness of God in all that they do.

In an interesting juxtaposition in Luke's gospel, the story of Mary and Martha follows immediately after the parable of the Good Samaritan. It was told in response to the question "who is my neighbour?," asked by a lawyer who wanted to "justify himself" (Luke 10:29). Jesus told his well-known parable in reply, explaining that one's neighbour is the person who goes out of the way to help others. The lawyer's need to "justify himself" is in sharp contrast to Martha's question about justice. The lawyer wants to look good; he had earlier asked Jesus what he needed to do to get eternal life (Luke 10:25), and seems mainly interested in legalistic answers that do not require transformation of the heart.

Martha, on the other hand, demands justice from Jesus not so that she will look good but because she thirsts for his presence. Like the Good Samaritan of the parable, Martha is passionately concerned with social imbalances. She feeds those who arrive and looks after their needs. Both stories resonate with an Eight's desire for justice and show that the activity of doing good must be rooted in mercy, love and the Divine Presence which transforms the heart. Martha's complaint against her sister embodies the Eight's concern for justice, and for challenging and empowering others. It arises from her self-assurance and her confidence in the validity of what she requests.

These characteristics are an important part of Martha's story but there is a more significant encounter that she has with Jesus later on, and for which she is less well remembered. It concerns her remarkable behaviour when her brother Lazarus dies. In the account of the events given in John's gospel, Martha goes forth to meet Jesus, rebukes him for not having arrived in time, and then is led to boldly profess her faith that Jesus is indeed the Christ (John 11:27). This declaration is overlooked by many people possibly because it is so similar to Peter's profession of faith which, historically, many Christians have taken to be of greater significance. In Peter's case, his profession of faith was drawn forth out of the leadership qualities of the Six. With Martha, her similar profession of faith provides us with an example of an Eight who is truly transformed.

As in the previous story from Luke's gospel, we again see her coming forth to complain to Jesus that events have not unravelled fairly. Again she exhibits the Eight's movement outwards against other people. She confronts him with her belief that had he been in Bethany sooner, she knows he could have prevented Lazarus' death. She and Mary had earlier sent Jesus a message that Lazarus was ill, yet still he did not come right away. John tells us that "Jesus loved Martha and her sister and Lazarus" (John 11:5). Mary is not even named at this point, thereby focusing the narrative primarily on Martha. She is placed in the foreground here, announcing to the reader that our focus should stay on her even before we look at what Jesus will do for Lazarus.

When Martha hears that Jesus is finally on the way, she goes out to meet him. Mary, on the other hand, remains at home (John 11:20). This pattern replicates the previous one from Luke's gospel, in which Martha was seen in the sphere of action in the kitchen while Mary remained quietly in the background. Here, she is much more forward, stubborn, even passionate in her encounter with Jesus. There is an impatience about her speech to him. The first thing she blurts out is that if Jesus had been there, Lazarus would not have died (John 11:21). The Eight's confrontational style is seen clearly in this meeting. There is no formality or beating around the bush. Jesus is called to account for his lateness in coming. Strange as it might seem to others, for Martha as an Eight, her bluntness is an invitation to intimacy as well as an affirmation of the intimacy she feels towards Jesus, showing him the confidence of a friend.

Martha also softens her accusation somewhat by quickly adding that she still knows that Jesus can do something about the situation. As a healthy Eight, Martha is transformed enough to know that all the activity and leadership do not need to come from her. She willingly gives over control of the situation to Jesus and she is able to simply be present to him and what he might say or do. Having spoken with the power of the Eight, she has also absorbed the 'Mary' part of herself which knows how to wait at the feet of Jesus.

In reply, Jesus assures Martha that her brother will indeed rise again. She assumes he is referring to "the resurrection on the last day" (John 11:23-4), an event located some time in the probably distant future. This is all she can imagine, and it is hardly consoling. But Jesus surprises her by saying that the resurrection is now, an event in the present. Just as the Woman at the Well had to shift from thinking that the Messiah was coming in the future to an awareness that he was already there in the present, so Martha needs to know that eternal life is not just something to work towards but also something which is of the moment. An Eight's concern to bring about justice in the future must not ignore the power of the present. The power of the resurrection merges life and death so that there is only one thing, and that is eternal life. Jesus tells her,

> "I AM the resurrection and the life. Those who believe in me, even though they die, will live, and everyone who lives and believes in me will never die. Do you believe this?"

> She said to him, "Yes, Lord, I believe that you are the Messiah, the Son of God, the one coming into the world."

> – John 11:25-27

Martha's response with her strong affirmation of belief in him as the Messiah marks the Eight's acknowledgment of where true strength lies. Her discussion with Jesus has not deprived her of power but has shown her the deeper and greater power of the life that never ends, and that is also hers right now in the present moment. Her confession of Jesus as the Christ and her belief in eternal life are the traditional marks of an apostle. Coming to that belief is the purpose for which John wrote his gospel.

Martha turns her new knowledge of the presence of the I AM in the world into action. She goes to get her sister Mary, thus performing her first 'apostolic' work of calling others to the newly-revealed Christ. She tells Mary 'privately' that Jesus has arrived and is calling for her (John 11:28). Eights do not like to display their tender side and, in her gentle calling of Mary, we can see that Martha has recognized her feeling center which has been awakened by her recognition of Jesus as the Christ, the I AM in their midst.

Allegorically, Martha has merged with Mary and it becomes clear that Mary has also absorbed her Martha part, for when she hears Jesus is in the village, she too goes out to meet him. In fact, she repeats Martha's words, that had Jesus been there sooner, Lazarus would not have died. She speaks her words while kneeling at his feet and weeping. The moment presents us with an icon of how she has experienced her own integration, for her words are similar to her sister's but her posture and attitude are her own. She has merged her stillness at the feet of Jesus with the action it took her to get there. There is no recorded dialogue between Mary and Jesus, for the two sisters have spiritually merged into the one person they have allegorically been all along.

The author of John's gospel clearly saw strength, conviction and leadership in the person of Martha. At a time when women were discovering with joy and amazement their own call to discipleship in the early Church, John erected a verbal memorial to this wise and active woman who learned how to integrate the action of the Eight with the stillness of waiting in the presence of God.

If we re-examine her earlier story in Luke, her serving of the meal to Jesus and those who were in her house may even take on a eucharistic significance. In the presence of Christ, she shares what she has and who she is. Her request for Mary to join her could indicate that the eucharistic meal presents us with the clearest path towards integration of our outer and inner natures. At the centre of it all is Christ, who is both the reason for the meal and the cause of the gathering.

Martha thus epitomizes the virtues of the self-reflective Eight who knows how to use her power for the good of others and within a context of relationship. She is thereby enabled to do great things for God and for others. She is equipped to use her forthrightness and her forcefulness to go forward on a mission of service to others.

Eights who have been presented with the figure of Martha can readily identify with her position as a woman out of place in her society because of her assertiveness and determination. They also recognize in her their own desire to be faithful and tender and to move forward in difficult situations when they know their cause is valid and just. They also know that her own energy must unite with the I AM which is its source to accomplish the work of bringing eternal life into the present moment.

Prayer in the Spirit of Martha
Psalm 126

When the LORD restored the fortunes of Zion,
  we were like those who dream.
Then our mouth was filled with laughter,
  and our tongue with shouts of joy;
then it was said among the nations,
  "The LORD has done great things for them."
The LORD has done great things for us,
  and we rejoiced.

Restore our fortunes, O LORD,
  like the watercourses in the Negeb.
May those who sow in tears
  reap with shouts of joy.
Those who go out weeping,
  bearing the seed for sowing,
shall come home with shouts of joy,
  carrying their sheaves.

The Canaanite Woman

"Woman, great is your faith!"

– Matthew 15:28

In the portrait of the Canaanite Woman, we have another picture of the Eight who confronts and challenges Jesus. Matthew's gospel says she is a Canaanite who comes to Jesus to ask for her daughter to be healed (Matthew 15:21), while Mark identifies her as a Gentile of Syrophoenician origin (Mark 7:26). The two accounts, both quite short, are very similar and, whatever her nationality might have been, she was definitely not a Jew. The point of the encounter hinges on her being, like the Woman at the Well, an outsider.

When the woman approaches Jesus to obtain healing for her

daughter, Jesus ignores her, but she will not go away and persists in her request. Finally Jesus tells her that he has only come for the people of Israel, not for outsiders such as she, who are like the family dogs trying to take the food from the children. In response, she says that Jesus is correct but goes on to point out that even the family dogs are allowed to satisfy themselves with the crumbs that fall under the table. Amazed at her faith and confirming the truth of her statement, Jesus announces that what she has sought, the healing of her daughter, has been accomplished.

In this synopsis, we see manifested the Eight's characteristics of directness, readiness for debate and a passion for justice. Matthew writes that she did not politely request an interview with Jesus but started shouting at him (Matthew 15:22). This image conjures up the presence of her strong body energy which continues through the entire scene. The Eight's presence is often perceived as physical power and is used to great effect when demanding fairness or justice in a situation.

The woman is not shouting at Jesus personally but shouting out her request for mercy in her distress because her daughter "is tormented by a demon" (Matthew 15:22), a common way of interpreting any mental or physical illness of the time. She is assertive in her movement 'against' Jesus and in claiming what she needs without showing any concern for public opinion, whereas a hostile Eight might have begun by berating Jesus for ignoring her and aggressively demanding he fulfil her demands.

As all the types of the assertive triad do, she aspires to mastery in the situation, not mastery over Jesus but control over her own outcast status. We can see this in the way she argues in her own defence and on behalf of her daughter. In an untransformed Eight, there might be a hostility towards others, the fear of being abandoned which arises from a general feeling of exclusion from life.[105] While this Canaanite woman indeed must have found herself excluded quite deliberately from the life and blessings of Israel, she is nevertheless not vindictive in her boldness towards Jesus. Her action arises from her clear conviction that her exclusion is an unjust barrier which is to be overcome. She does not appear to be anti-social (as some Eights may be), but sees it as her task to set things right and to demand fairness and justice. She certainly does not blame Jesus for his culturally conditioned exclusion of her.

Many readers of this story find it difficult to understand Jesus' complete ignoring of her, for "he did not answer her at all" (Matthew 15:23). Perhaps at first he is startled by her sudden shouting. She must have created quite a disturbance, for the disciples urge Jesus not just to "send her away" but to send her away with her request answered (the Greek verb used here contains both meanings), probably so that she would not return. The disciples suggest this as a superficial way to get rid of her; they are annoyed by her constant shouting, and saying that Jesus should give her what she wants does not come from their compassion or justice but is merely a pragmatic response to a social nuisance.

Jesus, too, might have been tempted to just give her what she wanted and send her packing. It is doubtful that he ignored her solely because she was a Gentile. Earlier in Matthew's gospel, he had healed the servant of a centurion in a situation which was remarkably parallel to this one. A Gentile had asked Jesus to come to his home on behalf of his ailing servant (Matt. 8:5-13). In that instance, too, Jesus had affirmed that the Abrahamic faith could also be found outside of Israel, and the servant was healed in accordance with the centurion's faith.

That the petitioner is a woman this time cannot be a cause of concern for Jesus either, because again earlier in Matthew's gospel, he had already encountered the faith of a woman with a 12-year hemorrhage who had crept up to him to touch his cloak. There is no indication that he was startled then and he immediately addressed her as "daughter" and announced that her faith had indeed healed her (Matt. 9:20).

The hemorrhaging woman was "unclean" because of her blood-contamination (Leviticus 15:25), the centurion was a Gentile — to be specific, a Roman — and hence unclean as well. In both cases, Jesus had compassion on their needs and granted their requests. Jesus did not seem terribly concerned with issues of ritual uncleanness. Just before the Canaanite woman accosted him, Jesus had in fact spoken to the crowd and to his disciples about this very subject. He pointed out that what was clean or unclean had to do with what was in a person's heart, not with ritual matters. Defilement consists of what emerged from a person's mouth and heart, what they say and do, such as "evil intentions, murder, adultery, fornication, theft, false witness, slander" (Matthew 15:19). Clearly, contact with those who were considered legally or ritualistically unclean was not a worry for Jesus.

It is more likely that Jesus was silent towards this woman because he did not quite know what to make of her. She is clearly both an outsider and a woman, yet she hails him under his Hebrew title of "Son of David," a title which might be assumed to belong to Israel alone. His silence might have meant he was surprised by her addressing him as Son of David, and not entirely sure what she meant. It is also possible that he was confronted with the possibility of a new and deeper awareness of what his ministry was. While he had previously welcomed a Gentile and an unclean woman, neither one had claimed, as this Canaanite woman does, that he act towards them in his capacity as Son of David. The woman is not only asking for something but is also putting herself under the umbrella of those who claimed an expectation of the Messiah.

This must be what gets Jesus' attention. He does not initially indicate any interest at all in the condition of her sick daughter, but is 'caught' instead by her recognition of him as Son of David. He responds to this alone, saying he "was sent only to the lost sheep of the house of Israel" (Matthew 15:24). The woman, however, simply redirects his attention. She does not want to argue theology with him but simply kneels before him and pleads from the heart, "Lord, help me."

This is a very difficult thing for an Eight to do. She physically abases herself and she requests help. An unhealthy Eight wants to hold on to her power at all costs but one who has moved in the direction of integration will readily use her power on behalf of others, in this case her daughter. She is bold and reaches towards Jesus without any guilt or remorse to have her need met. In her action she is indisputably an exemplar of assertive faith. Eights have big hearts. At their best they are protectors, especially of the weaker and the innocent. They will place their own protective bodies in front of the weak to struggle against any unjust odds.[106] This woman also clearly understands that the power of love is ultimately stronger than the lust of power. In kneeling before Jesus and asking him for a favour, she overcomes the Eight's basic fear of submitting to another and she also gives up the Eight's basic desire of remaining self-reliant.[107]

Jesus is not yet ready to accept her self-abnegation. He returns to what preoccupies him, that "it is not fair" to give the children's food to dogs (Matthew 15:26.). He responds to her in language which an Eight would immediately understand, for fairness is one of their deepest desires. His response might have been enough to deter any other ordinary person from pursuing her case, but not an Eight. The woman, kneeling at his feet and pleading for help, must have been jolted to action by his use of the word 'fair.' To an Eight this is a call for justice. She knows about fairness as readily as a child knows when to call out 'that's not fair!' For the moment, she even lays aside her plea for help and instead responds to Jesus' logical but, as far as she can tell, unfair statement, saying, "yes, Lord, yet even the dogs eat the crumbs that fall from their masters' table" (Matthew 15:27). She respects his position but appeals to an even greater fairness, a broader vision of who he is as Messiah. Even dogs are not left to starve when there are leftovers. She is also claiming that she does not require a large portion of what he can give, and that even a bite will contain all that she needs. Thus her faith is two-fold. She believes that Jesus will give her something and she also believes in a holographic universe in which even the smallest part contains the whole and suffices.

Through her words, Jesus comes to recognize a faith in God that transcends the narrow confines of the Jewish thinking of his culture and his own background, in which only the chosen people enjoyed the divine favour. Her persistence incites him to broaden his own perception of the divine design and the extent of God's movements in all people. The woman indicates that her belief is in a God who has crumbs even for the dogs, not just for the children of Israel. Even if God plays favourites, there is always enough leftover to satisfy everyone. So Jesus grants her the 'crumbs,' which amounts to no less than the fullness of healing her daughter at that very instant.

"Woman, great is your faith!" he exclaims (Matthew 15:28), recognizing and confirming the power that lies in the strong faith of the Eight and in the words of truth which she speaks. Her desire for fairness and justice has connected her with the innocence of the Eight and reminds us of our humanity as living beings who are part of an immense and natural order which is in perfect balance.[108] This order knows no divisions or dualities; Jew or Gentile, male or female, clean or unclean — all are fed from the divine hand.

As a Canaanite, the woman recalls the time when Joshua led the children of Israel into Canaan, the land flowing with milk and honey (Exodus 3:8). They settled there and enjoyed the fruits of the country, and it became their home. The woman identified as a Canaanite in Matthew's gospel allegorically suggests the descendants of the original inhabitants of the area. The Jews who were ancestors of Jesus were fed by her homeland and survived and prospered. She now claims from Jesus the food, or 'crumbs,' which are therefore rightfully hers as well. It is not a favour she requires as much as justice. We all are fed by others at some time in our lives and we all have an obligation to feed those who ask. There is no beginning and no ending to the cycle of compassion and justice.

In the ministry of Jesus, the physical food of Israel is now transformed into the spiritual food for all nations. There are eucharistic overtones to this brief encounter between Jesus and the Canaanite woman, for the spiritual 'crumbs' she receives provide healing and encouragement, and strengthen her faith. Even a crumb is a feast in the spiritual banquet in which quantity and quality are not measured by worldly standards. To reinforce this connection, the remainder of this section in Matthew's gospel states that after this encounter Jesus then healed great crowds and it ends with the account of his miraculous feeding of the four thousand. Faith, healing, nourishment, and the eucharist are all foreshadowed by Jesus' brief but unforgettable encounter with the Woman from Canaan.

Prayer in the Spirit of the Canaanite Woman
Psalm 35

Contend, O LORD, with those who contend with me;
    fight against those who fight against me!
Take hold of shield and buckler,
    and rise up to help me!
Draw the spear and javelin
    against my pursuers;
say to my soul, "I am your salvation."

You have seen, O LORD, do not be silent!
    O Lord, do not be far from me!
Wake up! Bestir yourself for my defence,
    for my cause, my God and my Lord!

Vindicate me, O LORD, my God,
   according to your righteousness,
   and do not let them rejoice over me.
Do not let them say to themselves,
   "Aha, we have our heart's desire."
Do not let them say, "We have swallowed you up."

Let all those who rejoice at my calamity
   be put to shame and confusion;
let those who exalt themselves against me
   be clothed with shame and dishonour.

Let those who desire my vindication
   shout for joy and be glad,
   and say evermore,
   "Great is the LORD,
   who delights in the welfare of his servant."
Then my tongue shall tell of your righteousness
and of your praise all day long.

Summary of the Eights

Both Martha and the Canaanite woman as Eights help us to enlarge our notion of what it is to be truly feminine to include the strength of conviction, clarity and fearlessness in speaking the truth. Martha demonstrates how it is acceptable to confront God and how in fact it is an act of faith to do so. She knows that her actions are just and, in her relationship to her sister Mary, teaches us how to appreciate the non-dual nature of all things. In the lives of the two sisters, we see an emblem of the active and the contemplative lives merged into one.

Martha knows she can speak without formalities to Jesus, and when her brother Lazarus dies, she is both blunt and direct in pouring forth her lack of understanding as to why he did not arrive sooner. Her openness enables her to realize that the resurrection which she thought would occur in the future is in fact an event which occurs in the present. As an apostle, she proclaims her faith in Jesus as the Messiah.

The Canaanite woman shows the Eight's forthrightness in not being concerned with public opinion when there are urgent things to be done. She shouts out her needs to Jesus and engages him in a respectful but not subservient manner. Her heart motivates her to become a protector of the weak and she demands of him that he show justice and fairness to all. She insists that everyone has a right to call him Son of David regardless of their birthplace or nationality. The history of her own people fed the children of Israel and now she asks Israel to share its crumbs with her and, by extension, with the entire world.

Type Three: Saul and David

> If I speak in the tongues of mortals and of angels, but do not have love, I am a noisy gong or a clanging cymbal.
>
> – 1 Corinthians 13:1

Threes are the achievers and the performers. They are energetic and self-assured, able to make just about anything they undertake look good. The ideal to which they must aspire is to take pleasure in who they are, not in their image, and to learn to live wholly out of the truth. Because they have a great need for acceptance, they may become deceitful and self-promoting, for without their achievements they do not feel they have any genuine worth. They are able to get a lot done and success is very important to them, sometimes even more important than their inner qualities.

As members of the assertive triad, the Threes, like the Sevens and Eights, have a misused Feeling centre. Like the other two types, they find it difficult to allow others to get very close to them, and have difficulty accessing their inner life. They also move against people, not to confront them but because they always feel they need to figure out what others want and at least create the impression that they can give it to them. Hence, they are not confrontational in their approach but are friendly and open. They do not, however, readily encourage intimacy. It is enough for them if their relationships look as if they are good ones, for the image may be more important than the reality despite their deep longing for real intimacy.

Although Threes are in the centre of the Heart space, their Feeling centre is also their misused centre. They interact with the outer world through their Feeling centre but then they are not able to process the information it gives them in a useful way. They will instead use their thinking and their doing to help them determine how to get the most favourable response from others.[109]

The one feeling they can clearly identify is the feeling of being successful. Even if Threes know that a particular project of theirs is flawed, they will know how to cover up its weaknesses and make it look good anyhow. At the extreme, Threes can get further and further away from any sense of self-awareness, lose touch with reality and forget entirely who their essential self is.

Like the Sevens and the Eights, Threes also try to get their needs met through mastery. The Sevens attempt mastery through self-gratification, while the Eights may do so through triumph or even vengeance. The Threes look for mastery or control through their ambitious pursuits and self-glorification.[110] Unlike the Ones, who really want everything to *be* perfect, the Threes are happy if they *appear* perfect in all situations. They wish to impress people and are very good at adapting their image to please whomever they are with at any given time. They are truly the chameleons in society.

In their work of transformation, Threes will practice overcoming their self-deceptions and learning how to live beyond the world of appearances. Instead of deceit, they will become emblems of truth, directness, and honesty. They will not mask their weaknesses or failures but will have learned to accept these as part of the human condition, not good or bad but just the way things are.

Their interactions and choices will no longer be based on how they satisfy the ego but will be set in a broader context of an objective view of reality. This means they will learn to understand their experiences without their being informed by the ego and its limiting concerns.[111] Success will then become not personal success but a contribution to the outcome of the universe and a part of its ongoing creative process.

Two biblical characters who occupy this space are Saul and David, the first and the second kings of Israel. Both Saul and David display the Three's characteristics of ambition, ability to motivate, and a desire for success, both within their kingdom and in their military encounters against their enemies. Both also have to face monumental failings in their royal careers. The overwhelming difference between the two kings ultimately leads to the failure of one and the success of the other. When Saul errs, he piles one mistake upon another and becomes preoccupied with his egocentric concerns. He falls victim to greater and greater deceit, until he does not know who he is.

David also makes errors during his life. However, when he realizes them, he does not try to cover them up but instead turns to God for help. He overcomes his egotistical self by acknowledging that he has failed. Recognizing their own fallibility and failure can be terrifying to unaware Threes but to those who are serious about the work of integration, it can be a very freeing experience. No longer must they find their identity through a deceptive self-image. True success will become for them an inner stance of knowing that all is well and that the universe is managing itself exactly as it is meant to.

While both characters dealt with here are kings, they are not set apart from ordinary life and can serve as mentors to all of us. Saul and David were not born to royalty but began their lives in rural families. They were called out of their homes by the prophet Samuel, who was acting on God's orders to anoint them as kings.

As archetypes, they represent the innate royal nature of every person, a royalty based not on blood-lines but on the high and noble calling of living as a full and aware human being. Saul and David present us with two options, one leading to destruction and the other to greatness. They demonstrate the worst and the best of the Three-space and offer us guidance as we attempt to move out of our own self-centredness and deceit and into a holy harmony with all that is.

Saul

> "I have been a fool, and have made a great mistake."
>
> – 1 Samuel 26:21

Saul was anointed the first king of Israel after a long period in which a series of judges ruled the nation, and the people began to clamour for a king so that they could be like other nations. After trying to convince them that a king would take their sons, their grain, and the best of their cattle, the prophet Samuel was told by God to go ahead and give them what they wanted (1 Samuel 8). The narrative immediately introduces Saul, son of Kish, a Benjaminite. Threes love to look good and have people admire them, and the reason Saul is singled out appears to be solely based on his appearance: "There was not a man among the people of Israel more handsome than he; he stood head and shoulders above everyone else" (1 Samuel 9:2). He looks the part of success and his father is "a man of wealth" (1 Samuel 9:1), attributes that a Three believes are important because they project a successful image. People know Saul and his family and think well of them.

At this early stage in the story, Saul is not out of touch with his Feeling centre. He has set off to look for his father's donkeys which have strayed and, not finding them after quite some time, he expresses concern that his father might begin to worry more about his missing son than his missing donkeys (1 Samuel 9:5). There is no preoccupation with success or with trying to cover up the failure of his mission here. On the other hand, at a young age a Three will often do things to make his or her family proud and it is possible that Saul, even though the donkeys had not been found, was proud of his attempt and knew his father would not be angry.

In addition, while a Three may often hide feelings of self-doubt either deliberately or unconsciously so that the projected image appears to be the real self, Saul seems genuinely surprised and humbled when Samuel tells him he is to be king:

> "I am only a Benjaminite, from the least of the tribes of Israel, and my family is the humblest of all the families of the tribe of Benjamin. Why then have you spoken to me in this way?"

> – 1 Samuel 9:21

Threes are very surprised when they discover that their self-image has become real. The surprise raises up in them the question of 'is this really me?' or 'can this really be happening to me?' In a truthful and humble way, they begin to see the value of their dreams and of the effort they have placed in achieving them.

Once he has anointed Saul, Samuel tells him that on his return home he will meet a band of prophets, will be "possessed" by the spirit of God, and will "be turned into a different person" (1 Samuel 10:6). This is the first of Saul's various personas and he acquires, or unveils, several more as his career moves forward. The first 'different person' he becomes is a gift from God, who "gave him another heart" (1 Samuel 10:9), and Saul prophesied with the prophets. When others notice this and comment on it, Saul seems to have some misgivings. Perhaps being in a prophetic frenzy made him look foolish. Certainly he seemed to want to put the matter behind him, for when he got home, he told no one about his newly anointed kingship or of his prophetic frenzy (1 Samuel 10:16).

The second time Samuel comes to declare who is to be the new king (in what could also be another account of the anointing of Saul), the lot again falls to Saul but he cannot be found. He is hiding among the baggage (1 Samuel 10:22). Hiding oneself is one of the chief characteristics of Threes, who wish to hide their vulnerability and fear of failure. Here we see it enacted quite literally as Saul tries to cover himself up. His new role, his kingship, has been declared but he does not want to be found. He is still at this point able to separate himself from his role as king but he soon merges into it and identifies with it.

As his story unfolds, Saul eventually identifies with his new role so entirely that he forgets he was the man who once hid among the baggage. This is of course a danger inherent in any role-playing. Playing at it long enough might make us actually believe in the role and forget the reality of the player. When some 'worthless fellows' resent Saul's anointing and wonder how he can possibly help them, Saul ignores them and "held his peace" (1 Samuel 10:27). He does not want to confront or remove the kingly self-image he is wearing.

However, Saul is tested about a month after his anointing and successfully defends Israel against the Ammonites. The rejoicing people are eager to seek out and kill those who spoke against Saul earlier but Saul decrees that no one shall be punished (1 Samuel 11). As a Three, Saul expresses a light conscience, that it is easy to forgive others and himself because he wants to be liked. He also exhibits how much the Three thrives on success, or at least on a successful image. Having both, as he now has, he has nothing to fear from what others might in the past have said about him.

Saul's military success continues against the Philistines but eventually the Hebrews find themselves in a dire situation. Saul falls victim to his own heightened image of his self-importance and believes that he can single-handedly rescue them, even though Samuel had told him to wait for him at Gilgal to offer a burnt offering. Samuel is delayed and we read that people began to "slip away from Saul" (1 Samuel 13:8). To appear successful at all costs, a Three will find or create any opportunity to make things work. To keep the people with him, and to retain the appearance of leadership, Saul decides to go ahead and offer the burnt offering himself.

As soon as he has done so, Samuel arrives and demands to know what Saul has done. Saul engages in an elaborate cover-up, rationalizing himself out of any culpability. His reasoning appears plausible at first: the Philistines were approaching and he wanted to win God's favour. But his explanation also contains an element of self-deception: "I *forced* myself, and offered the burnt offering," he explains (1 Samuel 13:12). A Three is consistently doing and finds it difficult to wait and be patient. Saul's rationalization is designed to cover up his deliberate choice of usurping the role of the prophet. Samuel does not fall for it. He reprimands Saul for being foolish and announces that his kingdom, which would have been established by God forever, will not continue.

Threes have a fear of failing and, his worst fear now realized, Saul responds from this point on as a degenerating and unhealthy Three. He begins to deceive himself more and more, shows signs of mental imbalance and falls into fits of rage. The narrative of his fall is intertwined with that of the rise of David, the one Samuel says will gain the kingdom instead, the "man after [God's] own heart" (1 Samuel 13:14). Saul becomes jealous of the successes and the popularity of David, so much so that he wants to kill him. He cannot endure not being the most successful in the eyes of the people. He is even prepared to kill his own son Jonathan who unknowingly violated his father's edict not to eat anything before evening, but the people rally in Jonathan's defence (1 Samuel 14:45). Saul wants so much to retain the regard of the people for his leadership and success that he is willing to kill the two men who are his strongest supporters.

Saul becomes more and more desperate as it appears his power and leadership are slipping. Even though Samuel guaranteed success for Saul over the Amalekites and told Saul to spare no person or animal in their rout, Saul still decided once again to take matters into his own hands and disobey. He was indeed victorious in the battle but he could not bring himself to destroy things of value as God had commanded. By setting himself up in place of God, Saul has reached a point in his self-deception which clouds his sense of reality. Confronted by Samuel, again he rationalizes and says that the soldiers took the valuable animals in order to sacrifice them to God (1 Samuel 15:21). When Samuel responds that God has rejected Saul as king, Saul admits what the Three in us often knows, that "I feared the people and obeyed their voice" (1 Samuel 15:24). His reputation was at stake and his fear of losing it overcame his conscience. Rejected by God, Saul pleads with Samuel to still return together with him so that the elders will see them in apparent harmony. Again, image is everything for the unaware Three.

With the rejection by God, Saul now experiences "an evil spirit" that torments him (1 Samuel 16:14). This has been interpreted variously as epilepsy, madness or depression. Whatever its manifestation, it symbolizes Saul's loss of his connection with his inner self. His feelings have been silenced by his concern for what others think of him and his need to keep a semblance of power and control. He is angry with the acclamation David receives from the triumph over Goliath and keeps an eye on him from then on (1 Samuel 18:9), even throwing a spear at him in a moment of inner torment (1 Samuel 19:10). In Saul's disintegrating state, he believes that someone else's power or popularity robs him of his own. He even tries to use his own daughter, Michal, as a "snare" for David so that the Philistines might kill him (1 Samuel 22:8). He believes others are conspiring against him and that no one tells him anything (1 Samuel 22:8). Everything becomes subject to the criterion of what will make Saul look good and, in a distorted Three, this can mean making everyone else look bad.

Even when David proves twice (by being in a position to kill

Saul and refraining from doing so) that he is not trying to kill the king, Saul is still not reassured of his own safety. He fears the army of the Philistines and, in the final chapter of his life, we see him succumbing to the traits of a truly disintegrated Three. The fear that he is failing and that his image is suffering leads him to his ultimate deceit. His desperation when God fails to respond to him causes him to seek the help of a medium at Endor. Having previously expelled and outlawed all mediums and wizards from the land, he now undermines his own work and seeks to consult one.

A desperate Three will do anything to hide his inner deterioration so that others will not know how troubled he is.[112] Literalizing this tendency, Saul physically disguises himself to visit the woman of Endor (1 Samuel 28:8). His outward covering up of who he is symbolizes the inner deception and mask that have increasingly dominated his life so that his persona is more real than his self. The woman does not know who he is, and neither, it seems, does Saul. When she finally recognizes him, she cries out what might be the theme song of his life: "Why have you deceived me? You are Saul!" (1 Samuel 28:12).

She calls him to account for his deception and she reminds him of his own identity, but he is not able to respond to her on either subject. His only concern is to call up the spirit of the recently deceased prophet Samuel to determine what to do. No longer does Saul have any inner authority or clarity of purpose. All that matters now is finding out what he needs to do to protect his image as king and to save his own life. Conscience has been cast aside and he relies on external tactics. But instead of telling him how to save himself, the spirit of Samuel announces to Saul that the next day he and his sons will be with Samuel in the land of the departed. This is to be Saul's ultimate unveiling. There is no way the Three can overcome death: no self-image or deception will protect him.

All Saul's skills of deceit fail him now and he becomes truly fearful. He has lost all control of himself: the woman as well as his servants have to remind him to eat and they force him to do so (1 Samuel 28:23).

The very next day the Philistines kill the sons of Saul and he himself is badly wounded. Fearful of being found by his enemies and slain, Saul commands his armour-bearer to kill him. It is not death he fears but being humiliated by his enemies. He would rather die than lose his self-image of success and distinction. But the armour-bearer fears murdering the king and does not help Saul perpetuate his image. He refuses the task, at which point Saul commits suicide with his own sword (1 Samuel 31:4). This is the ultimate desperation of the Three, a willingness to kill himself rather than suffer any form of humiliation or failure.

When Saul's body is found, the allegory is completed: his head is cut off and his armour removed. In other words, he was so separated in his life from his Feeling or relational centre, and had built up so many layers of deception that they were like metal armour protecting him. But at death those layers of armour are removed and his soul in its nakedness finally met both Samuel and God in its undisguised form. If our success is determined by the views others have of us, it must necessarily be short-lived since all lives, however long, are short against the backdrop of eternity.

Saul never learned to use his power and authority to help others. He was unable to let go of his competitiveness and he feared humiliation rather than seeking to discover humility. For the Three in us to be transformed, we need to learn to experience our inner identity as beings who are connected to the entire universe and love ourselves as part of that universe. As Almaas puts it:

> Until you know yourself to be completely Being, you are objectively helpless;... then this acceptance of helplessness, without defence, without judgment, without striving, becomes the point of entry into Being and its dynamism. (pp. 280-1)

Saul struggled against this knowledge for most of his life and his ending was tragic. His tragedy can be a lesson for the Three in all of us to work towards that which is life-giving and not a bearer of destruction.

Prayer in the Spirit of Saul
Psalm 53

Fools say in their hearts, "There is no God."
    They are corrupt, they commit abominable acts;
    there is no one who does good.

God looks down from heaven on humankind
    to see if there are any who are wise,
    who seek after God.

They have all fallen away, they are all alike perverse;
    there is no one who does good,
    no, not one.

Have they no knowledge, those evildoers,
    who eat up my people as they eat bread,
    and do not call upon God?

There they shall be in great terror,
    in terror such as has not been.
For God will scatter the bones of the ungodly;
    they will be put to shame, for God has rejected them.

O that deliverance for Israel would come from Zion!
    When God restores the fortune of his people,
    Jacob will rejoice; Israel will be glad.

David

> "The LORD does not see as mortals see; they look on the outward appearance, but the LORD looks on the heart."
>
> – 1 Samuel 16:7

We see the complexity of the Three most clearly in the character of David, one of the most rounded portraits in the entire scripture. He is shown in his many personas as a youth, a shepherd, a warrior, a loyal subject to King Saul, a loving friend to Jonathan, a king, a poet and psalmist, a musician, and an inspired dancer. He is also shown as a murderer, a victim of his own lust and a sometimes rather unskilled parent, but as a result of all this he is also a penitent. His full portrayal makes it possible for him to appeal to people in all stages of life and he is one of the most humanly portrayed characters in the entire biblical narrative. From his house and lineage arises the messianic line and his kingship becomes a prototype of the divine kingship later associated with the Messiah.

Given these many facets, it is not difficult to understand why David is best understood as a Three. Threes have many self-images and want to portray them all with success. With Saul, his failure to realize he was living out of his self-image and not his true self led to his downfall, for he never learned how to integrate failure into his inner growth and transformation. With David, however, we are able to trace his growth from a naive young shepherd to an old king of Israel and see how during his entire life he was able to keep connected to reality and to God.

Within the assertive triad lies the potential of narcissism. This is another way in which the assertive types can achieve the mastery they desire. It consists of being in love, like Saul, with one's idealized self-image.[113] In the Sevens, this is manifested as a belief in greatness, as with Solomon; in the Eights, it is shown through a powerful self-image, as with the Canaanite woman; in the Threes, we see an identification with perfect efficiency and success so that one *is* one's image. Saul recognizes David's core as a Three because it is so familiar to him. In his final words to David, Saul says, "Blessed be you, my son David! You will do many things and will succeed in them" (1 Samuel 26:25). From this moment, the power and success are transferred from Saul entirely onto David.

The story of David is in the genre of heroic narrative, the biblical parallel to the stories of Odysseus and King Arthur, in which the hero is a political figure who embodies the destiny of his country and is at the same time a person undergoing the archetypal human journey. David's complex personality combines many qualities which enable him to exemplify humanity in its many facets; his life of action as a king and a soldier is balanced by his contemplative and artistic side as a musician and poet. In a typical Three, the full range and depth of the emotions remains undeveloped,[114] because the Feeling centre is misused or underused. When a Three undertakes the work of transformation, however, access to the Feeling centre is opened and liberated. We see its effect in David's rich emotional life. Traditional composer of many of the psalms, David evidences in these poems strong, dramatic, and even violent feelings that traverse the entire emotional spectrum.

David's life at times shows a balance and at other times a tension between his restraint and his passion. Restrained, as when he twice refrains from killing his king Saul, he is a model of the Three who has learned to slow down and detach himself from his accomplishments. Impassioned, as when his lust for Bathsheba becomes obsessive and leads him to kill her husband, he shows the Three's tendency to act impulsively and to cover up his faults. Unlike his predecessor King Saul, however, David as king demonstrates over and over the reference point which keeps him from disintegration and madness: no matter what his circumstances, his life retains its spiritual centre, and his sins and mistakes are finally not excused and covered up but are repeatedly turned over to God. When he sees his sin, he knows it as sin against God; and when he triumphs, he sings the praises of God who has allowed it.

David is chosen to be king by the prophet Samuel,who inspects the seven sons of Jesse knowing that one of them is to be anointed. David is not among them, however, for his father thought him too young to be considered. Samuel insists that he is called in from keeping the sheep and pronounces him the one whom God has chosen. The theme of transformation for the Three is established right at the start of David's call to be king. Threes value the importance of appearances and David, we are told, is "ruddy, and had beautiful eyes, and was handsome" (1 Samuel 16:12).

But God has already told Samuel not to judge on the basis of appearances, for people "look on the outward appearance, but the LORD looks on the heart" (1 Samuel 16:7). In other words, God sees into the "essence" of a person. The work of the Enneagram, no matter which of its types we prefer, is to assist us in uncovering our own "essence" or real self, beyond the attributes of persona and ego, and David stands as a model of the process which may begin early in life and continue to our death. Once he is chosen by God's looking "on the heart," the spirit of God "came mightily" upon him from that day on (1 Samuel 16:13). God meets the Three directly in the Heart space, uncovering outward appearances and inner deceptions, and calls him into truth.

David's encounter with Goliath shortly afterwards enforces the power of essence over ego. Rather than adopt the bravado of a warrior, David goes to meet the Philistine strongman as an untrained lad. Saul cannot imagine success from this; he encourages David to at least wear some armour. Saul, a master of self-disguise and covered with armour at his death, does not understand David's reliance on God to save him. David tries on the various pieces of armour but, unable to walk in them, removes them and instead picks up five stones for his sling (1 Samuel 17:37-40). Weapons from the earth and the strength of its Creator are all that arm the young David. This dependence not on his ego or an image of success but on the reality of God's strength accompanies David throughout his life, even when he later makes miserable mistakes.

As a Three, David is also a master strategist and plays not only the parts that unfold in his life but he is also able to fabricate others. When he is fleeing from Saul and takes refuge in the house of King Achish, the servants recognize him and he fears betrayal. He immediately gets the idea to act the part of the madman and his behaviour both fools them and wins him safety (1 Samuel 18:1). Unlike Saul's disguise when he visited the woman at Endor, David's role-playing is not evidence of self-deception and loss of control but of his ability to confound his enemies and deceive *them*.

While Threes may have difficulty forming deep relationships because their Feeling centre is misused, David once again demonstrates how a potential weakness can become a great strength. When Threes are the recipients of genuine love, their hearts are awakened and they are open to being loved and loving in return.

David's friendship with Saul's son Jonathan is one of the deepest and most loving portrayed in the entire Bible. Their souls are "bound" to each other (1 Samuel 18:1), and Jonathan's death occasions one of the most poignant laments in literature:

> How the mighty have fallen in the midst of battle!
> Jonathan lies slain upon your high places.
> I am distressed for you, my brother Jonathan;
> > greatly beloved were you to me;
> > your love to me was wonderful,
> > passing the love of women.

> – 2 Samuel 1:25-26

Not only in sadness but also in joy does David experience his emotional centre unfolding. When he brings the Ark of God into the city, David rejoices in exuberant dance (2 Samuel 6:5, 14). He finds vitality and joy in his reign even amid its difficulties and political intrigues.

He also finds, however, that he is tempted to abuse his role as king. Perhaps his worst mistake is his behaviour towards Bathsheba and her husband Uriah. David had previously been able to show restraint towards a beautiful and clever woman, Abigail, who was married to Nabal, an ill-natured fool (1 Samuel 25:25). Abigail entreated David successfully not to take offence at her husband's insults and David had praised both God and Abigail, exclaiming, "Blessed be the LORD, the God of Israel, who sent you to meet me today! Blessed be your good sense, and blessed be you, who have kept me today from bloodguilt and from avenging myself by my own hand" (1 Samuel 25:32-33). On that occasion, David's response to personal offence by Nabal was contained in his thanking God for the encounter. He was able to sidestep an unhealthy Three's preoccupation with looking successful and give in to the pleading of a woman rather than kill her uncouth husband.

By the time he met Bathsheba, however, David had become king and tasted much success in his life. He does not appear to have hesitated in calling Bathsheba to him, even though he is told she is the wife of Uriah. His confidence makes him identify with his image of success and not consider the deceit he is undertaking. When Bathsheba becomes pregnant, David manifests the Three's tendency to try to cover up his mistake. He recalls Uriah from the battlefield to sleep with his wife in the hope that his adultery will not become known. Uriah, however, proves the more righteous, refusing to leave the palace since soldiers were required to refrain from relations with women.

David's arranging to have Uriah killed in battle is an extreme reaction to his panic at being found out. Threes do not necessarily need to be successful but they always want to look that way. Covering up adultery with murder is a desperate solution to David's dilemma, but his ploy is discovered by the prophet Nathan. Appealing to the nature of the Three to cover up the truth, Nathan covers up what he knows by telling David a parable. He tells him a story about a rich man who had many flocks but who nevertheless took the single loved lamb of a poor man to feed to a guest. David is outraged and demands restitution to the poor man. Nathan then reveals to David that the story is about him: "You are the man!" he exclaims (2 Samuel 12:7).

Here is an invitation for the Three to see himself as he really is, a flawed and deceitful person. The story has touched David's innermost life. He becomes emotional and determined to make amends. Through Nathan, a trusted friend and a prophet of God, God was able to reach David's heart so that he could access the horror, the pain and the remorse of what he had done.

It has been stated that Threes do not have a strong conscience but that fear of humiliation may keep their behaviour in check.[115] In Saul, fear of humiliation caused him to try even harder to cover up his misdeeds. But for David, the revelation of his sin moved him to proper humility, not out of fear but from an inner confrontation with the truth. In accepting his guilt, he can discover his own identity because he no longer needs to save face.

The child of David and Bathsheba does not live and David accepts even this terrible outcome as being from the hand of God. Before the child's death, he pleads with God and fasts; afterwards, he washes and eats, accepting that his prayers were not granted. He was not trying to project an image of a grieving father for the sake of others. His grief was genuine, as was his acceptance. He is even able to console Bathsheba. By letting go of his attachment to appearances and even to outcomes, David manifests a Three who is in touch with the reality of God's will and the belief that all is holy and that all is well. His turning to God in good times and in bad is a sign of his willingness to confront his fears and deeds in the light of the larger whole.

The narrative of David represents an unusual combination of the pastoral and the heroic forms of storytelling. Both lend themselves to the personality of the Three, for in the pastoral we find the image of a simple, peaceful life lived among people of the soil, and in the heroic we find the image of larger-than-life people who do great deeds. Both are fictions, for both models are idealized, but they suit the deceptive self-images of the Threes.

David inhabits both realms, starting his life as a shepherd and moving from the pasture to the royal court. While he adopts various personas during his lifetime, he is also engaged in the transformative work which seeks to find the truth. David's rural and royal roles can symbolize the balance he seeks between the active and the contemplative life. Just as Martha and Mary gave us a picture of that integration in the Eight space, so David combines in his single person the active leader of the people with the contemplative nature of the poet.

Threes can be clear in their vision and enthusiasm, or can be more concerned with simply making things into a good show. With David, we see an instance of clarity, and his life is one of action and accomplishment, and also of pulling back and resting in music and contemplation. His many changes of strategy and his developed skills as a motivator show him always ready to meet another challenge, yet he remains adaptable when his schemes do not materialize.

For instance, his great desire of overseeing the building of a house for God, a temple of worship, is denied him. David had projected onto God his own desire to make things look good and had assumed that God, too, would appreciate a nice cedar house to dwell in. But God tells David that he does not yet need a house, having wandered within Israel and never demanded any dwelling from its leaders. An unhealthy Three might see this as a rejection of his plans and an unfulfilled dream as a cause for making excuses. But there is no recorded protest by David, even though tying his name to the building of a temple would have given permanent success to his image.

David's silence in fact draws forth a greater promise from God: instead of David's building a house for God, God intends to build a house for David and not a house made with stone but a house of David's descendants, so that "your house and your kingdom shall be made sure forever before me; your throne shall be established forever" (2 Samuel 7:16). While David's dynasty did not in fact last forever, the promise eventually took on messianic significance, and the House of David came to be the family from which it was anticipated that the Messiah would spring. By giving up his concern with success for himself, David received instead an everlasting gift of having his name forever joined to that of the Messiah who would for all generations come to be known as the Son of David.

Prayer in the Spirit of David
Psalm 51

Have mercy on me, O God,
    according to your steadfast love;
according to your abundant mercy
    blot out my transgressions.
Wash me thoroughly from my iniquity,
    and cleanse me from my sin.

For I know my transgressions,
    and my sin is ever before me.
Against you, you alone, have I sinned,
    and done what is evil in your sight,
so that you are justified in your sentence
    and blameless when you pass judgment.
Indeed, I was born guilty,
    a sinner when my mother conceived me.

You desire truth in the inward being;
    therefore teach me wisdom in my secret heart.
Purge me with hyssop, and I shall be clean;
    wash me, and I shall be whiter than snow.

Let me hear joy and gladness;
    let the bones that you have crushed rejoice.
Hide your face from my sins,
    and blot out all my iniquities.

Create in me a clean heart, O God,
    and put a new and right spirit within me.
Do not cast me away from your presence,
    and do not take your holy spirit from me.
Restore to me the joy of your salvation,
    and sustain in me a willing spirit.

Then I will teach transgressors your ways,
    and sinners will return to you.
Deliver me from bloodshed, O God,
    O God of my salvation,
and my tongue will sing aloud of your deliverance.

O Lord, open my lips,
    and my mouth will declare your praise.
For you have no delight in sacrifice;
    if I were to give a burnt offering, you would not be pleased.
The sacrifice acceptable to God is a broken spirit;
    a broken and contrite heart,
O God, you will not despise.

Do good to Zion in your good pleasure;
    rebuild the walls of Jerusalem,
then you will delight in right sacrifices,
    in burnt offerings and whole burnt offerings;
then bulls will be offered on your altar.

Summary of the Threes

The tragic story of Saul offers us an opportunity to look at the dark side of ourselves. Not every biblical story is a success story, and in his downfall we see the tragedy of the Three who fell victim to his own deceit. By confronting the worst of the Three space, we come to know that whatever our own 'space,' we must be vigilant and stay awake so that we will not be caught sleeping like Saul and his soldiers. Saul tried to manipulate his way through life and became so enamoured with winning and overpowering others that he became his own victim. Saul teaches us to watch carefully our tendency, not limited to the Three, of self-deception and role playing, or the need to make others look bad in order to affirm our own shaky self-image. His poor choices remind us that, left to ourselves, we can fall victim to the desires of our ego and neglect the voice of our inner truth.

In contrast, David presents us with the opportunity to accept our personal guilt, as he does when confronted by the prophet Nathan. He does not cover up his deep inner pain with empty shows but faces it directly, as he does when his first son dies. The Three's virtue of Truth encourages us to seek friends who will speak as a Nathan to us if they see us seduced by vanity or passing pleasures, calling us back to an awareness of our true self. David is an archetype for us of the stages of growth in our own lives, as his story spans the time from his youth to his death. The archetypal human journey leads us to get in touch with and preserve our contact with our divine Centre, our Essence, to lead us unerringly in the way of transformation.

Group 3: The Withdrawing Types

Fours, Fives, and Nines

> Be doers of the word, and not merely
> hearers who deceive themselves.
>
> – James 1:22

The three types which form the withdrawing triad on the Enneagram are the Fours, Fives, and Nines. They are referred to as the individualists or romantics (Fours), the thinkers or observers (Fives), and the mediators or peacemakers (Nines). They are 'withdrawing' because in their relationships with people their natural movement is to step back, to move away from others. They are not necessarily shy, but they prefer to observe and process before they act.

The withdrawing types share a misused, or repressed, Doing centre. This does not imply that they are inactive or never do anything but that they often feel disengaged from what is going on around them. They move back from the outer world into an inner space where they feel more comfortable. In the Fours, this is manifested as an active imaginative life and a romantic shading of events that come their way. They are not overly concerned with shaping the external world, preferring to spend their time in their extraordinary inner world.

For the Fives, their misused Doing centre sends them into the world of their thoughts and ideas. They prefer to stand back in a group and gather information cerebrally rather than through their actions. They can get stuck in their ideas to avoid engagement with the outer world and make better planners than implementers.

The Nines are also internally disengaged from what is going on around them. When they act, their engagement is slow and deliberate. In contrast, they can also be inactive, or appear to be biding their time, and then suddenly be sparked into doing something non-stop.

The three withdrawing types often appear to be introverts, happier in solitude than in company. They are more comfortable dealing with their thoughts and feelings in the privacy of their own minds. They are not necessarily worried about showing their emotions in a public display, but just prefer to look within for what they might need.[116] Fours especially, while they often live in their internal fantasies, can become externally flamboyant and overtly dramatic. All the withdrawn types often have a rich inner life, imaginative and questioning. Yet under pressure, they tend to pull back from the public spotlight unless they have very strong internal motivations to step onto centre stage. If they find they need to do so, their reason is bound to be significant and, in such circumstances, they are able to forget their self-absorption and move with clarity and freedom.

Horney's characterization of this triad as showing "resignation" presents one way of understanding this aspect of ourselves. We may be said to be in our resigned Four, Five, or Nine space when our attitude towards something is "I'll just wait and see." There is little that can bother us while we remain in this internal stance. For those who do not normally find their Enneagram type in one of these three spaces, entering the space of withdrawal from action may sometimes signal and accompany a particular season in their lives, a time of mellowing or a detachment from our once-held desires or fears.[117] It can be a time of rest and retreat, one in which we pull back and observe what is happening in our inner life. Freedom from not doing anything is what is sometimes called holy indifference through which we are not invested in any one particular outcome but remain open and free to await the movement of the Spirit.

For the withdrawing types, it is a mistake to think that because they prefer to disengage from the outer world they will not experience struggle or pain as much as the other types do. They are characterized by their resignation through which they deliberately withdraw from the struggle or pain but they do not deny it. They present us with a picture of living their lives at a continuous "low ebb" in which there is no substantial friction but also no real zest.[118] They do not automatically react to a situation by trying to decide what they should do about it but prefer to wait it out, ponder deeply, observe it, imagine its possible outcomes, or wait for someone else to start the ball rolling.

Reality for these three types is found in their inner worlds. Unlike the assertive types, who are always jumping ahead into the future, the withdrawing types are more at home in the past. It is a more comfortable place for them to be since it does not — in fact, it cannot — demand anything from the Doing centre.[119] Everything is already accomplished there and, while we can always ruminate on the past and analyze whatever information we have about past events, these 'activities' do not allow us to change things.

As the previous two triads manifested the desires for love and for mastery, so this third triad is marked by its desire for freedom. For them, this is not the freedom to do something but the freedom from doing anything at all.[120] The withdrawn types are only inclined to do what they actually like. This is another way of understanding how having a misused Doing centre affects this triad. They might spend some time thinking about things they would like to do but they will never get around to actually doing them. They feel that they have no particular responsibility to effect change in either the external or internal world. They may even 'resign' from active living.[121]

The work of transformation for the withdrawing types consists of learning to show greater activity and participation in the world. Their very pitfalls can be transformed into great strengths. Observation and analysis can be used not only to understand the past but also to find solutions to problems in the present and future. Creative imagining can be brought from the past to the present and help move our world into its future way of existing. Patience and waiting can allow events to develop in a natural and unhurried way. In their transformative work, these types will therefore learn to use their imaginations to engage the world rather than to escape it.

Before the process of transformation begins, persons within this triad may have experienced life negatively as consisting primarily of things to be avoided. Life was defined in terms of things one did not want or did not want to do. Inner growth will lead them to feel less like onlookers and more like participants in the world. They will know how to live in the world with all its challenges and problems and be able to use their imaginations to effect positive changes. They will be able to use their observations and the information they have gathered to trust others more and also to trust themselves in their interactions. In so doing, they will come to know their own worth and not feel they need to wait to be better people before they can live their lives fully.

The biblical characters who represent the withdrawing types serve as mentors in teaching us how the Divine reaches them even though they have pulled back from certain aspects of the active life and seek the freedom of not doing. As a Four, Job encounters enormous personal tragedy and withdraws from life, sitting and complaining about his perceived sense of life's injustice. His encounter with God is dramatic and intense, awakening him into a more active relationship to the universe.

Mary Magdalene, another Four, withdraws from relationships when she goes alone to visit the tomb of Jesus, but her meeting with the resurrected Jesus transforms her into a woman of action and compassion. She is the first person to experience the risen Jesus after his resurrection and is immediately activated to run and tell the others, thereby becoming an 'apostle to the apostles.'

In the Five space, Joseph the Dreamer holds back from the

active engagement with life that his brothers have and, as a result, they hate him and arrange to get rid of him. God teaches him through his long ordeals of captivity and imprisonment how to move out of the dreaming state and into the realization that nothing that happens is to be avoided because all can be understood as cooperating with the divine purpose. The other Five described here, Nicodemus, is slow to move forward and out of his comfortable understanding of the world. His encounter with Jesus begins a process of slow transformation in him that ultimately leads him to embrace the suffering of the world and trust in the hope of redemption.

Finally, the two Nines discussed here have withdrawn from life through their waiting. Abraham has lived in the same place for 75 years when God abruptly calls him to begin a life-changing journey. He is catalyzed into motion, yet the story that follows still shows him patiently waiting for the fulfilment of God's promise to him. The Man at the Pool in John's gospel has been lying in the same spot for 38 years and has withdrawn physically and psychically from life. Jesus encounters him and offers him wholeness, and the man teaches us how difficult it can be to begin the process of transformation.

All of these stories show the possibility of growth for someone in the withdrawing triad who is transformed from stillness and inertia to fullness and freedom, not from participation in life but for the active living of an integrated and real life.

Type Four: Job and Mary Magdalene

"I am my beloved's and my beloved is mine."

– Song of Songs 6:3

Fours are the individualists and the romantics. They are dramatic, emotive and primarily focused on relationships. Fours are creative and sensitive, original and aesthetic. Fours appear to suffer more than the other types and often reflect a tragic quality in their lives. If they have an artistic bent, they might idealize their pain through their art. The virtue to which they aspire is equanimity and the passion to which they are most susceptible is envy.

Fours are in the Heart space of the Enneagram and they tend to put a lot of effort into their emotional lives and interpersonal issues. They feel deeply and spend a lot of time analyzing their emotions. Because, like the other withdrawing types, their Doing centre is misused, they will often feel about their relationships that there is really nothing that they can 'do' about them, but this will not prevent them from looking at them with intense scrutiny. Fours have a deep longing for identity. They might transfer this onto someone else and expect another person to fulfil them and make them feel whole.[122] They are also prone to envy others who may appear to be enjoying more fulfilling lives.

Fours believe that there is no one else like them. Of course they are right but for them it means more than simply being a unique human being. Because they feel so unique and individual, they think that no one else can possibly understand them or know what it is like to be in their shoes. The Four believes that our unique 'I' is somehow an identity separate from everyone and everything else. The concept of Holy Origin will teach them that "uniqueness is not specialness" but that all unique beings are expressions of the same divine Source.[123] To experience this reality means we have to let go of our ego-self with all its likes and dislikes and 'specialness' and sink into the deeper reality of our Essence. Coming to practice this through the work of transformation will be painful for a Four and some may prefer to hang on to their illusion of separateness.

Fours are often identified as artists and creative people. If they are locked into their ego-selves, their creativity could become self-absorbed and grounded in their own fantasy life. However, if they are working with their transformative energy, they will experience their creative instincts as an expression of the Creator.[124]

This is true of the two representative Fours considered here. The stories of both Job and Mary Magdalene begin and end with an attraction to the divine Centre. While both of them suffer great pain and loss in their lives, their connection with God keeps them from veering off into emotional breakdown, a possibility we could readily imagine happening were they not anchored in their spiritual connectedness.

As with all nine Enneagram spaces, there is also an inhibitor to growth for the Four. Focusing on what makes one different and unique feeds the ego at the necessary expense of one's spiritual growth. The more focused and isolated we become inside our own small awareness of 'me,' the less connected we become to other beings and to the larger universe in its seamless wholeness.[125] In the work of transformation, the truth of the Four is the remarkable discovery that "we are not *connected* to the Origin; we *are* the Origin,"[126] at least insofar as we are aware of our divine centre. Difference and uniqueness are matters of concern only if we are stuck in our ego-awareness. In the divine awareness, there is no multiplicity but only One: "Hear, O Israel, the LORD our God, the LORD is One" (Deuteronomy 6:4), a truth which calls out to us daily as the central affirmation of Judaism.

Fours invite us to share with them their natural capacity to see deeply within themselves with the eyes of the heart. When these eyes see clearly and openly, they see that the ways of the Divine are far beyond human comprehension. Job learns this from the mystery he encounters at the heart of the whirlwind. Mary Magdalene sees with the eyes of her heart when her human eyes are filled with tears at the empty tomb where Jesus had lain. In both instances, the touch which opens their eyes comes not from their own sufferings but directly from God. Having gone as far as they could go with their human passions and tears, both Mary Magdalene and Job have plumbed the abyss of despair and they emerge filled with hope and a new way of seeing.

Job and Mary Magdalene are two of the strongest individualists found in the Bible. Both of them, in very different ways, question their connectedness to the rest of the universe in both its macrocosmic and microcosmic dimensions. Job's agony and his immense suffering have often caused him to be considered a prototype of Christ, thus paradoxically giving him both uniqueness and universality. In the midst of his woe, Job longs for some revelation of the divine purpose to give meaning to his suffering. His dramatic story awakens him to the dangers of his earlier life of ease and plenty, a life which allowed him to coast along oblivious to the strong and mysterious forces at work in the created world.

The biblical accounts of Mary Magdalene are few but in the popular telling of her life there is a rich tradition associating her with several different portraits of women in the gospels. This gives her, like Job, an archetypal as well as a particular dimension. The historical Mary of Magdala has merged so completely with her tradition that they will probably never be separated. Thus, the Fours who believe that they are separate and special can learn from both Mary Magdalene and Job that by letting go of their need to be set apart and different, they can arrive at their true meaning through their union with the larger creative purpose. These two characters plumb the depth of emotions, question their relationships to others and to God, and suffer intensely. They are also ultimately led to a heightened awareness of what it means to live outside of their ego-concerns and see the vastness of the divine mercy and love.

Job

> "I had heard of you by the hearing of the ear,
> but now my eye sees you."

> – Job 42:5

The suffering of the Four finds no better example than that of Job. His suffering is initially physical but quickly becomes and remains spiritual and ultimately archetypal. Even people who know nothing of the more specific details of his story recognize Job as a symbol of the good man who undergoes unthinkable agony. His name has become a synonym for all undeserved suffering and pain in a world in which any proposed scheme of cosmic reward and punishment does not appear to make sense. His story raises the ultimate question for all religions and belief systems (Muriel Spark has called it "the *only* question" in her book of the same name), the theodicy of how we can reconcile the concept of a benevolent deity with all the apparently random and cruel suffering we experience in the world.

As a Four, Job is in the Heart space and he spends a lot of time examining and analyzing his feelings. His focus is on his small world which has been totally disrupted and destroyed. In this, he fits and epitomizes the tragic image of the Four. What he needs to learn is that speaking tragically and dramatically is part of a self-image that needs to be destroyed. It comes from a belief that things should be a certain way, namely, the way we want them to be. When things do not cooperate with what we want, we take it personally and feel that the universe is against us. Nothing could be further from the truth. As a withdrawing type, Job is oriented towards the past and the memory of his previous life of plenty. He needs to move into the present with all its trouble and pain and see that things are not good or bad, they just *are*.

In Job's seemingly endless questioning and railing, we hear raised the ancient and perennial questions of why there is suffering at all in the world, how we can possibly have a relationship with a God who allows it and whether we can in fact live a life of goodness and integrity in the face of suffering. After all has been suffered, can we accept the innate being of things as they are and not expect or receive any tangible reward, and even leave ourselves relaxed and open to the experience of pain and sorrow? The Four's transformative work shows us how we can do all this and push through suffering to an experience of equanimity and joy.

The Book of Job adds another ingredient to this provocative mixture: the character of the Satan, the Accuser (*ha-satan*, a title here which does not become a proper name until much later). The Satan appears as a member of the heavenly court and he asks God the same question we ask: has Job really been good and virtuous for nothing, or is his goodness a response to the good life he has been granted and enacted out of his fear of losing it? Take it all away, suggests the Satan, and see if Job continues to bless and worship God. Strangely, God gives the Satan permission to afflict Job, despite the fact that God has already announced his faith that Job will pass this odd test. The story as it is set up appears to be based on a wager between God and one of his courtly antagonists. Even before Job opens his mouth, the reader has good reason to be suspicious of a God who plays with his creation in this manner. Job's questions quickly become our own.

Job's story is long and intricate, consisting of a fragmented and difficult text with interpolated passages and more than a few linguistic difficulties. It opens with a fairy-tale quality, "There was once a man... " The narrative's dramatic structure announces to us that this drama, this tragedy, is not about a particular unique man but is about all of us. At the beginning of the story, Job is depicted as a virtuous man who does no wrong. In a sense, we all believe this of ourselves, for even though we make mistakes, we do our best and are not particularly wicked. Our lives go along as Job's did, eating and drinking in our houses, until one day something comes along to shatter them.

As a Four, Job is a withdrawing, resigned type, accepting what God has handed him via the hand of the Accuser. He represents the individualist in the Four, sensitive, intuitive, and very self-absorbed. He is at the opening of his story an example of what William James called a very sombre and sober religious person for whom danger hovers in the air. He is like a sparrow twittering in the air, unaware of the "imminent hawk" seated near him on the bough:

> Lie low, rather, lie low; for you are in the hands of a living God. In the Book of Job, for example, the impotence of man and the omnipotence of God is the exclusive burden of its author's mind.. . . . There is an astringent relish about the truth of this conviction which some [people] can feel, and which for them is as near an approach as can be made to the feeling of religious joy.[127]

This is an accurate expression of how Fours feel most of the time. Religious joy arises from knowing there is nothing we can do or know about anything compared to the vastness of God. Our response can be to see life therefore as tragic, or to plunge through its suffering and find equanimity. Certainly, the whole of the Bible refutes the former and embraces the latter. The Bible does not regard human life as tragic, though it has many unsavoury and painful elements in it. Dante called his great work on the journey of the human soul a divine comedy, not a divine tragedy, and the pattern of the spiritual life in all traditions would agree.

Job, however, does not regard his life as anything but tragic. His resignation is not life-giving but imprisoning for him, focusing on his calamity and loss. Even his wife urges him to "curse God and die," asking him, "Do you still persist in your integrity?" (Job 2:9). At first Job piously replies that if we receive the good from God, we should also be prepared to receive the bad. This sounds like a balanced Four but the text suggests that Job only says the words with his mouth, not his heart: "In all this Job did not sin with his lips" (Job 2:10). The sin of the Four is envy, and envy most often comes from the heart, not the lips. Job sees others like him who have not been afflicted and finally he yields to his wife's urging and replies with a curse. It is not a curse against God but against the day of his birth, that is, he curses his very life (Job 3:1). If he cannot have things the way he wants them then it would be better never to have been born.

Satan has asked God if Job fears God for nothing, for he suspects Job has a motive in his uprightness. The fear of God is an awareness of the awesomeness of the divine power or the divine wrath (for here they seem to be very closely connected). Thus we see the virtuous and upright Job before his calamity being very careful, so careful that he offers sacrifices on behalf of himself and his children just in case they might have sinned by thinking a bad thought in their hearts (Job 1:5). This is not the "self-renewing, redemptive, and revelatory" Four at work but the melancholy Four who hopes that his fragile status will "attract a rescuer and keep others away."[128] This becomes apparent later in the story when Job appeals directly for an advocate or a redeemer to take his part (Job 19:25).

In William Blake's *Illustrations for the Book of Job*, Job's attitude at the start of his story is seen not as heroic but as culpable. Blake depicts Job and his family shunning their creativity: while they piously read the scriptures, their children are kneeling, their musical instruments idly hanging above them on the trees. This picture is very similar to James' sombre and sober religious person. For Blake, Job's state represents a loss of imagination and not invoking their freedom of spirit and creativity is an insult, not an honour, to their Creator. The Four has a talent for creativity and imagination and Job appears, in Blake's work, to be ignoring his gifts. At the end of his series of engravings, after Job's restoration, Blake again depicts Job and his family but now they are standing and playing their lyres and harps, actively celebrating their participation in the divinely charged universe.

Blake did not know the Enneagram but his illustrations depict the transformation of the Four from melancholic listlessness to harmony. His interpretation serves as a useful commentary on the energy of the Four which Job demonstrates. Job is caught up in his own piety out of fear of giving offence and he needs to be shown that the universe will not negate or undermine its own creations, nor does it centre solely around him. Job's negativity is not a *via negativa* but borders on self-hate and ruins his relationship to his wife. Fours are sensitive to misery to the extent that they can lose themselves so much in their imaginations that they retreat into a private world of woe. In an unhealthy Four, this can lead to madness or even suicide, and while Job seems to fear suicide, he does at one point wish that someone would do the act for him: "I would choose strangling and death rather than this body. I loathe my life" (Job 7:15-16).

As has been stated, Fours are susceptible to envy, for they see themselves as somehow set apart and outside of the apparent goodness or ease with which others live. In this tale, the envy is seen in Job's questioning of why the wicked often prosper. He is distracted from his own inner work by looking over his shoulder at what everyone else is doing. He cannot see that his own friends envy *him* and even Satan seems to feel some degree of envy over Job's wealth and prosperity, enough to challenge it before God. Implied in all these accusations is an unspoken jealousy over Job's immense wealth, as Satan wonders, "Why you?" and his friends inwardly question, "Why not me?" Rarely do we reverse those questions and ask, "why me?" when something good befalls us, or "why not me?" if it is something unpleasant. This is precisely what Job needs to do for his transformation as a Four.

At the beginning of his tale of suffering, Job already knew that there is no connection between what you do and what you get, and he is adamant in his refusal to establish one. He resists any notion of a God who plays the human game of material rewards and punishments. In this, he has clearly begun to follow the path of a Four's transformation, for he already knows that his suffering is not connected to anything special that he alone has done. His desire for an explanation simply indicates that he has not yet seen the other side of the Divine which makes no distinction between dearth and abundance. In assuming that what he undergoes is wrong or evil, Job clearly does not believe that all is indeed well no matter how grim things appear.

Job's suffering also causes his friends to think he must have committed some terrible sin to be punished so miserably. Job knows that this is not so (and God appears to agree) and that his suffering is not punishment. This is a key element in his story. If there is no blamable cause for Job's pain, then our human systems of rewards and punishments do not operate in the cosmic realm and we do not get what we 'deserve' because we do not deserve anything. Expectations do not belong in the realm of Essence but are part of the ego's system of taking care of itself.

Job is the archetype of the melancholy Four, wondering why wicked people live long lives and achieve might and prosperity even while they ignore God (Job 21:7-14). When we are in a self-pitying and lamenting Four-space, we need to detach from negative feelings and refuse to identify ourselves with them. Job laments that even a cut-down tree has hope of sprouting forth new shoots but not so human beings (Job 14:7-10), but he is mistaken. In a transformed Four, the tree with its new greenery does not just represent but actually *is* the Four's new life. Both the person and the tree are sustained by the source of all being and the woe which Job expresses when he thinks of the sprouting stump only indicates that he has separated himself from the source of life and is so caught in his egoism that he cannot find joy in the life and unity of all things.

Granted, Job's suffering is extreme but once we begin to differentiate between degrees of suffering, we have already bought into the idea that suffering is something to be avoided at all costs. As the sages tell us, it is our desire to avoid suffering that gives it its control over us. Fours would do well to remember that, in the loving unity of the cosmos, "all is well, all is well," as the 13th century

English mystic Julian of Norwich reminds us so beautifully. The Holy Idea that belongs to the Four is Holy Origin, in which it becomes clear that all of human suffering is derived from our being disconnected from the Source.[129]

Job's moodiness, then (another characteristic of a Four), needs to be transformed into gratitude for his suffering which has allowed him to become the person he is at the tale's end as well as the archetypal Job we all know about.[130] His suffering was not meant as punishment for him but as enlightenment for us. His movement to wholeness consists of moving away from his heightened sense of injured individualism and ceasing to ask 'why me?' Instead, he must embrace a larger vision which sees that all is held in the unfathomable mind of God.

After many words which swirl around between Job and his friends without much clarity, God breaks into the story. Human analysis, pondering, questioning and complaining all cease when God speaks from out of the whirlwind. God does not answer any of Job's questions or complaints but tells Job that he has spoken "words without knowledge" (Job 38:2). As God outlines for Job the vastness of creation, he turns the tables and becomes the poser of questions to Job. Job, who wanted to affirm his importance and his uniqueness, is now left with no answers when God quizzes him about the morning stars and the way mountain goats give birth. The images of beauty and artistry which God speaks to Job are certainly ones which a Four would appreciate and relish. Job is being shown the magnificence of creation and God does not seem interested in talking about Job's hurt ego. Job's ego needs to be dissolved into the cosmic vision of unity, of "things too wonderful for me, which I did not know" (Job 42:3). Although Job spoke in ignorance, God also affirms that Job spoke rightly about him (Job 42:7), for unlike his friends, Job knew and accepted that our suffering may indeed come from God's hands. God does not rebuke Job either for his questioning or for his anger, but allows these very human responses to pain to be given a voice, and they are heard.

Job, a Four who was a melancholy individualist, had tried to justify himself by putting even God in the wrong: "Will you condemn me that you may be justified?" thunders the Voice from the whirlwind (Job 42:2). The God who speaks to Job is indeed a God of opposites and of contraries, and only by embracing them as a unity can the Four find wholeness. Fours need to know that God is the only uniqueness, not themselves. God is the only one from whom all else derives, and every thing and person "originates in Being and returns to Being" as the ground from which everything becomes manifest.[131]

Agonizing and moaning over life's situations indicates a lack of understanding. Job had tried to find meaning in his own situation. Instead, what he heard was the voice of the cosmic God thundering in his soul that the entire universe is indeed under control. Job's situation is not isolated from the rest of the cosmos. The mystery of why things are the way they are is swallowed up in the larger mystery of silence, as Job learns to listen and to see, but not to complain. His withdrawing stance ultimately becomes one of contemplation rather than one of resistance and rejection.

Job, through his long lament and pleas for justice and vindication, is finally able to move into the heart of the chaos. God speaks to him from the centre of the whirlwind, from the eye of the storm, which is stillness and calm. The Four hears of the vastness of creation from a God whom Jung characterized as "a totality of inner opposites" which gives him "his tremendous dynamism, his omniscience and omnipotence."[132] These "inner opposites" include both the masculine and the feminine creative elements of divinity. From the darkness of the divine womb, the seas and all of life burst forth (Job 38:8). God is also the father of the rain, as well as the one who gave birth to ice and frost. The images reflect both power and gentleness, as God controls the lightning and also watches like a midwife over the birthing of the deer and the mountain goats (Job 38-39).

At the end of the story, Job has learned the difficult yet comforting lesson that God "can do all things and that no purpose of yours can be thwarted" (Job 42:2). The origin of all can only be questioned if we are prepared to hear and accept the difficult answer we will hear. God's "purpose" can only be seen in the beauties and terrors of creation and in the light and darkness of the human heart. God asks if Job knows,

"Where is the way to the dwelling of light,
and where is the place of darkness,
that you may take it to its territory
and that you may discern the paths to its home?"

– Job 38:19-20

The consciousness ("dwelling of light") and the shadow ("place of darkness") of our personalities are both to be brought along the paths to the same 'home territory.' In discerning the path to this home, the Four in all of us needs to embrace all the parts of our being and to allow them to become a whole. The 'home' of the transformed self will then see only unity, fecund with diversity and life and also rich in fertile darkness.

What Job thought he knew about God, he had learned more by hearsay than by experience. It caused him to suffer but, in the experience of suffering, he also came to know the truth about the ways of God. He finally acknowledges to God that "I had heard of you by the hearing of the ear, but now my eye sees you; therefore I despise myself and repent in dust and ashes" (Job 42:5-6). The ultimate transformation does not come about because of what we *know* but because of what we have *seen* in our own personal experience, often borne out of immense suffering. The uniqueness which a Four may feel becomes caught up in a grander picture of the macrocosm of which he is a part. Yet in our holographic universe, the smallest part also contains the fullness of the whole and a Four's growth lies in this realization.

The story of Job ends not with his fortunes restored but with his fortunes doubled: he is twice as rich as he was at the beginning of his tale. If we see this only in material terms, we remain fixed in a belief system that sees material riches as a reward for something we have endured or a success we have had. But if we see the doubling of Job's wealth as a spiritual richness gained from his experience of a direct encounter with the God of all Being who knows no division, then we know that he is wealthy indeed. His belief in his own uniqueness which could not be shared or understood by anyone else has become lost in his knowledge of the only unique 'One who is.'

Prayer in the Spirit of Job
Psalm 130

Out of the depths I cry to you, O LORD.
    Lord, hear my voice!
Let your ears be attentive
    to the voice of my supplications!

If you, O LORD, should mark iniquities,
    Lord, who could stand?
But there is forgiveness with you,
    so that you may be revered.

I wait for the LORD, my soul waits,
    and in his word I hope;
my soul waits for the Lord
    more than those who watch for the morning,
    more than those who watch for the morning.

O Israel, hope in the LORD!
    For with the LORD there is steadfast love,
    and with him is great power to redeem.

It is he who will redeem Israel
from all its iniquities.

Mary Magdalene

As she wept, she bent over to look into the tomb.

– John 20:11

Mary of Magdala exemplifies the intensity and vulnerability of the Four, and at the empty tomb after the crucifixion, she also models for us the Four's deep longing to be rescued from her pain through a relationship. Like others in the withdrawing types, she watches events from a distance and does not act quickly. She is emotive and sensitive but, through her encounter with Jesus, she learns to activate her feelings into moving outwards to share them with others.

Mary Magdalene is a complex character to discuss since the tradition surrounding her confuses what may well have been two or three separate women. Over the years, Mary Magdalene has accumulated quite a diverse representation in both theology and art, encompassing the diverse roles of the prostitute, the penitent, the lover, and the bride. As a composite character, she offers us an archetypal richness.

Mary Magdalene was clearly one of the inner circle of women who were close friends and followers of Jesus, travelling with him and ministering to the needs of him and the other disciples. She was certainly one of Jesus' devoted followers, present at his crucifixion, and all four gospels name her as one of the first witnesses to his resurrection. Such rare agreement in the biblical narratives indicates the centrality of her role and the acknowledgement of her significance from the very beginning of the tradition. (There is even an apocryphal Gospel of Mary which dates from the second century.) Because the culture in which Mary Magdalene lived tended to downplay the status and even the possibility of women disciples (evident in the initial rejection of her testimony by the male disciples), the record of her witness in all four gospels becomes all the more forceful, as all agree that she visited the empty tomb and experienced the risen Christ before any of the others. This was a foundational fact about her character and her experience at the tomb overshadows everything else we know about her.

The oral and patristic traditions have combined the roles of Mary Magdalene, Mary of Bethany, and the sinner in Luke's gospel into one person. In Luke's gospel, we read that Jesus cast seven devils out of her (Luke 8:2), and from very early accounts she has also been identified with the woman "who was a sinner" and who anointed the feet of Jesus, weeping, and drying and kissing his feet with her hair (Luke 7:37). She has also been equated with Mary, the sister of Martha and Lazarus, who wept tears of distress and who anointed Jesus' feet with her hair when he came to their house in Bethany (John 11:12 and 12:3). Her tears, a hallmark of the Four, cause Jesus himself to weep over the death of Lazarus.

These separate accounts give us a composite picture of a woman who was dramatic, emotional, sensitive, and romantic. In Mary Magdalene, we also see demonstrated the intensity of the Four who has learned to withdraw to her inner life and who longs constantly to be in relationship with Jesus. This longing for relationship in the Four becomes, through the Four's transformational work, a longing for inner union with one's Essence and Mary needs to experience physical loss in order to begin to experience this.

As she weeps over the empty tomb after Jesus' crucifixion, Mary's posture becomes an icon for the introspection of the Four who bends inwards to face the inner emptiness of the soul longing for its absent lover. She waits, she weeps and she is finally given what her heart longs for, not in a physical way but in a spiritual way that she could never have foreseen. An early bishop of Rome,

Hippolytus (d. ca. 235 C.E.), identified her and her love-longing with that of the Bride in the Song of Songs. He even considered her to be the symbol of the Church, calling her the "Apostle to the Apostles."[133] She also became the New Eve, since in her recognition of Jesus in the garden she was able to reverse and redeem the sin of the original Eve, who separated herself from union with God in the Garden of Eden.

Desiring such special status and believing she has it is one of the traits of the Four. In the early traditions which equate her with the woman 'who was a sinner,' she clearly seeks such 'specialness' in her relationship to Jesus. In the account of her anointing of the feet of Jesus, she purchases extremely expensive perfume and makes a dramatic show of bestowing this gift on her special friend as she weeps and dries his feet with her hair (Luke 7:37-38). Jesus welcomes this gift of the Four, knowing that it is a genuine gesture which comes from her heart. When others in the room murmur about his being touched by a sinful woman, Jesus supports her action and does not reprimand her. He knows she is longing to touch him, to establish a relationship with him and has moved out of her normal withdrawing stance to do so. Of her action Jesus says, "she has shown great love" (Luke 7:47). Furthermore, he connects this love to forgiveness, adding that her many sins have been forgiven. He says this first to the people in the room and then directly to her, as he also commends her faith and sends her forth in peace (Luke 7:48, 50).

This interaction between Jesus and Mary encapsulates the transformation of the Four. Mary has been able to access meaningfully her Doing centre in her moving forward to Jesus. She discovers that she does not need to think of herself any longer as a 'sinner' but as a lover. In her acceptance by Jesus and in her own self-acceptance she is forgiven. She has experienced a real encounter in a real relationship, and her life is forever changed.

In the tradition which connects Mary Magdalene to Mary the

sister of Martha and Lazarus, we find her again focused on the person of Jesus. In Luke's account of the visit of Jesus to the two sisters (Luke 10:39)[134], Mary also acts like a Four as she interiorizes her experience of sitting at the feet of Jesus and listening to him, seemingly oblivious to the concerns of her sister Martha. Here, too, she longs for a special relationship with the Master and is reluctant to leave her favoured position of sitting at his feet. There may even be in these early stages a hint of clinging affection in her relationship with Jesus, as her own needs come before anything else, even practical necessities like preparing a meal. She must have felt supported and favoured when Jesus told Martha that Mary had "chosen the better part."

Though it was probably not the same person (Mary of Bethany would not have been called Mary of Magdala), tradition has also connected Mary Magdalene to the Mary who appears in the story of the death of Lazarus in John's gospel (John 11). As a Four in this story, she seems to be withdrawn even from the rest of the mourners who have come to her home. After her brother's death, there may even have been a touch of self-pity in her statement that her brother would not have died if Jesus had been there, not because he loved Lazarus but because he loved *her*. She may have fallen into the trap of believing that she was so very special that Jesus should have taken the initiative and come running as soon as he heard Lazarus was ill, not only to heal the man but also to alleviate her worry and her pain.

It would perhaps be a bit harsh to see in this a manipulative attitude, though a Four would certainly be capable of using self-pity to get what she needed. Jesus, however, moves to his own rhythms, arriving well after Lazarus has died. When he appears, Mary is able to abandon her withdrawing posture and get up to go towards him, a sign that her transformative work is underway. Jesus opens her eyes and the eyes of all those present to the unbelievable reality that death is not a disaster but a spiritual occasion.

He who is Life itself can call the spiritually (as well as physically) dead out of their tombs and into a new life. The lamenting at the tomb of Lazarus is but a foretaste of the weeping Mary will undergo at Jesus' own tomb and on both occasions she will learn in powerful ways that death gives way to life. Those who hear the voice of the 'one who is the Way' are called out of their egoistic consciousness, their soul-death, and into a new way of being, experiencing one's Essence so that eternal life is discovered in the *now*.

Mary's transformation as a Four demands that she accompany Jesus right to the cross itself, both literally and spiritually. The experience transforms her own sense of melancholy and pain into a larger understanding of what it means to die to self and all it entails, and how such a letting go is the prerequisite for the unveiling of the deeper inner life. The grieving and the pain of her ordeal scourge her soul, leaving it empty and waiting. Only from this new stance is she able to become a witness to the resurrection and its promise of new and eternal life. The empty sepulcher becomes for her both the tomb of her own death and the womb of her new birth.

In John's account, Mary Magdalene travels to the tomb twice. The first time, she sees that the stone has been rolled away. As a withdrawing type, Fours reflect and contemplate readily but their misused Doing centre often means that they only move outwards when told to do so by their emotions. At the empty tomb, Mary Magdalene's keenly felt pain and sadness activate her swift movement. She goes running from the empty tomb to tell the disciples that Jesus is gone. Peter and John run back with her, witness the empty tomb and return to their homes. Mary, however, remains there weeping, bending over to look within, pouring herself into the awful absence. As with that other Four, Job, her suffering arises from her heartfelt sense of disconnection from and loss of the source of life. Her gesture of bending forward, of leaning into the mystery, is the necessary posture of the yielding soul. It suggests the contemplative surrender to the emptiness which is at the heart of, and the source of, all fullness. For a Four, her bending forward into the emptiness represents the full presence of the heart-space to the inner darkness as it longs for union with its Beloved.

With Mary's movement of surrender, she is able to see two angels in the tomb. They address her as "Woman", a term only used previously in John's gospel by Jesus to address his mother. It is a formal word, separating the literal person from her symbolic role as Woman, as Mother Church, as Mother of the faithful, and as the New Eve. This title is now given to Mary Magdalene in her role as the Beloved, searching, like the bride in the Song of Songs, for her absent lover. She refers to Jesus as "my Lord" (John 20:13), claiming a personal relationship with him. Fours will often feel they need to personalize events, and so Mary collapses the events of the passion into the simple and individualized statement that "my Lord" has been taken away, almost as if he belonged solely to her and she is the one who feels his loss most grievously.

In reply, Jesus is suddenly standing next to her but she is unable to recognize him, "supposing him to be the gardener" (John 20:15). He, like the angels, calls her "Woman," and asks her two questions: why is she weeping, and whom is she seeking? In elevating her to metaphorical status as "Woman", the author of John's gospel is also addressing these two questions to the reader and to the whole church, all who feel life's suffering and seek a way out of it. The remedy for the weeping is found in the seeking, and the seeking leads to the finding. Mary thinks Jesus is the gardener because her weeping and her suffering have blinded her to the real presence of the one she seeks. Locked into her Four's sense of hurt, disappointment and possibly even self-pity, her loss and her desire cloud her vision, both literally and spiritually. She demands of Jesus the "gardener" that he tell her where he has placed the body of Jesus so that she can take him away (John 20:15).

The only way out of our suffering and our loss is to realize and experience that nothing has, after all, been lost at all and that our suffering is of our own making but in it is a gift. Jesus conveys this simple but awful truth just by calling her name: "Mary!" (John 20:16). In that naming, all is restored. Her Lover has returned to her and singled her out for a momentous and personal meeting. Yet she is not to hold on to that special meeting in the old way. Jesus tells her not to cling to him, for he has "not yet ascended to the Father" (John 20:17). The physical desire to hold on to someone or something is not what will keep him with her. In fact, union based only on physical presence must by its very nature come to an end. Mary needs to give up the desire for that precious tangible closeness and learn how to be in the presence of Jesus and in relationship with him, at every moment but in a new way. He is asking her not to detain him, and not to be afraid.[135] Jesus must move forward without delay into the embrace of the Godhead so that he can then send his Spirit. Any delay for whatever human reason, any "clinging" to his familiar appearance, could cause people to miss the reality of what has truly happened. Decisive action is required so as not to mislead his friends concerning how they are now to relate to him as the Risen One.

Mary Magdalene may well have been the first one to experience Christ as the Risen One. His ascension to the Godhead becomes for her also a descent into her own heart, where she will discover her own Essence and union with divinity. In that place (which is not really a place) the soul will always be united to its beloved even to death and beyond. In her yearning for relationship, Mary discovers through her encounter with the Risen Christ her unity with the Source.

No more of their conversation is recorded. The point has been made, not just for Mary Magdalene but for the reader and believer as well. Jesus is henceforth to be known not as a physical presence to which we cling, dreading his immanent or distant departure, but as present in the heart of the Father which is where our soul also resides. In this ascension to our true nature, death can have no power of separation between the Lover and the Beloved. Mary's response to her encounter is to go and announce to the disciples, "I have seen the Lord" (John 20:18). There is no hesitation or doubt in her proclamation. She tells the disciples what Jesus has told to her, becoming their teacher as well as earning her the title of "apostola apostolorum." Perhaps she was able to convey to them her new understanding of not-grasping and how her sense of loss had been converted to a permanent experience of divine union and love.

To the Four in us, Mary Magdalene demonstrates the persistence of love and its desire for the Beloved, and she shows us that in facing the dark reality of the empty tomb, we can learn to release our clinging nature and encounter the one who is both source and end of all our being. In union with the risen Christ, we begin to see with other eyes and sense in other ways the full reality of the human being. In ascending to the Divine, we also descend into our own hearts and are healed.

Prayer in the Spirit of Mary Magdalene
Psalm 45

My heart overflows with a goodly theme;
    I address my verses to the king;
    my tongue is like the pen of a ready scribe.

You are the most handsome of men;
    grace is poured upon your lips;
    therefore God has blessed you forever.
Gird your sword on your thigh, O mighty one,
    in your glory and majesty.

Hear, O daughter, consider and incline your ear;
    forget your people and your father's house,
    and the king will desire your beauty.
Since he is your Lord, bow to him;

the people of Tyre will seek your favour with gifts,
the richest of the people with all kinds of wealth.

The princess is decked in her chamber with gold-woven robes;
in many-coloured robes she is led to the king;
behind her the virgins, her companions, follow.
With joy and gladness they are led along
as they enter the palace of the king.

In the place of ancestors you, O king, shall have sons;
you will make them princes in all the earth.
I will cause your name to be celebrated in all generations;
therefore the peoples will praise you forever and ever.

Summary of the Fours

The story of Job as a Four helps us address the presence of suffering in the world and understand it in the context of a benevolent God who is the source of all existence and ultimately its answer. Job's sense of uniqueness needed to be put into a larger context in which he came to know that a belief in his own separateness prevented him from experiencing the enormity of God. When he learned to let go of his focusing on his own situation, he was able to embrace a vision of a cosmos in which all is well but mysterious. The artistry of the Creator spoke to the artistry of the Four and taught him to withdraw into contemplation and awe and not into his individuality.

Mary of Magdala is a composite portrait of a woman who embodies the Four's characteristics of being dramatic, emotional, sensitive, and romantic. She extravagantly anoints the feet of Jesus and weeps for her brother Lazarus but her pain is even greater when she weeps for Jesus as for an absent lover. Her story enacts the transformation of the soul into the Beloved and Bride of God. She experiences the meaning of the cross and leans into the heart of mystery at the empty tomb. Like Job, she learns that suffering and loss are only illusions if we dwell in the heart of God. Her encounter with the risen Jesus assures her that all longing will be satisfied, and that even death is swallowed up into the mystery of God.

Type Five: Joseph and Nicodemus

> Be still and know that I am God.
>
> – Psalm 46:10

"For who has known the mind of the Lord? Or who has been his counselor?" (Romans 11:34). Pondering those questions, a Five might inwardly reply, "Those are good questions, and I have been thinking about such knowledge for a long time. The process requires much study and there are many theories to research. I need to find out more about all of them." A Five's desire to know stops at nothing short of wanting to know everything. (Albert Einstein, a Five, wrote that all he wanted was to know the mind of God: all the rest was just details.)

Fives are the thinkers and the observers. Their ideal way of being is to observe without making a judgment, and to be immersed in reality and appreciate the wonder of creation. They are curious and insightful, and long to be capable and competent. Hence, their worst fear is of being incompetent or helpless.[136] Because they love to acquire information, the virtue to which they aspire is non-attachment, so that they do not feel they 'possess' what they know. The corresponding vice they need to avoid is therefore avarice, or hoarding all that they have learned and accumulated and not share it with the world.

Fives are in the Thinking space of the Enneagram and seek to become experts at something. They learn not by active involvement but through reading, observation, listening and accumulating ideas. Fives can think through all problems, analyze and synthesize information but they may find it difficult to engage the energy necessary to turn observation into action. They are adept at post-poning action on something in order to give it further intellectual consideration. This is because the misused centre for the Five is the Doing centre. Because they prefer to use their heads rather than their bodies, Fives are good at formulating strategies but might have difficulty implementing them. Still, knowledge is per-ceived to be the solution to filling any inner void and withdrawing in order to observe is one way in which knowledge is gained.

As withdrawing types, Fives prefer their inner lives to active socializing and in a group of people they would probably be happy just observing and gathering information about what is going on. The misused centres for all the types always cause an imbalance, and Fives perceive that to put their energy into motion requires an investment of themselves that they are generally not willing to make.

Much thinking, observation and analysis, while often a wel-come gift, could also be the source of the inherent difficulty of a Five. Because these processes require standing back, both men-tally and physically, Fives may begin to feel that they are truly isolated as individuals. While they are busy observing, they come to believe that they are unconnected to their observations and that the observer and what is observed are distinct and separate enti-ties. This is, of course, not just a mental habit of Fives. Many if not most people live out of their perception that they can somehow separate themselves entirely from what they see or experience.

In reality, this cannot ever occur. As Heisenberg's uncertain-ty principle has taught us, the very act of observing something changes it. We can never be a pure observer. The process of trans-formation, perhaps especially true for the Fives, demands that we mentally and viscerally experience the reality of the principle of "inter-being." Even though we may feel isolated and cut off, there are no forests without trees and when we believe we can be inde-pendent, we are like a pine in the middle of the woods insisting that it is a forest all by itself. It can remain a single pine tree but it cannot ever become a forest. Transformation is possible when that pine tree realizes not only its interdependence among all the trees but among all the other forest elements as well: the sun, the rain, other plants, insects and animals, equinoxes and solstices.

In their role of observers, investigators, and collectors of information, Fives may think they can remain onlookers at life's parade. Their detachment and non-participation often hinder them from forming emotional attachments and they can actually come to believe that they do not really need anything from anyone. A relationship might require a commitment of energy they are not willing to give and so Fives may tend to avoid any emotional expression. If another person begins to become so important that his or her loss would cause considerable pain, then the Five will often completely withdraw feelings from the relationship.[137] Fives unconsciously hold back energy and despite a deep inner longing, their fear of engagement causes them to withdraw from an active life to an inner world of speculation and 'what if's.' What may then come across to others as aloofness or bookishness may be a mask that keeps feelings at a distance and postpones the need to engage them in an active participation.

On the other hand, Fives make life-long friends if the friendship allows them independence and freedom, which all the withdrawing types long for, and they can connect with others on both abstract and non-verbal levels.[138] They are discrete and do not stir up emotional trauma and, while they are not social butterflies, they enjoy explaining ideas and theories to people.

The work of the Fives, then, consists of using their gifts of observation and curiosity for the betterment of the world. In their work of transformation, they will learn to use their emotions as well as their keen minds as another source of valuable information, and be able to act on their insights. The Five has a strong desire to be connected to the whole. As Brian Swimme and Thomas

Berry have pointed out so well, "the universe is a communion of subjects rather than a collection of objects," and "existence itself is derived from and sustained by this intimacy of each being with every other being of the universe."[139] We are all part of that community which does not end with the human species but includes all forms of life and non-living matter as well.

The two biblical Fives presented here, Joseph the Dreamer and Nicodemus, initially live in a world of disconnections and separateness. Joseph is literally separated from his family, and Nicodemus searches for his connection with the truth. Their stories reflect the growth which comes from a changed perspective. At the end of their narratives, both Joseph and Nicodemus arrive at a radical shift in their roles in their communities, roles which reflect interconnectedness rather than isolation. Joseph is able to forgive his brothers for their betrayal and provides food for them in the time of famine. Nicodemus has lost his status as a Pharisee but found his new connection to the community of disciples. Both men show us the way to move within the Five-space from detachment to integration of emotions, thoughts, and actions in order to focus on the wholeness of life.

Joseph

> So no one stayed with him when Joseph
> made himself known to his brothers.
>
> – Genesis 45:1

There are two Josephs in the bible: Joseph, the husband of the Virgin Mary, and Joseph who had the famous coat of many colours (more accurately translated as a robe of long sleeves). Both of them have been called Joseph the Dreamer, for both are recipients of prophetic dreams which provide directions for their lives and shape the future of Israel. The head is where dreams occur and both Josephs are in the head space of the Five on the

Enneagram. The earlier Joseph is the one dealt with here, though his character also provides insights into the Joseph we encounter later in the gospels.

In the Genesis narrative, Joseph is Jacob's favorite of his 12 sons. He was the first son born to Rachel, the most beloved of Jacob's four wives, and consequently enjoys special treatment from his father. Right from the beginning of his story (Genesis 37-50), Joseph demonstrates clearly the Five's sense of separateness. Though part of a large family, he is nonetheless detached from them. As a child, he does not go into the fields with his 10 brothers. He clearly does not feel any close fraternal connection to them, for the first thing he is recorded as doing in Genesis is bringing a bad report of his brothers to their father (Genesis 37:2). As Fives do, he has been watching them. What they did is not recorded but it is possible that Joseph was accustomed to observing them in the fields and tattling on them whenever possible. As a withdrawing type with a misused Doing centre, Joseph would have been quite comfortable sitting back and watching, while the only thing he thought he could 'do' was report the information he had gathered. His brothers hate him for his privileged status among them and so while he is an important part of Jacob's family, he is, even at 17, an outsider looking in. Joseph does not seem to be traumatized by his isolating experiences, for he is used to being a loner Five.

Joseph also has a pair of dreams which bolster his sense of superiority and specialness. In the first dream, he and his brothers are binding sheaves in the field when suddenly Joseph's sheaf rises up and those of his brothers bow down to it. In the second dream, the sun, the moon, and 11 stars bow down to him. He interprets both dreams as representing his father, mother and brothers doing homage to him. The imagery certainly highlights the Five's need to be set apart. While many people might keep such dreams to themselves, Joseph does what Fives do and analyzes the data and then interprets it. His ability to interpret dreams reflects the Five's desire to display his vast knowledge and to draw attention to unusual or exotic things, not the ordinary things most people know but the little-known detail or, in Joseph's case, the private revelation, the secret and unknown world of his dreams. This supports his feeling that he is special and has special abilities but it also feeds his brothers' hatred of him.[140] It also reinforces his uncomfortable position in his family.

As a Five, Joseph is able to find innovative solutions to his quite considerable problems. He does not take an insight or revelation as just an unconnected piece of information to be filed away with everything else he knows. He has mastered his interpretation of dreams and this makes him feel capable and strong.[141] Joseph sees his difficulties in his familial relationships as a problem to be analyzed and, by solving his problem through a dream which by its nature is a private piece of information, his privacy is secure. Dreams also offer him many options and ways of receiving new information about himself and about others. A more unhealthy response from a withdrawing type would be to acquire lots of information about oneself but to shut down avenues which would lead to transformation, believing that he was essentially unalterable.[142]

Joseph had to be flexible and find creative ways out of his difficulties. His entire story finds him moving from one impossible situation to another, with Joseph nevertheless triumphing over all the negative events of his life. He lands on his feet time after time mainly because, as we are told, God was with him (Genesis 39:2, 3, 21, 23). His first trial begins when his brothers, full of jealousy and hatred, conspire to kill him. Rather than do so outright, they instead throw him into a pit and then sell him to some traders who are passing by and who take Joseph into Egypt, where he is bought by Potiphar, an officer of Pharaoh. In his master's house, Joseph manifests the Five's talent of problem-solving to such an extent that he is very soon put in charge of the entire household. Fives are extremely good at finding solutions, largely because of their finely honed ability to look at many details and facts and accumulate enough information to make reliable forecasts. In the world of business and commerce, this can produce very profitable results. Because he possesses these skills, Joseph is consistently able to convert bad circumstances to good.

His second trial occurs when Potiphar's wife attempts to seduce him. The story does not even hint at Joseph's being tempted. His response to the wife is that of a disciplined Five who cites the evidence he has gathered about his trusted position – "Look, with me here, my master has no concern about anything in the house, and he has put everything that he has in my hand" (Genesis 39:8) – and flatly refuses to betray his master's confidence in him. When a Five finds a secure place in his world, he is happy to withdraw into it and take no risks of losing it. He does not want to engage his Doing centre and jeopardize his position. The woman, however, persists and when he continues to refuse her, she sets him up by tearing off his robe and then using it as evidence that he had attempted to lie with her. Her husband believes her story and Joseph is thrown into prison. There, Joseph finds himself in a secluded place and even though it is a prison, it is not entirely uncomfortable for a Five. He is at least for the moment away from any emotional strains of relationships, which a Five fears.

In this second 'pit' in which he finds himself, once again Joseph is able use the Five's skill at evaluating and solving problems. Within a few verses, we read that Joseph has been put in charge of all the prisoners, relieving the chief jailer of his cares just as he had relieved Potiphar of his household worries. In prison, Joseph also correctly interprets the dreams of two fellow prisoners. When one is released, he remembers Joseph's skill two years later when Pharaoh himself has two puzzling dreams which trouble his spirit and which none of his wise men can interpret. Joseph interprets the dreams as forecasting seven years of plenty followed by seven years of famine. He proposes a system of rationing and storing the food to provide for the lean years. As a result, Joseph once again rises above his situation as Pharaoh puts him in charge over his house and over the entire land of Egypt, and even gives him a priest's daughter in marriage.

The imagery of the seven years of holding back food to provide for the years of famine, of doing with less and minimizing the needs of the present, expresses Joseph's own inner reality as a Five of holding back to conserve and accumulate. At the same time it represents an invitation to him as he prepares for the ensuing seven years of famine. During the years of preparation, Joseph is called upon to properly activate his misused Doing centre, and to learn and practice both generosity and sensitivity to the needs of others.

In this first part of Joseph's story, he has been functioning as a healthy Five who uses his skills to make for himself a secure but detached place in his various unfriendly environments. In each situation, he is able to carve out a safe niche for himself, one which he obtains through his unique knowledge. He is also still able to maintain the Five's characteristic position as an outsider and observer, for he is quite literally a foreigner to the Egyptians and has special gifts which set him apart.

However, at 30 years old, as he goes about Egypt preparing for the oncoming famine, Joseph has also gotten married and fathered two sons. There is a sense of gentleness and softening in him as he enters these tender relationships. It is worth citing the explanation he gives for his sons' names:

> Joseph named the firstborn Manasseh, "For," he said, "God has made me forget all my hardship and all my father's house." The second he named Ephraim, "For God has made me fruitful in the land of my misfortunes."

> – Genesis 41:51-52

In naming them, it is clear that Joseph has not really forgotten either his hardship or his 'father's house.' He is claiming detachment from his past pain even while remembering it as his 'misfortunes.' While he longs for intimacy, he also fears it, but he now has another family which need not repeat the same unhealthy pattern he himself knew as a boy. Joseph is exhibiting the Five's tendency to rein in his emotions even while feeling them deeply, and to analyze them rather than to allow himself to genuinely feel them.[143]

Marriage and parenthood, however, often have a way of pulling someone out of isolation and into community. While Joseph's previous experience of his brothers in his own family was isolating and hostile, his creation of a new family in Egypt marks the transition in the narrative from Joseph's trials to Joseph's rise to power as the one who will be the saviour of many in the oncoming famine. His role as agrarian organizer places him in a position to encounter his original family when his brothers come to Egypt for grain. The rest of his story illustrates the transformative work of the Five as Joseph progresses from his lifelong emotional detachment to assuming his place in the fabric of life.

Jacob sends his sons, Joseph's brothers, to Egypt to buy grain during the famine. He does not allow his youngest son, Benjamin, to go with them. It appears that Benjamin has replaced Joseph as his father's favourite, being the second son of Rachel, who died in giving him birth. When the brothers arrive, Joseph recognizes them but does not reveal himself to them. He speaks harshly to them, accusing them of being spies (Genesis 42:7, 9). Joseph's treatment of his brothers reflects the Five's analytic tendency to dissect things in order to understand them, including the emotions and attitudes of his long-unseen brothers. He could also be concerned about being manipulated by them once more but perhaps their coming empty-handed to ask for food poignantly reminds him of his own inner emptiness and need to be filled.

At the same time, the shock of seeing his brothers propels him into acting impulsively, a sign that a Five is moving in a potentially unstable direction, since Fives think things through very carefully. Joseph demands that the brothers fetch Benjamin to prove their story that they have one younger brother at home with their father. Perhaps when they tell Joseph that, of the 12 sons of Jacob, "one is no more" (Genesis 42:13), he is emotionally undone but, as a Five and a withdrawing type, he cannot show his feelings to them. Though the "one who is no more" now stands before them, he cannot yet unleash his complex emotions at seeing them again. He has his brothers put into prison for three days, perhaps thinking that they must suffer just a small taste of what he himself went through when he arrived in Egypt more than 10 years earlier.

Part of the transformation of Fives consists in moving out of impulsive or secretive actions into the freedom to act out of their own mastery of what they know. Joseph had already moved in this direction when his insights and analyses of dreams catapulted him out of prison and into authority in the Egyptian kingdom. His analytic mind is still hard at work when he devises a scheme for testing his brothers. The scale of this project, while small compared to saving all of Egypt from famine, is to Joseph much larger. It touches his core issues as a Five who fears emptiness and the rejection he knew as a boy and who now covers it up with knowledge and cleverness. He insists that one of them be left behind while the rest return to Canaan and bring Benjamin back with them.

The brothers, not knowing that Joseph could understand their native language, for they had been using an interpreter, decry their earlier action of ignoring the cries of the young Joseph when they threw him into the pit. They believe they are now paying the penalty for their hardness of heart (Genesis 42:21). At this sign of their own anguish, Joseph, the emotionally distant Five, "turned away from them and wept" (Genesis 42:24). His tears signal a transformative moment for him, for even though he turns aside so that no one will notice, he is finally able to shed the tears which have been locked inside him for so long. This is the first of three times, in "a clear crescendo pattern,"[144] in which Joseph weeps over his brothers.

Yet Joseph is not done with his scheming. He sends the brothers home, having kept Simeon behind. He must know that when they return to Jacob and demand Benjamin accompany them back to Egypt, it will tear his father apart. In testing his brothers, Joseph is still acting out of his sense of separateness and feeling isolated. He does not regard himself as part of his family and, while he can observe their anguish and imagine his father's pain, he is detached from these feelings. His moment of weeping and his love for his own two sons indicate the direction in which he needs to move for his own transformation to continue. As he becomes more aware of his emotional life, he can then begin to integrate it into his mental world and move beyond scheming and planning for smaller more personal goals to becoming an instrument of a greater pattern in the human community. As yet he is unaware of the connection between his emotions and his higher purpose but the rest of the story teaches him, and the reader, how the divine omniscience works. With the Fives, we come to realize that everything that happens is intimately connected to everything else and that separateness is an illusion which keeps us trapped in our own egotistic consciousness.

When the brothers return to Joseph accompanied by Benjamin, the sight of his youngest brother once more causes Joseph to be overcome with emotion and he goes into a private room to weep unseen (Genesis 43:30). This second time of weeping gives us more details than the first: after withdrawing, still needing to hide his inner state, Joseph washes his face and returns to the room "controlling himself" (Genesis 43:31). He has expressed his emotions but then covered them up again by literally and symbolically washing himself free of them.

Joseph has one more test with which he can observe his

brothers. Unknown to them, he has had a silver cup planted in Benjamin's sack and he then accuses the brothers of stealing it. They are grieved when the missing cup is discovered and Joseph the keen observer watches their reaction. Here is an opportunity for them to do to Benjamin what they did to Joseph, to turn him over for theft and be rid of him forever. However, they know that to do so would be the certain death of their father and, to Joseph's surprise, they refuse to leave Benjamin behind. Instead, Judah, the brother who had suggested selling Joseph to the traders in the first place, offers to take the place of Benjamin and remain Joseph's servant for life so that Benjamin can return in safety. Apparently, Judah knows that his absence will not affect Jacob as greatly as did the loss of Benjamin and Joseph.

Joseph, who has been so much in control all along, can finally "no longer control himself" (Genesis 45:1). The push to connectedness proves to be stronger than the pull of withdrawal. The previously detached and unemotional Joseph sends everyone else away and makes himself known to his brothers, weeping so loudly that the entire household hears it (Genesis 45:2). He no longer turns aside to weep, but weeps openly. The Five has moved from the world of mental theories into rich and total connection with humanity. He tells his brothers, "Come closer to me" (Genesis 45:4). The distance between them closes and his isolation evaporates. He allows himself not only to be seen by them but to be touched, as his body also learns to express its long locked-up emotions. He experiences the new sensation of being seen instead of feeling invisible.

Only then does Joseph realize the full truth of the Five's transformation: that all is connected in a whole which does not isolate its members but utilizes their gifts for the benefit of the community. Joseph tells his brothers that even though they sold him into Egypt they need not be distressed, "for God sent me before you to preserve life" (Genesis 45:5). Once he is able to step outside of his belief that he must control all things in such a way as to keep his inner security intact, Joseph understands his role as a vehicle through which the divine work can be accomplished. All he has experienced can now be seen as part of a larger scheme which he does not need to try to control. God is able to bring about good not because of but despite the contrivances and hurts which humans inflict on themselves and each other.

In this new way of seeing, Joseph can even assert that it was not his brothers but God who sent him into Egypt. He sends for his father with great haste, kisses his brothers, weeps with them and talks with them. After three times of weeping alone, Joseph is finally able to weep *with* his brothers. When his father Jacob arrives, Joseph weeps "a good while" with him (Genesis 46:29). When his father dies in Egypt, Joseph again throws himself upon Jacob, weeps over him and kisses him (Genesis 50:1). He weeps again when his brothers fear that Jacob's death will cause Joseph to turn on them (Genesis 50:17). This is indeed a picture of a Five who has emerged from his perceived isolation into communion, from being one who has knowledge to one who has arrived at understanding. He reasserts that "even though you intended to do harm to me, God intended it for good, in order to preserve a numerous people, as he is doing today" (Genesis 50:20). As an observer of life, Joseph has come to one of the greatest observations a Five can make: that all is connected as part of the divine web of being, and that knowledge of this frees the individual from feeling isolated from or on the outside of reality.

Joseph becomes the first model of the biblical theme of the Suffering Servant when he learns that suffering, though not intended or demanded by God, can be used to fulfil the divine purpose. It is a remarkable theological breakthrough in this narrative, and it only occurs when the Five is able to accept that he does not have to know everything, for God will act in such a way that all needs will finally be met. The death of Joseph in the final verses places all of human life and suffering in the larger context of the divine wisdom. Ultimately all is contained in the divine knowing in which we share when we move out of our false sense of separateness. Joseph moves into this Holy Omniscience, "a very beautiful condition in which you retain your humanity without losing your divinity,"[145] that is, without losing the knowledge that at our core we are forever bound to God in a reality that is deeper than, yet includes, all that it means to be human. It is a fitting end to Genesis, the first book of the bible, for it establishes a basis for understanding all that is to follow.

Prayer in the Spirit of Joseph
Psalm 105

O give thanks to the LORD, call on his name,
    make known his deeds among the peoples.
Sing to him, sing praises to him;
    tell of all his wonderful works.
Glory in his holy name;
    let the hearts of those who seek the LORD rejoice.
Seek the LORD and his strength;
    seek his presence continually.
Remember the wonderful works he has done,
    his miracles, and the judgments he uttered,
O offspring of his servant Abraham,
    children of Jacob, his chosen ones.

He is the LORD our God;
    his judgments are in all the earth.
He is mindful of his covenant forever,
    of the word that he commanded, for a thousand generations,
the covenant that he made with Abraham,
    his sworn promise to Isaac,
which he confirmed to Jacob as a statute,
    to Israel as an everlasting covenant,

saying, "To you I will give the land of Canaan
   as your portion for an inheritance."

When they were few in number,
   of little account, and strangers in it,
wandering from nation to nation,
   from one kingdom to another people,
he allowed no one to oppress them;
   he rebuked kings on their account,
saying, "Do not touch my anointed ones;
   do my prophets no harm."

When he summoned famine against the land,
   and broke every staff of bread,
he had sent a man ahead of them,
   Joseph, who was sold as a slave.
His feet were hurt with fetters,
   his neck was put in a collar of iron;
until what he had said came to pass,
   the word of the LORD kept testing him.
The king sent and released him;
   the ruler of the peoples set him free.
He made him lord of his house,
   and ruler of all his possessions,
to instruct his officials at his pleasure,
   and to teach his elders wisdom.

Nicodemus

"How can these things be?"

– John 3:9

In Nicodemus we meet a Five who, at least at the beginning of his story, seems to be well-situated in the Head space. Since he is a withdrawing type, we know that he has a misused Doing centre. As for all Fives, involvement for him is tentative except at the mental level, and uncertainty often prevents him from action because he thinks he must keep accumulating information until he can grasp and understand it, and then act on it. Fives need to feel competent, and this can take a long time. It may in fact never reach the stage in which they feel they finally know enough not only to make a decision but to act upon it as well. Nicodemus provides us with a model of how a Five can be touched in such a way that his acquired information together with his wisdom ultimately enable him to act both clearly and feelingly.

Nicodemus is a Pharisee, one of the respected leaders of the Jewish people and a teacher of the Law. As a Pharisee, he is respected for what he knows. His character occurs only in John's gospel, a gospel which explicitly states its purpose for the reader: it is written to encourage belief in Christ and through this belief to lead a person to abundant life (John 20:21). Every person who encounters Jesus in John's gospel serves as a model of what it means to come to such belief, as well as the stages and choices which the process entails. The story of Nicodemus outlines for us three stages of that journey towards faith: questioning, pondering, and, finally, acceptance. These outer stages which Nicodemus passes through resemble the traditional three stages often spoken of in the contemplative life, namely, the purgative, the illuminative, and the unitive.[146] Undergoing them signifies the soul's transformation and union with God.

Nicodemus experiences this growth in three episodes strategically placed at the beginning, the middle, and the end of John's gospel. After the first, which is his introduction to Jesus, his subsequent two appearances create the effect of an incremental repetition in which his personal journey to belief progresses and deepens, indicating for the new or potential believer what may lie ahead for all of us if our initial encounter with Jesus is taken seriously.

Nicodemus initially comes to Jesus "by night" (John 3:2). To come by night means to come in the dark. To come by night for a

Five is also to come when it is safest. No one will see him and he can literally stay in the shadows until it feels safe. It may well actually have been nighttime when Nicodemus arrived. At every turn, however, John's gospel invites us to go more deeply into its details and look at what lies beneath a purely literal reading. In this instance, we are asked to recall that just a short time earlier in the gospel Jesus had been referred to as the Light which had come into the world (John 1:4-5). He is the Light and Nicodemus is in the dark. Nicodemus has already investigated and found out certain things about this rabbi – "we know that you are a teacher who has come from God" (John 3:2) – but as a Five, he needs to get more information before he is willing or able to do anything with his knowledge. For Fives, insufficient information suggests an inner emptiness and void. As well, commitment until understood is hard for them, and they would much rather stand back and observe than get involved in any potentially risky action. Nicodemus therefore needs to see the big picture and to do what he first needs to get more information.

Jesus responds to Nicodemus with his well-known statement that anyone who wishes to see the kingdom of God needs to be born anew from above (John 3:3). Despite its familiarity to many people today, this is still a very puzzling statement. It puzzles Nicodemus, who asks how anyone can actually be reborn: can he indeed return to his mother's womb to be born again (John 3:4)? Nicodemus has good reason to question, for here was a totally new concept. Because there is an aspect of the Five which is out of touch with the body, this talk about birth and rebirth is especially difficult. If we feel disconnected from our body, we need to learn how to sense our own aliveness and physical existence to grasp any concept of rebirth. A Five does not live well with such paradox. Paradox is too open-ended and slippery and defies the desire to know at least enough to come up with a workable theory. For a Five, where there is paradox, more information is needed.

After presenting him with the paradox of a grown man being reborn, Jesus then tells Nicodemus,

> "The wind blows where it chooses, and you hear the sound of it, but you do not know where it comes from or where it goes. So it is with everyone who is born of the Spirit."

> – John 3:8

In both the Greek and the Hebrew, the words for 'wind,' 'spirit,' and 'breath' are the same. In this statement, then, even the words which Jesus uses defy single meanings for Nicodemus. Both the wind and the Spirit blow through creation, giving the breath of life to all who are born once, and then born anew. Jesus' metaphor is deliberately suggestive and elusive. It requires reflection and most of all individual experience to be grasped. It is not understood solely at the level of the head, yet it invites deep thought and study in order to better open up its truth. It is rich food for Nicodemus to try to digest. His only response to Jesus is, "How can these things be?" (John 3:9). Jesus meets him right in his head space by challenging him with, "You are a teacher of Israel, and yet you do not understand these things?" (John 3:10). This is a question sure to provoke a Five and possibly send him away to do more research.

As a teacher of the teacher Nicodemus, Jesus knows how to engage him. His response to Nicodemus is complex and not simplistic. He knows that Nicodemus needs lots of information and time to ponder it. He also respects Nicodemus' need for inner privacy and meets him well within his comfort zone of intimacy. Jesus probably relished the intellectual questioning of Nicodemus and, instead of brushing him off, he went to great lengths to be present to his curiosity and his real desire to understand. One way to support a Five is to be present in just such a way and to offer one's time and energy, as Jesus does for Nicodemus.

Nicodemus' question of how such things could be is a very good question for a Five to ask. Nicodemus wants to understand, to add to his knowledge of what it means to be a good Pharisee who teaches the people about God. But the things Jesus says are beyond his expertise. Jesus speaks in paradoxes, riddles and metaphors and, while these appeal to the intellect of the Five, they also frustrate any attempts at solidifying their meanings. Yet a Five who is open to transformation is also open-minded. Nicodemus' question of "how can these things be?" is not uttered either skeptically or dismissively. A learner and a teacher, he really does want to understand even while he is unable to perceive the depths of what Jesus is saying. He goes off to ponder these things and to gather whatever additional information he can about Jesus and his teachings.

Many people on a spiritual path would likely agree that some form of dying is necessary before a rebirth and a new awakening can occur. But Jesus suggests a different pattern in this encounter with Nicodemus. The correct order, he seems to be saying, is to awaken, then to die, and finally to be reborn.[147] Nicodemus is not yet aware of the first step, of 'waking up.' He comes in the dark when a person is still asleep. Hence he has difficulty understanding the second and third steps, for only when one is 'awake' can one then die and be reborn. Nicodemus learns what it entails to 'wake up' the next time we encounter him.

Nicodemus' second appearance in the gospel occurs near the middle, at the time when Jesus has begun stirring up considerable controversy among the people and among the Jewish authorities. He has just lost a number of followers because of his claim to be the 'Bread of Life' (John 6:35). Many responded to him by saying, "This teaching is difficult; who can accept it?" (John 6:60). Their question sounds a lot like the earlier one of Nicodemus, "How can these things be?" Both questions present a choice between two responses: to go into them further, or to walk away.

Many of Jesus' disciples did in fact turn back at his words (John 6:66). The subsequent events tell us that Nicodemus was not one of them. The crowd debates whether Jesus is the Messiah: some claimed that he was while others said the Messiah could not possibly come from Galilee (John 7:41). Nicodemus gets caught up in the controversy. The chief priests and Pharisees have asked the police to arrest Jesus but they have not yet done so. As a Pharisee, Nicodemus is among them when the police return empty-handed. They report they could not arrest Jesus because of the way in which he spoke. The Pharisees say that only the uneducated crowd pays any attention to Jesus and that none of the Pharisees have believed in him. At this point, Nicodemus steps forward, not to claim belief (for that would be premature for the Five who is still gathering information) but to point out that their law requires that a person receive a hearing before being condemned. He relies on his knowledge of the law to put forward a tentative defence of Jesus. We can only assume that since his initial meeting with Jesus 'in the dark,' Nicodemus has been searching for answers to the question he had asked, "How can these things be?"

In the stages of his journey to belief, Nicodemus retains the Five's need to collect data and to observe what others are saying and doing. Clearly, his Feeling centre is also engaged as his knowledge becomes more and more personalized and less detached from pure facts. It is able to help him resolve his inner vagueness about Jesus and the paradoxes he offers. By reminding the council of priests and Pharisees that Jesus deserves a fair hearing, Nicodemus is also stepping into the sphere of Doing, the misused centre of the withdrawing types. Fives armed with research and trust enter into justice-making like no other type. They are fearless, competent, and clear.

Nicodemus' generous treatment of Jesus, despite the scorn of his peers, is an important step in his spiritual growth. It is important to note that his transformation is still not complete. He is here identified not just as one "who had gone to Jesus before" but also as being "one of them," meaning one of the Pharisees who wish to arrest Jesus (John 7:50). He must have felt somewhat estranged, trying hard to be a part of two opposing communities. The Pharisees, in an ironic echo of Jesus' earlier question to Nicodemus, tell him to "search and you will see that no prophet is to arise from Galilee" (John 7:52). Telling a Five to search is redundant. In the case of Nicodemus, it is what he has been doing all along. The Pharisees assume his searching will lead him to agree that Jesus cannot be the Messiah but Nicodemus has already undertaken his questioning with an open mind and an open heart and his search leads him back to the one he had sought in the dark. There is no account of what happened to Nicodemus after that council meeting and he exists only in the shadows of the gospel until the very end.

The final stage of Nicodemus' transformation takes place off-stage, which is where a Five prefers to be, withdrawn from the main action but keenly observing all that is going on. Jesus has finally been arrested, tried, and put to death. Following the account of the crucifixion, the gospel goes on to say,

> After these things, Joseph of Arimathea, who was a disciple of Jesus, though a secret one because of his fear of the Jews, asked Pilate to let him take away the body of Jesus. Pilate gave him permission; so he came and removed his body. *Nicodemus, who had at first come to Jesus by night, also came, bringing a mixture of myrrh and aloes, weighing about a hundred pounds.* They took the body of Jesus and wrapped it with the spices in linen cloths, according to the burial custom of the Jews.
>
> – John 19:38-40

Nicodemus appears with Joseph of Arimathea who is identified as a secret disciple. The other gospels add that Joseph of Arimathea was rich (Matthew 27:57) and, more importantly, "a respected member of the council" who was waiting for the kingdom of God (Mark 15:42). We also know that he was a good and righteous man who, although he was a member of the council, "had not agreed to their plan and action" (Luke 23:50). Nicodemus would have known him as a fellow member of the council. The friendship between these two men must have been nurtured by the secrecy of their discipleship. Secrecy is considered to be one of the characteristics of a Five, for it means holding in all the data and not pouring it out randomly. We can infer that, like Joseph, Nicodemus had also not agreed to the council's decision to arrest and kill Jesus. Now he comes forward to claim and wrap the body of Jesus. Surely this action became known and unfavourably sealed his future with the council. He could no longer observe their deliberations but would now be one who was himself watched.

This is a bold place for a Five to be, out of the shadows and into the limelight. The movement indicates the transformative work Nicodemus has undergone. The most important thing for Fives to do is to connect themselves with the real world and test their ideas in it.[148] Nicodemus, after much pondering and information gathering, was finally able to move his ideas and knowledge about Jesus into that arena of testing them. This would only have been possible because Nicodemus had connected personally with Jesus, first in the dark, then in the shadows, and finally into the light. He has now chosen to carry his light into the public realm. His detachedness has yielded to pure connectedness as he touches and wraps in spices the lifeless body of Jesus. His gesture creates a pieta which in its sadness and in its fragrance transcends all words and rests in the silence, the hope, and the beauty of what is to come.

The man who had been full of questions now comes in silence. He has no final speech with which to end this gospel. Nicodemus the withdrawn thinker has been transformed into Nicodemus, still the thinker but now also the man of free action. His questions and arguments are useless as he holds the lifeless body of Jesus. The paradox he has wrestled with has taken on bodily form: the light and life of the world now lies lifeless in the dark of the tomb.

Having shared the rich questioning of his mind with Jesus, Nicodemus now shows rich generosity to the body, wrapping it in a hundred pounds of spices. The claiming of the body is the final symbol in the story of Nicodemus. He literally returns to the body and to feeling beyond the thinking mode. His body holds his Essence as here he holds Jesus. He is indeed reborn as a result of Jesus' dying.

Prayer in the Spirit of Nicodemus
Psalm 23

The LORD is my shepherd, I shall not want.
　　He makes me lie down in green pastures;
he leads me beside still waters;
　　he restores my soul.
He leads me in right paths
　　for his name's sake.

Even though I walk through the darkest valley,
　　I fear no evil;
for you are with me;
　　your rod and your staff –
　　they comfort me.

You prepare a table before me
　　in the presence of my enemies;
you anoint my head with oil;
　　my cup overflows.
Surely goodness and mercy
　　shall follow me
　　all the days of my life;
and I shall dwell in the house of the LORD
　　my whole life long.

Summary of the Fives

Joseph as a Five teaches us to trust in God in the midst of whatever trials beset us. He endures betrayal, slavery and temptation yet divine Providence surrounds and sustains him in every circumstance. Joseph moves out of isolation and into communion by not giving in to his natural self-centredness and he manifests the Five's desire to be both capable and competent. He learns how to use his talents for the benefit of the community, and in so doing he saves his own family as well. Joseph experiences his suffering as part of a larger divine purpose and as this unfolds he perceives the connection between all events and God's loving plan for humanity. He becomes a wise teacher of his brothers and develops the Holy Omniscience of the Five, as he retains his very human qualities but grows in divine insight.

Nicodemus is a Five who moves from a withdrawn, questioning and uncertain position regarding Jesus into the fullness of communion with him. His transformation unfolds in the gospel in three stages, as he comes to Jesus in the dark, both literally and spiritually, and gradually moves more and more into the light. Jesus becomes a teacher to the Five who wants to learn and to know. The secretiveness and distance Nicodemus showed at the beginning in his encounter with Jesus give way in the end to clarity, commitment and trust, as he comes forward to claim Jesus' body and to anoint it, no longer himself in the dark but having come into the presence of the 'Light of the World.'

Type Nine: Abraham and the Man at the Pool

"Peace I leave with you; my peace I give to you."

– John 14:27

The Nines are the mediators and the peacemakers. The true nature of the Nine is to be a limitless flowing source of love and universal benevolence. Nines are comforting, unselfish, and accommodating. They long for peace and stability not just in themselves but in their surroundings and so they avoid conflict and are accepting and tolerant. The virtue to which they aspire is action and the vice to which they are most prone is indolence or sloth. Nines are at the centre of the Body triad of the Enneagram.

Like the Four and the Five, the Nine is also one of the withdrawing types, and has a misused Doing centre. For the Nine, however, the Doing is also the preferred centre. What this means is that, while Nines interpret the world through their Doing centre, they are also slow to process and make sense out of what needs to be done, and they often lack the self-confidence to do it.[149] For Nines, the freedom which is valued and sought by all the withdrawing types is best expressed as a freedom *from* rather than a freedom *for*.[150] Such freedom allows the Nine to preserve an inner life while at the same time withdrawing both from inner conflicts and from "active living" and active inner growth.[151] Nines will tend to do what they like, the way they like to do it, and when they like to do it. They convey a sense of control of their energy, moving deliberately and sparingly.

Nines are characterized by inertia – either the inertia of rest or the inertia of motion. This is another way of looking at the Doing centre's being both favoured and misused at the same time. The inertia of rest makes Nines appear slothful and passive, hoping a problem or situation will just go away without their having to do anything about it, a sort of playing dead in order to stay alive. For them, sloth may also be *accidia*, a kind of laziness about spiritual matters which causes them to put off paying attention to their inner growth and to delay the work of transformation. For Nines, this is a relinquishing of their identity, denying their wants and needs and dreams, avoiding decisions and especially commitment to those decisions and all in the name of keeping the peace or maintaining the status quo. The inertia of motion, on the other hand, gives them momentum, creating the stamina and perseverance to keep at a task and stick with it until it is done.

Nines make excellent mediators and counsellors because of these traits. They have no investment in themselves, so they can listen, understand and accept others without feeling they have to exert any of their own power.[152] Because they merge with others and live vicariously through them, Nines can also be in tune with another person's sense of being and are able to draw forth from them the deepest meaning of living. The inner life of the heart and soul of another is more readily accessible to Nines than their own inner lives. Nines are consequently gentle, unassuming, good-natured, helpful and sympathetic.

As Nines undertake the work of transformation, they will learn to face conflict within and outside of themselves, become more aware of their potential and begin to live out of it, and come to a state of peacefulness about themselves and about the world. Their inertia will give way to increasing energy.[153] They will increasingly feel more connected to the universe by engaging with it rather than withdrawing from it, a freedom *for*, not a freedom *from*. They will be peacemakers, not because they wish to avoid conflict but because deep down they perceive that there *is* no conflict and no duality when they live out of their Essence.

We see both types of the inertia of the Nine represented in the two biblical characters presented here as Nines. Abraham embodies the inertia of motion: his story begins with a call to leave his home and to keep going until he arrives at a new place. The Man at the Pool in John's gospel manifests the inertia of rest, having been paralyzed and unable to move from his spot for 38 years. Both of them are led through transformative stages of growth because of their encounter with the Divine Presence, which calls them to leave their places of comfort and familiarity and begin living in new ways. Until their experience of God within them, decision-making was difficult as it meant moving out, letting go, changing and abandoning the comfort of their anonymity. Above all, it meant reconnecting with themselves and with their lives.

Abraham's narrative is extensive and detailed; the Man at the Pool's story is quite brief, with very few details. Both stories are equally useful in understanding the Nine, for they complement each other well. The story of the Man at the Pool gives us a clear, undistracted outline and Abraham's story fills in some useful details spanning an entire lifetime.

The Nine-point on the Enneagram has been regarded as 'the seminal Point in the Enneagram map.' This is because it represents Holy Love, that which is the fundamental expression of all of reality. For this reason, the other eight points may all be said to flow out from Holy Love. Holy Love is at the heart of the experience of knowing that all of reality is good and loving and benevolent and that nothing can separate us or be separate from that Love.[154] It is not static but dynamic, breaking down barriers of perceived separateness and making it impossible for us to identify with our ego-self. In fact, we discover, much to our amazement and delight, that we do not even *have* an ego-self but that we have at our core Holy Love itself.[155] The peace and harmony experienced are utterly unrelated to the quality of one's external circumstances and we are neither for nor against anything but are simply at peace with everything around us.

Of course, this realization can also be achieved through the other eight points of the Enneagram, any one of which can be a starting place for our own transformative growth. Holy Love, as seen in the Nine, is not a *feeling* of love but a "quality of existence that makes that existence lovable."[156] Perceived through such Holy Love, all moments and all experiences are wonderful. This is what Julian of Norwich meant in her famous assertion that "all shall be well." A Nine who learns to look within will discover this truth resides in the individual soul as well as in the entire cosmos.

Abraham

"Here I am."

– Genesis 22:1

The first real 'character' in the Bible, Abraham is known as the "Father of Faith" to three world religions: Judaism, Christianity and Islam. He is the 'first real character' in the literary sense which demands some biographical details as well as motivations for the decisions the character makes during his or her life. While Adam and Eve, Cain and Abel, and Noah are all important literary and psychological archetypes, none of them has the depth of character associated with Abraham. He gives us the first full-length portrait of a human being who is engaged in an ongoing encounter with, and experience of, God.

Abraham's story begins in Genesis 12 when God tells him to leave his country and family to go to a land which God will show him (Genesis 12:1). This call is probably more difficult for a Nine to respond to than for anyone else, for a Nine likes to do what he wants and prefers things to remain as they are. On the other hand, because Nines do not like to rock the boat, they will often go along with things they do not really want to do just to keep the peace. In the account of the calling of Abraham, Abraham does not say a word in response to the huge demand that has just been put on him to leave all that is familiar. All we are told is that he "went, as the Lord had told him" (Genesis 12:4). A structure has been provided for him from outside and this empowers Abraham with energy and security. Of course this does not mean that Abraham did not want to obey God and do what he had been asked but there is a danger for him, as a Nine, to lose touch with what he really wants to do. Here he seems to have had no doubts whatsoever.

Interestingly, in Hebrew God's command to Abraham to "go" (Gen. 12:1) could also be translated as "go you" or even, more provocatively, as "go to you" or "go to yourself."[157] This second reading which, to be fair, is not the primary linguistic sense of the command, suggests the tantalizing possibility that God's call to Abraham is also a call to journey into himself, to begin the inner pilgrimage of transformation. The call for all of us, whatever our type, is always a call to the self, to move towards the essence of the divine that is within us.

Added to this is the fact that we are also told that Abraham is 75 when he hears God urging him to get on with his life. As a Nine it is not surprising that he has lived in one place for 75 years. What is surprising is the suddenness of his response. He does not deliberate or ponder or wait to think things through. For Nines, in small matters indecision can reign but, strangely enough, in matters of life-changing importance, a Nine can break the pattern and respond instantly from the gut and simply say 'yes.' Recognition of the right decision can be made in an instant. Abraham's previous inertia of rest is transformed instantly into an inertia of motion and he begins the long journey to an unknown place.

Abraham and his wife Sarah, though they are childless, are told they will have an heir and descendants as numerous as the stars in heaven. Despite this promise, Abraham is quick to let Sarah leave him when he anticipates trouble. As they enter Egypt, he tells his wife to lie and say she is his sister. This is because he fears she will be desired as Pharaoh's wife and the Egyptians will kill him so that they can have her. His fears are realized: Sarah is taken into Pharaoh's house but Abraham's life is spared. Abraham is treated well on account of his supposed sister. We again see Abraham wanting to keep peace at all costs but may wonder if this scheme was going too far. Abraham seems to be more concerned with pleasing the Pharaoh and attending to his wishes than he is to his own desires. The Nine's tendency to avoid conflict at all costs is apparent in this dangerous arrangement.

Sarah is finally released because Pharaoh's house is afflicted with plagues and Pharaoh realizes what has happened. The narrative shows Pharaoh to be genuinely concerned with moral goodness and in sending Abraham on his way, he allows him to keep all the goods he had been given. Two things can be said about this episode: perhaps Abraham was not merely trying to avoid conflict but knew that the God who had called him out away from his home and promised him land and children would somehow see the thing through. If so, Abraham shows amazing trust in God and confidence that he need not fight any battles since God will fight (and win) them for him.

The second important aspect of this episode is its similarity to the story of Moses in Egypt. In both stories, plagues are visited upon Pharaoh and his household on account of the chosen man of God. And in both, it is God who fights on behalf of the chosen people. As Moses tells the Israelites, God is the actor and they are the spectators in the divine drama:

> "Do not be afraid, stand firm, and see the deliverance that the LORD will accomplish for you today;. . .The LORD will fight for you, and you have only to keep still."

> – Exodus 14:13-14

It would appear that Abraham operates on the principle that if someone else will do the hard work for him, then he need not get involved in the conflict himself. We can read Abraham's non-involvement, then, either as pure reluctance to act or as solid faith that God is the sole actor in Abraham's life. Or we can say that both, in fact, are true, and that God meets the Nine where he is and gradually leads him into transformation.

There are other moments in Abraham's story in which he chooses not to involve himself, or tries to avoid a conflict. His nephew, Lot, is travelling with him and when it becomes clear that the land cannot support both of them, because of their many flocks and possessions, Abraham says to Lot, "Let there be no strife between your herders and my herders" (Genesis 15:4). He asks Lot to choose which portion of the land he wants, and Abraham will go in the other direction. Lot chooses the Jordan plain, and Abraham settles in Canaan. Abraham either does not care which parcel of land he gets, or else he knows that whatever Lot chooses will accomplish God's purpose. As before, to avoid strife Abraham lets another make the decision but again, his withdrawing also indicates his firm belief that all shall be well.

Abraham and Sarah are still childless, however. Abraham reminds God of this and is told that they will indeed have an heir of their own (Genesis 15:4). Abraham believes God, and yet when Sarah begins to complain that they are still childless, he gives in to her request that he father a child by her slave-girl Hagar. He is willing to merge with, and to give in to, her wishes to avoid a confrontation. It is unlikely that he trusts Sarah more than he trusts God but here again he acts in a way that will keep the peace and stop Sarah's nagging. A son, Ishmael, is born, and again Abraham listens to Sarah when she wants to drive Hagar and her son away, since Sarah has become unhappy with the arrangement. This could be an instance of a Nine saying 'yes' to something he does not really want in order to avoid domestic strife, yet the morality of the action is indeed questionable. Perhaps Abraham is here manifesting the Nine's apathy and tiredness over his long waiting period. Perhaps, too, this is part of the inner journey to which he has been called and which entails allowing himself to be pushed beyond the limits of normal tolerance. It is a good instance of how slowness of transformation befits a Nine.

Abraham's waiting continues. He is 86 when Ishmael is born; he waits another 13 years and when he is 99, God again appears to him and promises to make him the ancestor of "a multitude of nations" (Genesis 17:5). All together, he therefore waits a quarter of a century for the promised son to be born. While not deliberate procrastination on his part, the waiting suits the Nine's temperament.

In contrast, Sarah is less patient, and her asking for a son earlier had forced Abraham to abandon his patience and give in to her request that he take Hagar as a wife.

Before the birth of Isaac, however, we see yet another instance of Abraham's acting as peacemaker and mediator. Learning that God plans to destroy Sodom, Abraham bargains with him to spare the city for the sake of 50 righteous people (Genesis 18:24). He becomes a self-appointed referee, appealing to God's sense of justice. In fact, he is able to bargain with God enough to reduce the number of necessary just people from 50 to 10. The story is an excellent example of how God meets people where they are. God is willing to bargain with Abraham, which indicates that God accepts Abraham's sense of himself as a mediator. He does not confront Abraham and accuse him of arrogance. There is no whirlwind theophany such as Job experienced to put Abraham in his place or show him his own ignorance of things divine. Instead, God meets him as an equal at the bargaining table and they haggle over the number of just souls it will require to spare the city. The wonderful irony here is that, while Abraham appears to have struck a very good deal, Sodom is nevertheless destroyed. God encourages Abraham's skill as a mediator by allowing him to have his way and then enacts the rest of the divine plan.

Isaac, the child of the promise, is finally born when Abraham is 100 years old (Genesis 21:5). His patience has resulted in an heir to the covenant he made with God. What follows is one of the most difficult passages in all of scripture: while Isaac is still a boy, God tells Abraham to take him to the mountains and offer him as a burnt offering to God (Genesis 22:2). The command used is the same form as God's earlier call to Abraham to go out from his country. The two moments are connected as the pinnacles of examining Abraham's relationship to God. Without a word of objection or reply, Abraham gets up early the next day and prepares for the awful journey. In his quick and silent reply, there might be hidden an instance of the Nines' stoicism which can be used to suppress their anger.[158] Anger is one of the most frightening emotions for a Nine, for it threatens to destroy their inner peace. Yet their anger can also be used to help them connect with their inner power and "burn away" their inertia.[159]

Another way to understand Abraham's willingness to obey so readily is to see it through the lens of the Nine's dominant characteristic of merging with another. Merging allows him to put aside his emotions and individual objections in order to avoid a heart-rending conflict. If we read the story this way, then it becomes clear that the one Abraham is merging with here is actually God.

As earlier, there is again an ambiguity in Abraham's words. When Abraham takes Isaac up the mountain and tells the others to wait behind, he says, "we will worship, and then *we* will come back to you" (Genesis 22:6). Perhaps he is trying to throw them off the scent here but it is also possible that he has no intention of killing Isaac and knows that somehow God will allow them *both* to return. After all, God rescued Sarah from the Pharaoh and spared Hagar and her son Ishmael from anticipated death. Surely God will do something similar here.

And God does. As Abraham takes the knife to kill his son, God intervenes and tells him not to do so. Abraham has passed the "test" of not withholding his son. Yet something does not sit quite right with the reader. Surely God had no need to test Abraham further. Abraham has left everything and obeyed God faithfully. After the bargaining over Sodom, God even seems to have accepted Abraham as a partner.

Perhaps another way into this episode is through Abraham's actions as a Nine. Maybe Abraham's merging with God is more a merging with his own *idea* of God and what God would, in Abraham's understanding of things, desire from a devoted and grateful servant. As he gets to the actual moment of sacrifice, the repressed anger comes rushing to the surface, screaming at him that this is *not* what God wants of him. Having set out on the journey, inertia keeps Abraham moving but, having reached the summit, the place of rest, both his body and his heart refuse to cooperate any further. Abraham learns to trust himself, and in so doing, realizes that what his deepest self wants is also what God wants. He makes what feels like an independent decision, something which Nines find difficult to do. His autonomy becomes real. The decision not to kill Isaac turns out not to be an isolated moment but the very means by which Abraham reconnects to his humanity and, ultimately, to divinity.

There is a midrashic, or oral, tradition which says that before Abraham's call, he was a maker of idols. An idol is an image of a lifeless god, and stands between us and our own divine nature. It substitutes a cold object for a warm presence and displaces the possibility of an unmediated confrontation with the divine. It also allows us to keep our emotions at a safe distance from our beliefs. If we look at this symbolically, we see that Abraham's transformation necessitated his leaving behind a world of idols, one which avoided direct confrontation with God. By leaving behind his false gods, he was forced to undertake the spiritual work of Nines, to listen to the inner voice of their soul.[160] The voice he finally heard, from his soul rather than from his mind, told him not to sacrifice his beloved son. He knew then that not only was Isaac beloved of God but that he too was loved by God. Instead of withdrawing from the situation and allowing the sacrifice to proceed, God entered the moment profoundly and demanded the task not be carried out. Abraham thereby learns that withdrawing must always be accompanied by a corresponding willingness to engage wholeheartedly in actions which show God's love and which show our own desire to be a part of the love and the struggle of human life. Abraham and Sarah's journey is our own, giving up the familiar lands we know and moving to a place of trusting and connecting with our true selves and with God, a new land where the human truly and forever connects with the divine.

Prayer in the Spirit of Abraham
Psalm 40

I waited patiently for the LORD;
    he inclined to me and heard my cry.
He drew me up from the desolate pit,
    out of the miry bog,
and set my feet upon a rock
    making my steps secure.
He put a new song in my mouth,
    a song of praise to our God.
Many will see and fear,
    and put their trust in the LORD.

Happy are those who make
    the LORD their trust,
who do not turn to the proud,
    to those who go astray after false gods.
You have multiplied, O LORD my God,
    your wondrous deeds and your thoughts toward us;
    none can compare with you.
Were I to proclaim and tell of them,
they would be more than can be counted.

Sacrifice and offering you do not desire,
    but you have given me an open ear.
Burnt offering and sin offering
    you have not required.
Then I said, "Here I am;
    in the scroll of the book it is written of me.
I delight to do your will, O my God;
    your law is within my heart."

May all who seek you
    rejoice and be glad in you;
may those who love your salvation

say continually, "Great is the LORD!"
As for me, I am poor and needy,
    but the LORD takes thought for me.
Your are my help and my deliverer;
    do not delay, O my God.

The Man at the Pool

Jesus said to him, "Do you want to be made well?"

– John 5:6

Whereas Abraham showed us a Nine on a physical and spiritual journey, the unnamed man at the side of the pool in John's gospel represents another type of the energy of the Nine, the inertia of rest and inaction. The man cannot walk. His withdrawal from life is literal as well as symbolic: he has been lying by the pool for 38 years (John 5:5). He probably feels that he is nobody special and is content to stay camouflaged in the background of all the activity around the pool. It is a comforting way to be, for it creates no expectations and therefore experiences no disappointments.[161]

When Jesus sees the man lying there, he asks him, "Do you want to be made well?" (John 5:6). Jesus knew exactly what question to ask this Nine who, as a true exemplar of his type, finds it difficult to make a decision but still likes to be consulted. He has been asked an undisguised and straightforward question but he cannot answer it with a simple 'yes' or 'no.' He is repressed not only in his physical limitations (symbolizing his misused Doing centre) but in his inner development as well. As a Nine, he is a creature of habit who may have felt that non-interference was the best policy and that eventually things would somehow work themselves out. He is proof that postponement is something that Nines are good at.

The man's outer helplessness is a symptom of his inner inability, or perhaps just reluctance, to help himself. By being dependent on the assistance of others, he can avoid conflict and maintain at least superficial relationships. He may even be denying his serious illness, trying to create for himself as well as for others the illusion that everything is okay.[162] For when Jesus asks the man if he wants to be healed, the man deflects the question, and replies,

> "Sir, I have no one to put me into the pool when the water is stirred up; and while I am making my way, someone else steps down ahead of me."
>
> – John 5:7

He tells Jesus that when he moves, he moves very slowly, inching towards the healing waters of the pool. The tradition connected with the pool is that when the waters are stirred up by an angel, whoever is first to enter the pool will be healed. But the man can never move quickly enough because of his handicap. He offers this excuse to Jesus in response to Jesus' asking him whether he wants to be made well. His reply is a good example of the 'spiritual sloth' of the Nines which keeps them from engaging with reality in an active way.[163] Possibly it also contains some of the repressed anger of the Nine who might feel here that he is not worth being loved.

His excuse might also be a call for help but a veiled one. Perhaps in his mind his answer avoids a potential confrontation and possible disappointment too, for if he said he wanted help, Jesus might not have been able to do anything anyway. Worse, though, is the possibility that Jesus could indeed do something and, if he did, the man's life would be forever changed in a moment. Because Nines do not like change, especially sudden, traumatic change, the man is faced with a real dilemma: resist change and stay immobilized, or risk change and suddenly have many decisions to make and relationships to alter.

The withdrawing types often restrict their wish-making and believe that it is a good thing not to really wish for anything at all or to expect anything. For the Nine, this belief is often accompanied by a pessimistic outlook on life in general and an attitude that nothing ever comes of anything anyway so why bother making futile efforts?[164] It takes a lot to motivate a Nine such as the Man at the Pool to take up his bed and walk when the bed is so comfortable and he has been lying in it for so many years. Walking in this instance is an invitation to the man to wake up. It has been said that Nines have an inner "snooze button" that makes them postpone their spiritual waking up,[165] and this man seems to keep hitting his. The fulfilment of his wish to walk is perceived as a burden, not a freedom.

Perhaps by this stage the man does not really care if he is healed or not. He has been on the sidelines all these years and his inability to move has drained his energy. While others might leap at the chance for healing, Nines do not leap at anything. The lameness of the man at the pool is metaphorical as well as literal, for he cannot leap either in body or in spirit.

For the Nine to be motivated into action, it takes a colossally strong impetus from within or, if that is lacking, from without. Jesus, who knew what was inside of people, knew that the man did not wish to be bothered or given the immense choice of his own healing. As soon as the man gives his indirect response, avoiding the question of whether he does in fact want healing, Jesus wastes no more time indulging the man's equivocation. The very next verse tells us that "Jesus said to him, 'Stand up, take your mat and walk'" (John 5:8). Immediately the man is healed, takes up his mat and begins to walk. Some people are bothered that Jesus intrudes on the man's wishes and does not wait for a clear invitation from the man to heal him. Jesus' intervention is exactly what a Nine needs, however, and when we find ourselves surrounded by the inertia of our Nine energy, we too often need a divine jolt to get us up and moving into wholeness.

A person's transformation can be upsetting to others who are then challenged to examine their own lives to see where they themselves might be paralyzed. The religious leaders in Jerusalem immediately confront the man because his healing has occurred on a sabbath day and he is carrying his mat which constitutes a violation of the sabbath prohibition on work. They are not able to see beneath the literal level of the law and celebrate the divine healing which has occurred in their midst. The man's response to them shows us that he has been changed in more than a physical way. His earlier indecisiveness gives way to assertiveness and confidence, and he finds new energy in the virtue of right action. When they challenge him for carrying his mat, he replies that he was told to do so by the man who made him well. He does not back down from the conflict as a Nine might be expected to do. When asked who that man was, he says he does not know; he cannot point out Jesus to them, for Jesus had disappeared into the crowd.

Consistently in the gospels, being touched by Jesus and having one's life changed can get one into trouble. Jesus may disappear into the crowd but he does not abandon the man he has just healed. He finds him in the temple and pointedly connects the inner and the outer work which has been begun in him: "See, you have been made well! Do not sin any more, so that nothing worse happens to you" (John 5:14). This is not a threat or warning that God will get even if the man ever sins again. It is simply a statement of fact: if the man turns back to his life of inaction and passivity, he will be worse off than he was before.

The man now knows who has healed him and he returns to tell the temple authorities. Some might choose to interpret this as trying to pass the buck, to tattle on Jesus. But this would not be consistent with a Nine's transformative actions. It is far more likely that the man returned to the temple because he was no longer afraid of conflict or confrontation. He is now able to assert himself and is willing to enter into a situation of potential conflict instead of trying to avoid it. Possibly he could still see himself as a mediator or peacemaker between Jesus and the authorities. It is equally likely, however, that he needed to make a decisive statement about who had healed him, thereby aligning himself with a controversial public figure in a way that might cost him a further price. He is no longer withdrawing or trying to escape from making a decision but is willing to take a stand. His basic desire for inner stability and peace of mind has been fulfilled.[166] He is fully engaged with life and has opened himself to a continuing relationship with Jesus.

The culmination of this healing story is reached when Jesus replies to the authorities, when questioned about his working on the sabbath, "My Father is still working, and I also am working" (John 5:17). On the surface, this is a direct reply to their accusation and breaks through their literal legalism to point out that God's ongoing activity of holding creation together does not cease on the sabbath. On a deeper lever, it is a summary of the man's healing, of the divine awakening of the Nine from sloth to action and from indifference to passionate caring. The ongoing work of transformation does not cease on the sabbath day, or on any day. Showing someone the path to healing can never constitute an opposition to the divine laws. The sabbath is fulfilled when the ongoing work of God is absorbed into the human heart so that no one is separate from the love and creativity of God.

To understand work in this way is to move beyond economic and monetary concepts. All along, this book has been referring to the 'inner work' of our transformation and how the Enneagram can help point us in helpful directions towards that transformation. Distorting economic values so that they become the measure by which we judge others and ourselves can mean that the value of our material possessions often defines our personal worth. Nothing could be further from the biblical understanding of work and its purpose. The work of God, which Jesus tries to set forth in his words to the authorities, suggests that the inner work is indeed the only 'real' work we do. It is not transient, and it is life-giving. The healing of the Man at the Pool becomes an icon for the perfecting of creation in all its aspects. The man's body is healed, but so too is his soul, filled now with the water of life which the pool at Bethzatha could not provide.

Thus the Man at the Pool's story is not told in isolation but is woven into the beautiful metaphor of Jesus as the Living Water. The motif is found in John's gospel in the story of the wedding at Cana, at which Jesus turns water into wine (John 2:1ff.). It continues in the encounter between Jesus and the Woman at the Well when Jesus offers the woman living water which will well up from within and bring eternal life. While the Man at the Pool waits for an angel to stir up the sacred waters to enable healing, Jesus the living water comes to him to show him that genuine healing is not primarily external but internal. The Man at the Pool (like the Woman at the Well) is not named in order to remind us that he represents everyone who is willing to undertake the work of inner healing. His transformation is an example of how our own paralysis of spirit is encountered by the divine presence which offers us new life.

The Spirit of God which brooded over the waters at the start of the first creation story in Genesis is now present not in the stirring of the waters of the pool but in the person of Jesus. The Man at the Pool had been lying beside the pool waiting for 38 years when the Spirit of Jesus came to hover over him and breathe new life into his lame and broken body. He and all those who feel stranded in their waiting have the opportunity to discover that with the presence of Jesus, healing occurs. The helpless body of the Nine is activated and drawn out of its lifelong lethargy.

Two chapters later in John's gospel, Jesus cries out, "Let anyone who is thirsty come to me and let the one who believes in me drink. As the scripture has said, 'Out of the believer's heart shall flow rivers of living water'" (John 7:37-38). Belief in Jesus is, as has been noted earlier, the motive for John's gospel, and belief opens the heart so that the living water is not kept in and hoarded but flows freely outwards to all creation. For the Nines who prefer withdrawal yet long for freedom, Jesus' words encourage them to move from holding back to flowing forth. As with all the types of the Enneagram, movement forward in love holds the key to transformation. Head, heart, and body will work together in Holy Love once the divine Source has been unlocked within.

Prayer in the Spirit of the Man at the Pool
Psalm 46

God is our refuge and strength,
   a very present help in trouble.
Therefore we will not fear, though the earth should change,
   though the mountains shake in the heart of the sea;
though its waters roar and foam,
   though the mountains tremble with its tumult.

There is a river whose streams
   make glad the city of God,
   the holy habitation of the Most High.
God is in the midst of the city; it shall not be moved;
   God will help it when the morning dawns.
The nations are in an uproar, the kingdoms totter;
   he utters his voice, the earth melts.
The LORD of hosts is with us;
   the God of Jacob is our refuge.

Come behold the works of the LORD;
   see what desolations he has brought on the earth.
He makes wars cease to the end of the earth;
   he breaks the bow, and shatters the spear;
   he burns the shields with fire.
"Be still, and know that I am God!"

> I am exalted among the nations,
> I am exalted in the earth."
> The LORD of hosts is with us;
> the God of Jacob is our refuge.

Summary of the Nines

Abraham as a Nine is called to move out from his place of rest and into a journey with his wife Sarah that will transform him and create a new nation as well. As a peacemaker, he yields to outside influences such as the Pharaoh who has his eye on Sarah, which might disturb his equanimity. He wants to avoid conflict at all costs, even to the point of sending away Sarah's servant Hagar because Sarah is unhappy with her. When his much-awaited son Isaac is finally born, Abraham faces his worst fear when he hears God telling him to sacrifice his son. Abraham's transformation, which has been going along slowly (as befits a Nine), reaches its high point when Abraham does not go through with the sacrifice. He learns that God rejects human sacrifice in any form and that never does it glorify God's name. He also learns that Holy Love does not cause suffering and he realizes his true nature as a Nine is to be not a source of death but a limitless flowing source of love and universal benevolence.

The Man at the Pool in John's gospel is lame and cannot move. His inertia as a Nine is both physical and spiritual. Like Abraham, he has been in the same place for a long time when he is called forth from it by God. He does not respond readily as Abraham did, for he has withdrawn almost completely from life, and is not sure he wants to be pulled back into it. Jesus jumpstarts his transformation by healing the Man at the Pool before he can postpone his engagement with life any longer. Having been touched and healed by Jesus, the Man's life is no longer the same. He has encountered the Living Water and no longer fears conflict or confrontation with the authorities over being healed on a sabbath day. He is invited to join with Jesus and his Father to continue the creative work that does not cease on sabbaths or at any moment in our lives. Through his connection to Jesus he becomes a channel for the Living Water to be poured forth in abundance to the world.

The Spiral of Transformation: From Thinking to Mysticism

"So work away on your side: I guarantee
that God will not fail on God's side."

– Cloud of Unknowing, ch. 26.

The stories contained in the Bible are among the most compelling and meaningful known to humankind. They have been narrated and retold countless times, enriched by the accumulated wisdom of centuries. They provide a mirror in which each one of us can find our reflection of the divine image. The biblical characters express the breadth and depth of human emotions. They scale the peaks of ecstasy and they languish in the dungeons of despair.

This final chapter offers some possible applications of opening the Bible and using its insights and stories, along with the gift of divine grace and help, to assist in transformative work. With the author of the letters to Timothy, we can hope to discover from within our own experience that "All scripture is inspired by God and is useful for teaching, for reproof, for correction, and for training in righteousness" (2 Timothy 3:16). When we apply this to the various biblical characters and regard them as our spiritual mentors, we find that even our simple daily gestures can take on new meaning. Our personal contact with these archetypes can help us understand God, ourselves and others in fresh and rewarding ways.

Assisting this understanding is the Enneagram, a useful tool for helping us in our spiritual transformation. After we have understood its outline and its energies and after we have explored how various biblical characters fit into its nine different spaces or types, we need to ask ourselves if it has come alive inside of us. Have we been engaging in an exercise which is intellectually interesting and spiritually challenging but which has not really affected our lives in any notable way? Is our spiritual transformation helped at all by what we have been considering or is this just one more book that tries to put things together in a clever new way?

To find some way of realizing with our whole being all that has been delivered to our intellect, we need to address again the entire process of personal transformation and ask ourselves what it entails and, ultimately, what its purpose actually is. The message of Christ is that we need to lose ourselves in order to find ourselves (Matthew 10:39). This paradox invites us to examine closely what is the self that we must lose and what is the self which we will then find. Over the centuries, the lives and the writings of such people as Augustine, Teresa of Avila, John of the Cross, Julian of Norwich, and Therese of Lisieux have witnessed to and taught the importance and the example of a person's undertaking this journey to holiness and wholeness through loss of self and finding of true self. In our own time, more contemporary writers such as Thich Nhat Hanh, Anthony de Mello, Brian Swimme, Thomas Berry, Joan Chittister and Deepak Chopra, have also identified the process of movement to wholeness, including spirituality, communal growth and the interrelationships between humans and the cosmos. They have written and spoken and, with their own lives, witnessed to the effect of the human person on peace and harmony in the soul and in the universe. It is time to take seriously Jesus' statement that "the one who believes in me will also do the works that I do and, in fact, will do greater works than these, because I am going to the Father" (John 14:12). 'Going to the Father' or returning to the source makes even greater things possible for us because we too are connected to the source at our divine centre, and in recovering our Essence we have complete access to its creative and regenerative energy at all levels of being. Jesus' return to the Godhead anticipates our own return which we can begin in this life when we undertake the work of conversion and transformation.

Anyone who reflects on his or her life for even a few moments will readily acknowledge that growth occurs in several directions at once, and that spurts and setbacks follow one another in no apparent order. Sometimes it seems as if we have been in the same spot for a long while and other times it seems as if we have taken more steps backwards than forwards. Then, for no apparent reason, things switch around and we find we are moving speedily to a new place, for a short or a long while, until we settle again on another plateau. In the natural world, the days and months march along in an irreversible sequence yet, at the same time, they repeat themselves in an endless round of seasons and years. Similarly, the process of our learning and the experience of inner work is not linear, nor is it simply cyclical. This union between straight and circular movements is best described by the pattern of the spiral which circles around and pushes forwards and outwards at the same time. It is the pattern of the galaxies. The spiral of our own life also swirls about and reaches ahead even though some of its turnings seem retrograde. Yet its movement strives for harmony: it dances rather than marches.

This dance or spiral of transformation circles around our true centre or essence. Realizing our essence entails letting go of our illusions about our false self. Instead of clinging to the accidents and choices of personality which have shaped us since birth, we are encouraged to align ourselves with the Source which preceded birth and continues after death. The Enneagram encourages exploration of the false identification we make with ourselves through its nine types. This false self is closely connected to, and may even be the equivalent of, our ego-self, the sense we have that 'this is me and there's nothing I can do to change it.' By identifying who we 'are' with the qualities suggested by one of the Enneagram's nine spaces, we may unwittingly lock ourselves into a pattern which resists growth and assumes that we cannot change our basic nature. Unlike the electron mentioned at the beginning of this book, we may prefer to stay in one orbital shell and never respond to the impulse which makes us jump into a higher level of energy. We march when we could dance, forgetful of our creativity and our freedom.

Life is dynamic and change is its only constant. In its application, the Enneagram does not represent a static form but a dynamic motion. As with the rest of the universe, it is more energy than matter, more movement than substance. We cannot arrest the energy it represents any more than we can stop the sun from shining. The diagram of the Enneagram is a picture of a process, not the process itself, and we can continue to look at it from the outside without its ever impacting our lives. Reading a book or a menu is not the same as having the experience it describes. Once we accept the form of the Enneagram as simply a model or a blueprint which depicts the transformational process, we can then begin to release its potential for helping to unlock the self that must be given up in order for the true self to be found. What it later teaches us as well is that, once this 'new' self has been found, it too must finally be given up as something we can possess, for it cannot be located in any 'place' nor can it be pinned to any particular form of being. It is universal and permeates the universe.

Quantum physics has, through Heisenberg's uncertainty principle, taught us that the very act of looking at something we are trying to observe and measure changes the behaviour of what we are seeing. The result is that we cannot measure two things at once, nor can we separate ourselves completely from our observation and think that we are seeing something 'objectively.' This principle has strong theological implications, for it suggests that we cannot see ourselves, the world or God objectively, that is, as an 'object' with an independent life. To see anything that way, we would need to be outside of it, and we can never be outside of the universe. We participate in the act of observing and are neither a unique subject or object but both at once. As the mystics of all ages have tried to tell us, the seer, the thing seen, and the act of seeing are all somehow mysteriously entwined. The Enneagram functions much like the Eastern metaphor of Indra's net, which is woven full of gems in such a way that the facets of each gem within it reflect every other gem in the net. All are interconnected and none exists without reference to all the others. Like Indra's net, the Enneagram is not about isolated traits but is about the whole of human existence and, by extension, the whole of existence itself. It is not objectified and cannot be studied apart from our own involvement with it.

Practicing Transformation

Beginning or continuing our work of transformation does not require extra time, nor is it time-consuming. When people say they have no time to start something new, they usually imagine that it would require taking time away from something else. But when we are speaking about transformation, this is not the case. We may find that we want to undertake something new once we have begun the work but the practice of transformation only asks that we be conscious at every moment of our life. We are to heed the call of scripture to stay awake at all times and to "pray without ceasing" (1 Thessalonians 5:17):

> "Sleeper, awake!
>   Rise from the dead,
> and Christ will shine on you."

> – Ephesians 5:14

These words refer not to actual sleep but to a spiritual sleep and a spiritual death which can become our normal condition in this life. People who are 'asleep' are still able to function in their ordinary lives but their lives are on automatic pilot and most of the day is spent thinking about things which have happened recently or long ago or things which are about to happen later in the day or some time down life's road. Rarely are such people consciously aware of what is actually going on around them in the actual present. Only when something alarming or surprising happens are they woken up and brought back to the moment.

Perhaps the greatest difficulty in practicing an awareness of the present moment is remembering to do it! We start off with all the best intentions and within minutes our minds have drifted away into unfocused inner chatter. Many people spend most of the day practicing escapism: dreaming, pretending, indulging in wishful thinking, criticizing, deflecting, taking refuge in abstract 'spiritual practices' that do not actually nurture the divine in us. Such practices can easily become habitual and a substitute for the awakened life which presents us with opportunities for suffering and for compassion and, hence, for transformation. If we prefer sleepwalking through life, we will miss the joy that lies waiting for us in each moment.

Praying without ceasing does not mean 'saying our prayers' all day long but keeping ourselves centred on the divine presence within us. All day long, our three centers of Head, Heart, and Body are being bombarded by external events. If we are not awake, then we become like "children, tossed to and fro and blown about by every wind of doctrine" (Ephesians 4:14). Our day is spent reacting to events in an automatic way without inner awareness. It is as if we have been hypnotized into behaving in the same way all the time. If we identify with our mechanical reactions, we are still asleep while, if we realize them, we undergo a moment of consciousness.[167]

This book has referred to three triads of personality types: withdrawing, compliant, and assertive. Each of these stances has something to offer in the work of spiritual transformation. The Fours, Fives, and Nines, in their withdrawing and waiting, point us to the *via negativa*, the "negative way" in which we choose to give up all things, whether they be salutary or harmful. This is undertaken not as an act of masochism but as a choice which allows us to experience the paradox of which all the mystics tell, that in the nothingness we attain the All. It is a return to the "formless void and darkness" which preceded the work of creation in Genesis (Genesis 1:2), and from which everything arises. It represents our getting out of the way, that is, getting our ego out of the way so that the divine creativity can push through. The withdrawing triad provides us with our home base when we wish to experience this inner dynamic.

In the spiritual life, the negative way is balanced by the positive way, the *via positiva*, in which we choose to embrace all things, whatever they are, as a means through which we can approach God. This way is best represented through the Enneagram by the compliant triad, for in the Ones, Twos, and Sixes, we find the drive towards perfection, loving relationships and faithfulness which manifest the divine in the created realm.

The third group, the assertive triad, completes the picture by challenging the status quo and looking towards the future. In the Sevens, Eights, and Threes we find the expansiveness of the self aching for fulfilment beyond the present concerns of the ego.

The work which the Enneagram enjoins upon us is to develop and balance all three centres so that we are not one-sided or acting out of our own obsessions or preferences but awake to our true self. As part of the journey, we need to remember who we are. One of the oldest admonitions in the Western world is the command to 'know thyself.' To know that we are mortal, to know that we have a divine source and destination, to know that we carry divinity within – are all part of self-knowledge. We are in a sense hypnotized by the material world and need to wake up to its illusory nature.[168] Hand in hand with this awakening is our great need to forgive and be forgiven, to let go of the past, and not hold grudges against others or our self for things done or undone. "Forgive us our debts," reads one translation of the Lord's Prayer, using the language of cancelling a debt to reinforce the fact that as long as we feel the world owes us something, we are trapped in the ways of the world and inhibiting our spiritual growth.[169]

In this debt-forgiving part of the work, each of the nine types can learn to cancel its own particular kind of debt. The things we think we need or are owed represent our unhealthy distortions of reality. Riso and Hudson assign the following distortions to each type: critical perfectionism (One), the need to be needed (Two), chasing after success (Three), self-indulgence (Four), useless specialization (Five), attachment to beliefs (Six), frenetic escapism (Seven), constant fighting (Eight), and stubborn neglectfulness (Nine).[170]

It is not difficult to see how each of these is to be relinquished if we are to grow spiritually. What is harder to see is that as well as our aversions, we also need to let go of our preferences, some of which may be very wholesome but which we often allow to define ourselves. We can become identified with the healthier traits or virtues represented in each of the nine spaces and this is a more subtle attachment which also must be left behind if we are to behave as active subjects rather than as passive objects. For example, the Three who tries to give up the desire to feel accepted and recognized may feel as if she has fallen into an abyss of worthlessness; the Five who decides he will no longer try to be totally knowledgeable may become terrified at feeling incapacitated and useless. And so it is with all nine types. Self-forgiving, letting go and purging our thoughts requires much work and persistence and sometimes seems to bring very little reward. St. Teresa of Avila's metaphor of watering a garden likens this early stage to the hard work of carrying water to the garden in buckets which have been filled by hand.[171] There is a lot of work involved and it takes a lot of effort, and not very much is given in return.

But as we make the effort, it becomes a preparation for further stages of growth. In St. Teresa's garden metaphor, the result is described as watering our gardens by means of irrigation, which is less work than hauling water in buckets and also provides more water to the garden.[172] The water comes from a spring or river which only needs to be directed. The spring is already there; it only requires a bit of attention to be seen and its purpose understood. We finally 'see' the wisdom of what we have been working with and discover it is not an arbitrary pattern of traits and dependencies and virtues, but an archetypal whole that is greater than the sum of its many parts and both includes and transcends them. Like so many paradoxical truths, the real meaning is both inside and outside the thing we are looking at.[173] As long as there is a perceived separation between ourselves and what we are observing, we are not yet at the last stage of contemplation which is finally able to break down the barrier of separateness.

The diagram of the Enneagram becomes not a series of points, lines, and arcs but a unified whole which suggests movement and integration. It functions like the ruby (or silver)[174] slippers for Dorothy in *The Wizard of Oz*: through wearing them, she always had the power to return home whenever she wanted. But she had to journey a long way before she learned this. The journey for her began on a road which was depicted as a spiral, starting right at her feet and spiralling outwards to the Emerald City. Her journey away from her home was ultimately her journey back to her home. It shares with other mythical and literary journeys the pattern of finding oneself away from home, struggling against many obstacles and finally returning to where we belong.[175]

What we were looking for was right under our feet all the time. We had to travel a long way to discover what was ours from the beginning, our true self as a whole person who carries within the spark of divinity. Once we know this truth, it takes only the click of our heels and we are home. We see ourselves not as identified with one number or space or direction of movement on the Enneagram but as the dance of the whole which is bigger than its separate movements.

Practice and Purpose of the Thinking Centre

The types associated with the Thinking centre are the Fives, Sixes, and Sevens. These types, which belong to the Head space, see the world in terms of reflection, analysis, and planning. However, in the Ones, Twos, and Sixes (the Compliant types), these aspects of thinking are misused and underdeveloped. The Compliant types do not use their thinking for purposes of organization and action, but generally find that their thinking, while it may be abundant, is often unproductive. These types will find it helpful in their work of transformation to 'practice' using their Thinking centre.

The Thinking or reflective centre includes the difficult task of self-observation, which is essential for arriving at self-knowledge. Nicoll explains the connection well:

> Without self-observation there can be no self-knowledge. People, of course, imagine they know themselves and live in this illusion. It is precisely this illusion that prevents them from realizing that they do not know themselves and that in place of self-knowledge they have imaginary pictures of themselves which do not resemble themselves as they really are and which only complicate their lives with pretences and lead them in a hundred and one wrong directions. Nursing these pictures of themselves, as it were, like precious dolls, they rarely catch even a glimpse of themselves and, if they do, they hug their dolls more closely.[176]

It is difficult to see ourselves without all our acquired layers of pretence and illusion but we must begin to do so if we ever wish to leave our old selves behind and be born to a new way of being. Self-observation does not mean simply labelling our thoughts and feelings and believing we have been observant. It usually entails peeling back layer after layer to discover what lies *beneath* our thought or feeling or action and, then again, what lies beneath *that* discovery, and so on and so on, until we arrive at something quite different from all the images of our self we have built up. We catch a glimpse of our unity with the divine source and false idols of self fall away.

The archetypes in this centre showed Nicodemus aspiring to truth and light; Joseph translating his dreams to reality, and the woman at the well's agile mind and openness causing her to change her life. Solomon's wisdom, the fruit of the thinking center, enabled him to evaluate and to build; the Maccabean mother courageously tolerated the mystery in its deep ambiguity; and Peter confessed his mistakes and moved on. Thus it is in this Thinking centre that we are able to see a big picture, to balance our ideas and to celebrate diversity.

Practice and Purpose of the Feeling Centre

The types included in the Feeling centre are the Twos, Threes, and Fours. These types of the Heart space perceive the world relationally in terms of feeling and of being connected to others. In the Assertive types, that is, the Threes, Sevens, and Eights, the energy of the Feeling centre is misused. The misuse is actually an underuse, either through over-intensity, lack of sensitivity, denial of feelings, or not being present to the emotional atmosphere of a situation. Their practice as they work towards wholeness is to value their Feeling centre and learn to use it productively.

The Feeling or relational centre includes detachment from persons, things, and ideas and a fuller opening to the enlightening or illuminating work of the Spirit. It continues the work of letting go of our false self, our fixations and our passions. It is actually a combination of the Head and the Heart, for the ideas, concepts, and illusions of the Head are examined in the light of the purpose and intelligence of the heart. The heart ponders the values of love and trust, of relationships, and the presence of mystery.

The biblical archetypes of the Feeling centre offer us the stories of their lives and experiences which touch the heart. They are shown in their relationship to themselves and others, as well as to the source of their being. Job received and responded to love and affection from God; David found a companion on his journey, and produced deeply evocative poetry; Mary Magdalene cried from her heart searching for her soul; Ruth integrated new values and gave her life to a new people; and Saul awakened to the hardness of his heart. All these characters may have suggested that being in relationships is the road to intimacy.

Practice and Purpose of the Doing Centre

The types included in the Doing centre are the Eights, Nines, and Ones. These types belong to the Body space and perceive the world in terms of moving, creating, and surviving. The Doing centre is misused in the withdrawing types — the Fours, Fives, and Nines — who often feel unconnected to what is going on around them. In their practice they will seek to develop their Doing centre and participate more fully in the world, engaging with it rather than escaping from it.

It is the synergy of the creative elements of the body which brings forth a new reality and a new creation. This energy connected to the Heart centre is transformed into positive actions towards oneself, other people and the world. It is seen in all the efforts being made to honour the earth, to overcome geographical and political boundaries in the name of our common purpose and to bring justice to the oppressed. In this state, as Paul described it, there are no more barriers which separate, divide or obstruct: "There is no longer Jew or Greek, there is no longer slave or free, there is no longer male and female; for all of you are one in Christ Jesus" (Galatians 3:28). The psalmist also described it well in writing, "steadfast love and faithfulness will meet; righteousness and peace will kiss each other" (Psalm 85:10).

Our creative centre is also a crucial element in our being whole. For years the body has been seen as a nuisance and a barrier to personal and spiritual growth. Contemporary wisdom is urging humanity to consider the body as gift. It is for some a vessel of the soul and, for others, the soul enfleshed.

The body occupies both space and time and is a miraculous blend of quantum energy. Being present to the body's moving towards, moving against, or moving away from something or someone is the most reliable way to discover where one's attention is focused. Including the body in our work accepts its connectedness to the earth and to the Creator who saw that "it was very good" (Genesis 1:31).

The archetypes of John the Baptist and Paul actively and intensely used the energy of their bodies to achieve their goals. The Canaanite woman unabashedly sought justice for her child despite the prevailing system which worked against her. Martha blended her doing with her being in her relationship to Jesus. Abraham and the Man at the Pool, at rest in their bodies, were both open to moving into new adventures.

Nurturing the Centres

Some practices lend themselves more fruitfully to the work of a particular centre, while others can nurture all three. If we need to develop our Thinking centre at a particular time in our life, we can look to such things as journaling or other forms of writing, discursive meditation and *lectio divina*. We can try to build up our knowledge and learning, which will educate us to greater awareness of the immensity of our world. We can learn from everything which occurs when and just as it happens and be open to new patterns of thought. We can make the search for truth a strong value in our lives, believing that the truth will make us free (John 8:32). In seeking the truth we will become aware of our inclination to seek simple solutions for complex questions or to offer stereotyped answers instead of finding solutions which emerge out of deep reflection on reality and our own experience of essence.

If our Feeling centre is calling for attention, we can turn to one of the art forms and draw, make music or listen to it, or read some of the world's great poetry. All these can be undertaken with a desire to do them consciously and to let our hearts open to the vastness of emotions and feelings. We can give particular attention to a relationship in order to practice giving and receiving love. We can become more awake in noticing how we feel and where that feeling arises, and allowing our hearts to unfold and expand to encompass everyone we encounter. The different communities in which we live and work also offer ample opportunities to develop our relational centre as we grow in our understanding of how the universe is a web of interconnectedness. One of the first things God says in Genesis is that it is not good for a person to be alone, (Genesis 2:18) and human contact is a constant reminder of our need to be in relationship with others.

Our Doing centre also needs to be supported, and we can assist its growth by being deliberate about taking care of our bodies. Exercise of all sorts – sports, dance, yoga, walking – stimulates our Doing centre and integrates our body into the rest of our life. Also helpful are being gentle with ourselves, taking a day of rest, being aware of our breath and the pulse of our heart, fasting to free space for the spirit and to discipline the compulsions. We may sometimes feel that we are bearing our body but we need to remember that in fact it is our body that is bearing us. The many miracles of healing reported in the gospels attest to the honour that is given to the body and the compassion to be shown to those who suffer. The body becomes a useful ally when we notice all the signals it gives us of when we are falling out of awareness. Used consciously, our Doing centre is not in opposition to our awareness of 'being.' Like Martha and Mary, Doing and Being exist in the same household of our body and work together when we are aware. We do not then 'do' things out of our natural compulsions or personality but remain awake to the ways in which that personality tries to kidnap our mindful attention. Such distractions arise constantly and challenge us to hold on to our deeper sense of essence.

While each centre can be deliberately exercised and strengthened, it must always be borne in mind that the purpose of focusing on one centre over the others is solely to bring about a balance among all the energies described by the Enneagram. This requires that we turn off the internal commentary which runs through us all day long in order to relax our body, quiet our mind and open our heart to accept with compassion whatever affects us. We can learn to cultivate the awareness that each moment is the only moment, a gift to be attended to and received joyously. A perfect balance among our centres would become manifest as our perfect presence to our Essence, to others, to the earth, to the universe, and to God. Such presence would touch the Source of our life and enliven our dancing within the spiral of transformation.

Mysticism: Coming Home

Our encounter with the biblical characters in the sacred narratives of the bible provides us with a template for our lives. Through their stories, we learn how their souls struggle and grow, and how God encounters them in a full spectrum of situations in order to offer them life, healing, and wisdom. Following in their footsteps, and accompanied by divine grace, the mystics of the Christian faith have written extensively about what it means to lose one's self in order to find oneself in the work of transformation. They speak in metaphors and images in their attempt to convey the unimaginable. The forms of prayer they write about are all ways of coming home, that is, of returning to the Source of our being which we encounter in the experience of conversion and prayer.

Mysticism is not limited to a few highly developed spiritual souls. In fact, contemplative experiences are really quite normal in all humans, though most would not call them that. They are part of our natural sphere of behaviour. These experiences teach us that it is indeed possible to shut down our "grasping machines,"[177] the attitudes and reactions we habitually hold on to and which become part of our inner chatter. When even the 'ordinary' person in normal circumstances sinks more deeply into the inner self, the experience of God is purer, more intense, and clearer than before. As a result of a sustained practice, experiences of the Spirit become clearer, more explicit and more normal. Distinctions between inner and outer presences dissolve and the reality of the lived moment becomes the point of contact with the divine reality.

In this state all three centres of our being — head, heart, and body — come together in perfect balance. As we reach balance in our lives, the movement from point to point on the Enneagram becomes a mystical dance which never ceases. We enter the ancient and cosmic dance of the spheres. This phenomenon can be described as a merging of the true self with God. It dissolves any sense of the self acting independently from God. Jesus expressed this when he prayed "not my will but yours be done" (Luke 22:42). Likewise, it fulfils the statement of John the Baptist when he referred to the nature of his relationship to Jesus: "He must increase, but I must decrease" (John 3:30).

As this occurs, it is, as St. Teresa of Avila described it, as if we have a garden which is watered through no efforts of our own but by the rains which fall freely from the heavens and saturate all they touch.[178] Our stance becomes one of openness and receptivity and we are receptive to nothing but God.[179] We allow ourselves to be acted upon by a reality greater than our own selves. As Meister Eckhart understood it, there is a single goodness in everything and that is where we know ourselves and where we live.[180] We cannot make this experience happen, but can strive to create the environment in which it will arise from within as the work of God. The provision for a sabbath or day of rest in our lives allows us to cease our outer work and attend more deeply to the inner.

Journeying to that place is the work which we freely undertake. It is called 'work' because it is not easy but it is also the delightful sort of work which we do when we dance. It might even look like a form of play, just as Lady Wisdom played creation into being, delighting in God and in the human race and "rejoicing in the inhabited world" (Prov. 8:22-31). Work done from our centre, our Source, will always be meaningful and never alienating.[181] In fact, it will not be 'our' work but the work of the divine within us, as Jesus said: "the Father who dwells in me does his works," and "My Father is still working and I also am working" (John 14:10; 5:17). It is apparent that Jesus did not mean the work that enables us to acquire material things: the work in which he invites us to participate is a work not to acquire something we do not have but to get rid of something which we do have.[182] Working to clear away our ego attachments and aversions makes a road and prepares the way in our personal wilderness so that the divine may find an unobstructed path in us.

"See, I am making all things new," says the one called Alpha and the Omega, the beginning and the end, in the book of Revelation (Rev. 21:5). *All* things are made new, not just some things. In the transformed life of the New Jerusalem, nothing is the same as before. A new way of being is envisioned, not a return to the Garden of Eden but an ascent to a City. The City includes nature (it has a river and trees) but is based on a community of those who have been called to the marriage feast (Rev. 19:7). This final image in the Bible gives us a picture of total transformation. The marriage between God and humanity is anticipated and celebrated in the work we do here and now of uniting all opposites and bringing our body, mind, and heart into alignment and balance.

Using the modern compass provided by the Enneagram, the Bible becomes an even more effective guide for our journey into wholeness. The inspirations and challenges it offers are unchanging yet ever new. The stories of personal transformational experiences resonate with our own as we learn from those who have traveled the road before us as mentors and guides. All the energies of the Enneagram manifest themselves in the scriptural stories, to which we can return time and time again, always finding in them glimpses of our own story and help along the way.

When we have moments of encounter with the Real Presence of the divine in our lives, all else seems illusory and fading. Nothing exists apart from God, and no action can be begun or completed without the divine consent: "in God we live and move and have our being" (Acts 17:28). There is no other reality. If God is All, then when we claim a feeling or a desire or a thought or an action is 'ours,' our owning it as part of ourselves indicates precisely where we are *not* connected to God. The loss of 'our' attachments, both sensual and spiritual, leaves room for the 'no-thingness' which can not and does not resist God.[183] As well, inasmuch as we remain attached to 'our' number or type on the Enneagram, we may be clinging to a barrier to our spiritual growth and transformation. Discovering the no-thingness which underlies all being throws us back into the world of being with new sight. As the eastern saying goes, "Before Enlightenment, chop wood and carry water. After Enlightenment, chop wood and carry water." Nothing changes, yet everything changes: "See, I am making all things new." As T.S. Eliot wrote in his famous lines from *The Four Quartets*,

> We shall not cease from exploration
> And the end of all our exploring
> Will be to arrive where we started
> And know the place for the first time.

If we see our number or type as the place from which we start, we have already begun our journey. It will return us to where we have been all along, only we did not know it. Our coming home is a coming home to our true self, which has always been there waiting to be awakened. The small resurrections born from daily discipline prepare the way for the ultimate resurrection when we will discover our true Essence in all its radiant beauty.

The Bible remains a great source of wisdom and inspiration for all time. The many people whose stories it contains show us how we may meet God in our own lives and be transformed by the encounter. By providing us with such wise mentors, who in their various and surprising ways teach us how to integrate the thinking, feeling, and acting centres of our being, it generously pours forth its riches into our own souls, assuring us that we do not walk the path of transformation alone and that our work will bear much fruit for ourselves and for our world. Our relationships with the Divine, with others and with ourselves can be enriched beyond our wildest dreams. We are invited to penetrate, to probe, and to experience in new ways the patterns of divine communication with human beings in all their complexity, frailty and strength, sinfulness and amazing potential, and ultimate grandeur. Nothing less than intimacy with the Divine awaits us if we let the energy of the inspired Scriptures captivate our hearts and minds and move us forward towards our final destiny. Let us not be detained from this work.

Notes

Notes for Chapter 1: The Bible and the Enneagram

1   Richard Rohr and Andreas Ebert, *The Enneagram: A Christian Perspective* (New York: Crossroad, 2001).

2   D.W. Robertson, trans. *On Christian Doctrine* (New York: Bobbs-Merrill, 1958), p. 75.

3   Dei Verbum, 3.12. *The Sixteen Documents of Vatican II.* (Boston: Daughters of St Paul, n.d.), p. 382.

4   *Cloud of Unknowing*, trans. Clifton Wolters (New York: Penguin, 1978); rpt. 1987, chap. 3–6.

5   See especially Maria Beesing, Robert Nogosek, and Patrick J. O'Leary, *The Enneagram: A Journey of Self-Discovery*; Helen Palmer, *The Enneagram: The Definitive Guide to the Ancient System for Understanding Yourself and the Others in Your Life*; Don Richard Riso and Russ Hudson, *The Wisdom of the Enneagram: The Complete Guide to Psychological and Spiritual Growth for the Nine Personality Types*; Richard Rohr and Andreas Ebert, *Discovering the Enneagram: An Ancient Tool for a New Spiritual Journey*; and Kathleen Hurley and Theodorre Dobson, *What's My Type?*

6   Harvey D. Egan, S.J. Karl Rahner: *The Mystic of Everyday Life* (New York: Crossroad, 1998); and Richard R. Gaillardetz, *Transforming Our Days: Spirituality, Community, and Liturgy in a Technological Culture* (New York: Crossroad, 2000).

7   Egan, p. 55.

8   Egan, p. 88.

9   Alexander Pope, "An Essay on Criticism." In *The Works of Alexander Pope* (Hertfordshire: Wordsworth Edition, 1995), l. 298, p. 74.

10 Walter Brueggemann, *Finally Comes the Poet* (Minneapolis: Fortress Press, 1989), Introduction.

11 Augustine. *The Confessions of St. Augustine.* Trans. F.J. Sheed. (New York: Sheed & Ward, 1943). Book 13, chap. 11, p. 328.

12 Egan, p. 197.

13 William James, *Varieties of Religious Experience* (New York: New American Library, 1958), p. 127.

14 Pope John Paul II, "A Dynamic Relationship of Theology and Science," *Origins*, vol. 18, no. 23 (Nov. 17, 1988), p. 378.

15 C.K. Jung, *Collected Works*, trans. R.F.C. Hull (Princeton: Bollingen Series, 1966), vol. 15, p. 82.

16 Brueggemann, *Finally Comes the Poet*, pp. 5–6.

17 Diarmuid O'Murchu, *Quantum Theology* (New York: Crossroad, 1997), pp. 178, 199. See also Peter A. Pitzele, *Scripture Windows* (San Francisco: Torah Aura Productions, 1998).

18 Aloysius Pieris, S.J. *The Christhood of Jesus and the Discipleship of Mary*, Logos series, vol. 39, no. 3. p. 82.

19 Pieris, *The Christhood of Jesus*, pp. 82–83.

20 Pieris, *The Christhood of Jesus,* p. 112.

21 Virgil Howard and Patricia LeNoir, "Unleashing the Power of the Bible," in *The International Bible Commentary*, ed. William R. Farmer. Collegeville (Minnesota: Liturgical Press, 1998), p. 37.

22 Brian Swimme, *Hidden Heart of the Cosmos,* VHS (Mill Valley, CA: Center for the Story of the Universe, 1996).

23 O'Murchu, p. 133.

24 Gary Zukav, *The Dancing Wu Li Masters: An Overview of the New Physics* (New York: Bantam, 1979), p. 193.

25 O'Murchu, p. 114.

26 Throughout this text we have adopted the conventional use of B.C.E. (Before the Common Era) and C.E. (Common Era) to indicate historical dates.

27 Anthony DeMello, *Awareness* (New York: Doubleday, 1990), p. 136.

28 Quoted in R.A. Markus, *Gregory the Great and His World* (Cambridge: Cambridge University Press, 1997), p. 47.

29 Sogyal Rinpoche, *The Tibetan Book of Living and Dying* (New York: Harper Collins, 1993), p. 130.

30 Don Richard Riso and Russ Hudson. *The Wisdom of the Enneagram* (Toronto: Bantam Books), 1999, p. 20.

31 Rohr and Ebert, p. 11.

32 Rohr and Ebert, p. 15.

33 We are indebted to Dr. David Leeming at the University of Victoria for the explanation and examples.

34 Robin Amis, *A Different Christianity: Early Christian Esotericism and Modern Thought* (Albany: State University of New York Press, 1995), chap. 10.

35 A.H. Almaas, *Facets of Unity: The Enneagram of Holy Ideas* (Diamond Books: Berkeley, 1998), p. 140.

36 Almaas, p. 6.

37 Quoted in Rinpoche, p. 49.

38 Pope John Paul II, *Novo Millennio Ineunte* (January 6, 2001), Article 23.

39 Amis, p. 212.

40 Maurice Nicoll, *Psychological Commentaries on the Teaching of Gurdjieff and Ouspensky*, 6 vols. (York Beach, Maine: Samuel Weiser, 1996), p. 1007.

41 Karen Horney, *Neurosis and Human Growth: The Struggle toward Self-Realization* (New York: W.W. Norton & Co., 1950); rpt. 1991.

42 Kathy Hurley and Theodorre Donson, *Discover Your Soul Potential* (Lakewood, Colorado: Windwalker Press, 2000).

43 Riso and Hudson, *Wisdom*, pp. 59–63.

44 In mathematics, the Law of Trichotomy confirms this. In its simplest form, the Law says that if you are given two real numbers a and b, then exactly one of the following statements is true about these two numbers:
    i. a < b
    ii. a = b, or
    iii. a > b

   If a and b are any two of the three centres on the Enneagram, a will either be repressed (<b), preferred (>b), or both repressed and preferred, as occurs at the Enneagram points of Three, Six, and Nine. (Thanks to Dr. David Leeming of the University of Victoria.)

45 James, p. 160.

46 Augustine, *Confessions*, Book Eight, chap. 5, p. 165.

47 Augustine, *Confessions*, Book Eight, chap. 11, p. 176.

Notes for Chapter 2: The Compliant Types

48 Horney, p. 222.

49 The Basic Fear and Basic Desire for each type are taken from Riso and Hudson's *The Wisdom of the Enneagram*.

50 The passion or sin associated with each type is that named by Oscar Ichazo.

51 Horney, p. 223.

52 Horney, p. 217.

53 Horney, p. 222.

54 John Dominic Crossan, *Jesus: A Revolutionary Biography* (San Francisco: Harper SanFrancisco, 1995), p. 167–8.

55 *Varieties of Religious Experience*, p. 192.

56 Sean Kelly and Rosemary Rogers, *Saints Preserve Us!* (New York: Random House, 1993), p. 222.

57 Riso and Hudson, *Wisdom*, p. 119.

58 Nicoll, p. 1487.

59 Riso and Hudson, *Wisdom*, p. 122.

60 De Mello, p. 19.

61 James, p. 172.

62 Riso and Hudson, *Wisdom*, p. 135.

63 Riso and Hudson, *Wisdom*, p. 136.

64 Riso and Hudson, *Wisdom*, p. 136.

65 Horney, p. 227.

66 Riso and Hudson, *Wisdom*, p. 134.

67 Horney, p. 228.

68 Don Riso, *Understanding the Enneagram* (Boston: Houghton Mifflin, 1990), p. 46.

69 Riso and Hudson, *Wisdom*, p.198.

70 See, for instance, Genesis 16:4, 29:23, 29:30, 30:4, 38:18.

71 Riso, p. 47.

72 Horney, p. 227.

73 See Genesis chap. 38.

74 June Jordan, "Ruth and Naomi, David and Jonathan: One Love." In *Out of the Garden: Women Writers on the Bible*, eds. Christina Büchmann and Celina Spiegel (New York: Fawcett Columbine, 1994), p. 87.

75 Hurley and Donson, *Soul Potential*, p. 122.

76 Hurley and Donson, *Soul Potential*, p. 121.

77 See Matthew 16:16; Mark 8:29; Luke 9:20; John 6:69.

78 Horney, p. 227.

79 Riso and Hudson, *Wisdom*, p. 254.

80 Riso, pp. 64–5.

81   2 Maccabees 7:1–42 and 4 Maccabees 8–18.

82   We are considering the apocryphal books, which contain the Books
     of the Maccabees, as part of the scriptural canon since they were
     used and known by the early church and are still read in many
     branches of Christianity today. They were part of the Septuagint
     and were considered canonical at least until the 4th century but
     rejected by some during the time of the Reformation.

83   2 Maccabees 6:1ff.

84   Horney, p. 217.

85   4 Maccabees 17:4.

86   2 Maccabees 7:9, 14, 17.

87   James, p. 275.

88   See further on Abraham below, where he is discussed as a Nine.

89   James, pp. 265–6.

Notes for Chapter 3: The Assertive Types

90   Horney, p. 192.

91   Almaas, p. 162.

92   *Hochmah* in the Hebrew, and *sophia* in the Greek.

93   Almaas, p. 163.

94   Horney, p. 194.

95   Horney, p. 194.

96   See 2 Kings 17:24ff.

97   Horney, p. 193.

98   Horney, p. 203.

99   Hurley and Donson, *Soul Potential*, p. 150.

100 Horney, p. 192.

101 Almaas, p. 96.

102 Horney, p. 200.

103 *Cloud of Unknowing*, p. 85.

104 Claudio Naranjo, *Ennea-Type Structures: Self-Analysis for the
     Seeker* (Nevada City: Gateways, 1990), p. 134.

105 Horney, p. 211.

106 Helen Palmer, *The Enneagram: Understanding Yourself and Others
     in Your Life* (San Francisco: Harper Row, 1988), p. 306.

107 Riso, p. 74.

108 Riso and Hudson, *Wisdom*, p. 312.

109 Hurley and Donson, *Soul Potential*, pp. 78–9.

110 Horney, p. 192.

111 Almaas, p. 255.

112 Riso and Hudson, *Wisdom*, p. 161.

113 Horney, p. 194.

114 Riso, p. 148.

115 Riso, p. 148.

Notes for Chapter 4: The Withdrawing Types

116 Hurley and Donson, *Soul Potential*, p. 188.

117 Horney, p. 259.

118 Horney, p. 260.

119 Hurley and Donson, *Soul Potential*, p. 188.

120 Horney, p. 274.

121 Horney, p. 259.

122 Hurley and Donson, *Soul Potential*, p. 93.

123 Almaas, p. 197.

124 Riso and Hudson, *Wisdom*, p. 54.

125 Riso and Hudson, *Wisdom*, p. 191.

126 Almaas, p. 191.

127 James, p. 74.

128 Riso and Hudson, *Wisdom*, p. 188.

129 Almaas, p. 202.

130 Riso and Hudson, *Wisdom*, p. 204.

131 Almaas, p. 187.

132 C.K. Jung, *The Portable Jung*, ed. Joseph Campbell (New York: Penguin, 1971), p. 531.

133 Susan Haskins, *Mary Magdalen* (London: HarperCollins, 1993), p. 63.

134 For discussion of Martha as an Eight, see above, "Assertive Types".

135 John Marsh, *Saint John* (New York: Penguin, 1968; rpt 1972), p. 637.

136 Riso and Hudson, *Wisdom*, p. 208.

137 Horney, p. 264.

138 Palmer, p. 232.

139 Brian Swimme and Thomas Berry, *The Universe Story* (San Francisco: Harper SanFrancisco, 1992), p. 243.

140 Riso and Hudson, *Wisdom*, pp. 208–9.

141 Riso and Hudson, *Wisdom*, p. 216.

142 Horney, p. 268.

143 Éilis Bergin and Eddie Fitzgerald, *An Enneagram Guide: A Spirituality of Love in Brokenness* (Mystic, Conn.: Twenty-Third Publications, 1995), p. 96.

144 Robert Alter, *Genesis: Translation and Commentary* (New York: W.W. Norton, 1996), p. 248.

145 Almaas, 107.

146 For further discussion of these stages, see chapter 5.

147 Nicoll, 510.

148 Hurley and Donson, *Soul Potential*, p. 116.

149 Hurley and Donson, *Soul Potential*, p. 162.

150 Horney, p. 274.

151 Horney, p. 285.

152 Palmer, p. 365.

153 Riso and Hudson, *Wisdom*, p. 337.

154 Almaas, p. 288.

155 Riso and Hudson, *Wisdom*, p. 340.

156 Almaas, p. 209.

157 Alter, p. 53.

158 Riso and Hudson, *Wisdom*, p. 333.

159 Riso and Hudson, *Wisdom*, p. 336.

160 Hurley and Donson, *Soul Potential*, p. 172.

161 Riso and Hudson, *Wisdom*, p. 324.

162 Riso and Hudson, *Wisdom*, p. 334.

163 Riso and Hudson, *Wisdom*, p. 326.

164 Horney, 263.

165 Riso and Hudson, *Wisdom*, p. 331.

166 Riso and Hudson, *Wisdom*, p. 316.

Notes for Chapter 5: The Spiral of Transformation

167 Nicoll, p. 603.

168 Nicoll, p. 1482.

169 Nicoll, p. 253.

170 Riso and Hudson, *Wisdom*, p. 33.

171 Teresa of Avila. *Collected Works*, 3 vols., trans. Kieran Kavanaugh and Otilio Rodrigues, (Washington, D.C.: ICS Publications, 1976), vol. 1, p. 114.

172 Teresa of Avila, *Collected Works*, vol. 1, p. 147.

173 O'Murchu, 35.

174 Frank Baum's text calls them silver, but most people are more familiar with the ruby slippers in the Hollywood film version.

175 One thinks of *The Odyssey, Tom Jones, The Divine Comedy*, numerous fairy tales, and Arthurian legends, to name just a few.

176 Nicoll, pp. 1210–11.

177 Nicoll, p. 54.

178 Teresa of Avila, *Collected Works*, vol. 1, p. 161.

179 Meister Eckhart, *Essential Sermons, Commentaries, Treatises, and Defense*, trans. E. Colledge and B. McGinn (New York: Paulist Press, 1981), p. 286.

180 Eckhart, p. 210.

181 Mathew Fox, *The Reinvention of Work* (San Francisco: Harper Collins, 1994), p. 23.

182 Nicoll, p. 1654.

183 John of the Cross, *Collected Works*, trans. Kieran Kavanaugh and Otilio Rodriguez, (Washington, DC: ICS Publications, 1991), p. 13.

Bibliography

Addison, Howard A. *The Enneagram and Kabbalah: Reading Your Soul.* Woodstock, Vt.: Jewish Lights Publishing, 1998.

Almaas, A.H. *Facets of Unity: The Enneagram of Holy Ideas.* Diamond Books: Berkeley, 1998.

Alter, Robert. *Genesis: Translation and Commentary.* New York: W.W. Norton, 1996.

Amis, Robin. *A Different Christianity: Early Christian Esotericism and Modern Thought.* Albany: State University of New York Press, 1995.

Augustine. *The Confessions of St. Augustine.* Trans. F.J. Sheed. New York: Sheed & Ward, 1943.

_____. *On Christian Doctrine.* Trans. D.W. Robertson. New York: Bobbs-Merrill, 1958.

Beesing, Maria; Robert J. Nogosek; and Patrick O'Leary. *The Enneagram: A Journey of Self-Discovery.* Denville, N.J.:Dimension Books, 1984.

Bergin, Éilis, and Eddie Fitzgerald. *An Enneagram Guide: A Spirituality of Love in Brokenness.* Mystic, Conn.: Twenty-Third Publications, 1995.

Berry, Thomas. *The Great Work: A Way to the Future.* New York: Bell Tower, 1999.

Bloom, Benjamin; Max D. Engelhart; Edward J. Furst; Walker H. Hill; and David R. Krathwohl, *Taxonomy of Educational Objectives.* New York: David McKay, 1956.

Bowker, John, ed. *Oxford Dictionary of World Religions.* Oxford: Oxford University Press, 1997.

Brandt, Charles A.E. *Meditations from the Wilderness.* Toronto: HarperCollins, 1997.

Brown, Raymond. *Reading the Gospels with the Church.* Cincinnati: St. Anthony's Press, 1996.

_____. *Introduction to the New Testament.* New York: Doubleday, 1996.

Brueggemann, Walter. *Finally Comes the Poet.* Minneapolis: Fortress Press, 1989.

_____. *The Psalms and the Life of Faith.* Minneapolis: Fortress Press, 1995.

Campbell, Joseph. *The Hero with a Thousand Faces.* Princeton: Princeton University Press, 1949.

Chabreuil, Fabien and Patricia. *Comprendre et gérer les types de personnalité.* Paris: Dunod, 2001.

Chittister, Joan. *The Friendship of Women: A Spiritual Tradition.* Franklin, Wisc.: Sheed and Ward, 2000.

Chopra, Deepak. *The Seven Spiritual Laws of Success.* San Rafael, Calif.: Amber-Allen, 1993.

Cloud of Unknowing. Trans. Clifton Wolters. New York: Viking Penguin, 1978.

Conlon, James. *Pondering from the Precipice: Soulwork for the New Millenium.* Leavenworth: Forest of Peace, 1998.

Crossan, John Dominic. *Jesus: A Revolutionary Biography.* San Francisco: Harper SanFrancisco, 1995.

Dei Verbum, 3.12. *The Sixteen Documents of Vatican II.* Boston: Daughters of St Paul, n.d., p. 382.

DeMello, Anthony. *Awareness.* New York: Doubleday, 1990.

Douglas-Klotz, Neil. *Prayers of the Cosmos: Meditations on the Aramaic Words of Jesus.* San Francisco: Harper, 1990.

Eckhart, Meister. *Essential Sermons, Commentaries, Treatises, and Defense*. Trans. E. Colledge and B. McGinn. New York: Paulist Press, 1981.

Egan, Harvey D., S.J. *Karl Rahner: The Mystic of Everyday Life*. New York: Crossroad, 1998.

Eliot, T.S. *The Complete Poems and Plays*. New York: Harcourt, Brace and Company, 1952.

English, John J., S.J. *Spiritual Freedom: From the Experience of the Ignatian Exercises to the Art of Spiritual Guidance*. Chicago: Loyola Press, 1973.

Farmer, William R., ed. *The International Bible Commentary*. Collegeville, Minn.: Liturgical Press, 1998.

Fatula, Mary Ann. *The Holy Spirit: Unbounded Gift of Love*. Collegeville, Minn.: Liturgical Press, 1998.

Fleming, David L., S.J. *The Spiritual Exercises of Saint Ignatius*. St. Louis, Missouri: Institute of Jesuit Sources, 1978.

Fox, Matthew. *The Reinvention of Work*. San Francisco: HarperCollins, 1994.

Frye, Northrup. *The Great Code: The Bible and Literature*. New York: Harcourt, 1982.

Gaillardetz, Richard R. *Transforming Our Days: Spirituality, Community, and Liturgy in a Technological Culture*. New York: Crossroad, 2000.

Gallares, Judette A. *Images of Faith: Spirituality of Women in the Old Testament*. Maryknoll, N.Y.: Orbis Books, 1992.

Gotch, Carol Ann, and David Walsh. *Soul Stuff: Reflection on the Inner Work with the Enneagram*. Winnipeg: Inscapes, 1994.

Haskins, Susan. *Mary Magdalen*. London: HarperCollins, 1993.

Hillman, James. *The Soul's Code: In Search of Character and Calling*. New York: Random House, 1996.

Horney, Karen. *Neurosis and Human Growth: The Struggle toward Self-Realization*. New York: W.W. Norton & Co, 1950; 1991.

Howard, Virgil, and Patricia LeNoir. "Unleashing the Power of the Bible", in *The International Bible Commentary*. Ed. William R. Farmer. Collegeville, Minnesota: The Liturgical Press, 1998.

Hurley, Kathy, and Ted Dobson. *The Hurley/Dobson Breakthrough Enneagram Seminar Booklet*. Lakewood, Colorado: Enneagram Resources, Inc., 1985.

Hurley, Kathy, and Theodorre Donson. *Discover Your Soul Potential*. Lakewood, Colorado: WindWalker Press, 2000.

_____. *Enneagram for the 21st Century*. Lakewood, Colorado: Windwalker Press.

_____ *What's My Type?* San Francisco: Harper, 1991.

James, William. *The Varieties of Religious Experience*. New York: New American Library, 1902; 1958.

John of the Cross. *The Collected Works*. Trans. Kieran Kavanaugh and Otilio Rodriguez, Washington, D.C.: ICS Publications, 1991.

John Paul II. "A Dynamic Relationship of Theology and Science." *Origins*, vol. 18, no. 23 (Nov. 17, 1988), pp. 375–8.

Johnson, Luke Timothy. *The Writings of the New Testament: An Interpretation*. Rev. ed. Minneapolis: Fortress Press, 1999.

Jordan, June. "Ruth and Naomi, David and Jonathan: One Love." In *Out of the Garden: Women Writers on the Bible*. Eds. Christina Büchmann and Spiegel. New York: Fawcett Columbine, 1994, pp. 82–87.

Julian of Norwich. *Revelations of Divine Love*. Trans. E. Spearing. London: Penguin, 1998.

Jung, C.K. *Collected Works*. Trans. R.F.C. Hull. Princeton: Bollingen Series, 1966.

_____. *The Portable Jung*. Ed. Joseph Campbell. New York: Penguin, 1971.

Kelly, Sean, and Rosemary Rogers. *Saints Preserve Us!* New York: Random House, 1993.

Maitri, Sandra. *The Spiritual Dimension of the Enneagram: Nine Faces of the Soul*. New York: Putnam, 2000.

Markus, R.A. *Gregory the Great and His World*. Cambridge: Cambridge University Press, 1997.

Marsh, John. *Saint John*. New York: Penguin, 1968; rpt. 1977.

Metzger, Bruce M., and Michael D. Coogan, eds. *The Oxford Companion to the Bible*. Oxford: Oxford University Press, 1993.

More, Thomas. *Care of the Soul: A Guide for Cultivating Depth and Sacredness in Life*. New York: Harper Perennial, 1992.

Naranjo, Claudio. *The End of Patriarchy and the Dawning of a Tri-une Society*. Oakland: Amber Lotus, 1994.

_____. *Ennea-Type Structures: Self-Analysis for the Seeker*. Nevada City: Gateways, 1990.

Nicholl, Maurice. *Psychological Commentaries on the Teaching of Gurdjieff and Ouspensky*. 6 vols. York Beach, Maine: Samuel Weiser, 1996.

Nouwen, Henri J.M. *The Return of the Prodigal Son*. New York: Doubleday, 1994.

O'Murchu, Diarmuid. *Quantum Theology*. New York: Crossroad, 1997.

Palmer, Helen. *The Enneagram: Understanding Yourself and Others in Your Life*. San Francisco: Harper Row, 1988.

Pearsall, Paul. *The Heart's Code: Tapping the Wisdom and Power of Our Heart Energy*. New York: Broadway Books, 1998.

Pearson, Carol S. *Awakening the Heroes Within*. San Francisco: Harper, 1991.

Pieris, Aloysius, S.J. *An Asian Theology of Liberation*. New York: Orbis, 1992.

_____. *The Christhood of Jesus and the Discipleship of Mary*. Logos series, vol. 39, no. 3.

Pitzele, Peter A. *Scripture Windows*. San Francisco: Torah Aura Productions, 1998.

Pope, Alexander. *The Works of Alexander Pope*. Hertfordshire: Wordsworth Editions, 1995.

Rinpoche, Sogyal. *The Tibetan Book of Living and Dying*. New York: HarperCollins, 1993.

Riso, Don Richard. *Understanding the Enneagram*. Boston: Houghton Mifflin, 1990.

Riso, Don Richard, and Russ Hudson. *Personality Types: Using the Enneagram for Self-Discovery*. Rev. ed. New York: Houghton Mifflin, 1996.

_____. *The Wisdom of the Enneagram*. Toronto: Bantam Books, 1999.

Rohr, Richard, and Andreas Ebert. *Discovering the Enneagram: An Ancient Tool for a New Spiritual Journey*. New York: Crossroad, 1990.

_____. *The Enneagram: A Christian Perspective*. New York: Crossroad, 2001.

_____. *Experiencing the Enneagram*. New York: Crossroad, 1992.

Rolheiser, Ronald. *The Holy Longing: The Search for a Christian Spirituality*. New York: Doubleday, 1000.

Satir, Virginia; John Banmen; Jane Gerber; and Maris Gomori. *The Satir Model: Family Therapy and Beyond*. Palo Alto: Science and Behaviour Books, 1991.

Schüssler Fiorenza, Elisabeth, ed. *Searching the Scriptures*, Vols. I & II. New York: Crossroad, 1993.

_____. *Wisdom Ways: Introducing Feminist Biblical Interpretation*. Maryknoll, N.Y.: Orbis Book, 2001.

Severin, Gérard, and Françoise Dolto. *L'Evangile au risque de la psychanalyse*, I and II. Paris: Editions du Seuil, 1978.

Soelle, Dorothy. *The Silent Cry: Mysticism and Resistance*. Minneapolis: Fortress Press, 2001.

Stuhlmueller, Carol, ed. *The Collegeville Pastoral Dictionary of Biblical Theology*. Collegeville, MN: Liturgical Press, 1996.

Swimme, Brian. *Hidden Heart of the Cosmos*. VHS. Mill Valley, CA: Center for the Story of the Universe, 1996.

Swimme, Brian, and Thomas Berry. *The Universe Story*. San Francisco: Harper SanFrancisco, 1992.

Teresa of Avila. *Collected Works*. 3 vols. Trans. Kieran Kavanaugh and Otilio Rodriguez, Washington, D.C.: ICS Publications, 1976.

Vanier, Jean. *The Scandal of Service*. Ottawa: Novalis, 1998.

Wagner, Jerome. "Karen Horney Meets the Enneagram." *Enneagram Monthly*, April 2001, 8.

Wilber, Ken. *A Brief History of Everything*. Boston: Shambhala, 1996.

Zukav, Gary. *The Dancing Wu Li Masters: An Overview of the New Physics*. New York: Bantam, 1979.

For more information

Contact Diane Tolomeo, Pearl Gervais or Remi De Roo for information about their retreats or workshops at:

Enneagram Applications
P.O Box 37032
20-3200 Island Highway
Nanaimo, B.C.
Canada V9T 4N6
Telephone (toll free) 1 (877) 743-0235
Fax (250) 729-0132
e-mail ea@enneagram-applications.com
Web site: www.enneagram-applications.com